Long Way from Adi Ghehad

Long Way from Adi Ghehad

A biography of
Dr Teame Mebrahtu

STAN HAZELL

SHEPHEARD-WALWYN (PUBLISHERS) LTD

First published in 2017 by
Shepheard-Walwyn (Publishers) Ltd
107 Parkway House, Sheen Lane,
London SW14 8LS
www.shepheard-walwyn.co.uk
www.ethicaleconomics.org.uk

British Library Cataloguing in Publication Data
A catalogue record of this book
is available from the British Library

ISBN: 978 0 85683 518 6

Typeset by Alacrity, Chesterfield, Sandford, Somerset
Printed and bound in the United Kingdom
by Short Run Press, Exeter

Contents

List of Plates

Foreword

Stories of outstanding people, who overcome great adversity, encounter almost impossible odds in rising from humble beginnings in remote villages to become noteworthy citizens of the world, form part of the most uplifting areas of literature. Such individuals and their life experiences in following a powerful mission to improve human-kind, provide exemplars of how to live a truly good life. This account of the life of Teame Mebrahtu is undoubtedly part of that pantheon of biographies.

As a colleague at the University of Bristol, I first came to know Dr Mebrahtu twenty years ago as a respected fellow academic who led postgraduate courses in Education, directed principally at students from the developing world. As we became better acquainted, it became evident that his commitment to the students was both to inspire and equip them to be knowledge leaders in the often poor but proud countries of Africa and South America. He also saw it as his duty to care for them as individuals, who were studying in an unfamiliar culture, at a prestigious university with high expectations. His own experience was fundamental to the time and concern he gave them, which often extended to representing their interests to governmental agencies, to support when there were deaths in their families, to meals at his home and all too often to giving his own money to aid them.

This level of humane engagement was well beyond the expectations of the University, and no doubt it was seen by some of his colleagues as unwise and a diversion from his obligations to research and publish, to ensure career progression. It was only as our friendship slowly

developed, that fragments of his personal encounters with the problems afflicting some of his students emerged. As this powerful account
of his life reveals, Dr Mebrahtu is profoundly modest, routinely
dismissive of praise, generous to a fault and genuinely selfless.

So, it was a long time before the detail of his origins in the timeless
hilltop village of his birth, his struggles to gain an education, the
impact of political upheavals in Ethiopia and Eritrea, and his ultimate
enforced asylum in Bristol were revealed. In more recent years we
have talked a good deal of his love of Eritrea and desire to play a part,
again, in its development. Only then did I learn of his remarkable
father's determination to give his firstborn son the education he was
denied. The story of the mule journey (recounted in Chapter 2) made
a deep impression on me. It has biblical resonance. Like Abraham and
Isaac, it tells of painful partings, self sacrifice, great vision and a
lifelong honouring of the gift.

The author of this splendid book, Stan Hazell, has also known
Teame for a long time. We shared a view that the full version of this
story should not be left untold. Our individual and joint represent-
ations to him to 'write it all down', resulted in reluctant agreement,
wrapped up in the overwhelming modesty that ensured its progress
was small. Stan, a journalist who learned his craft as a writer for
newspapers in South Wales and later for many years with ITV in the
West of England, went a crucial stage further and offered to write
down Teame's telling of his past. What we see in this volume is the
result of an impressive partnership of skill and trust.

Once Teame agreed to the project, he and Stan met every week for
two and a half years, to unearth this personal and professional
biography. This extended dialogue, with Stan as the systematic
interlocutor, released a wealth of recollections that may have lain
silent without his professional capacity for searching out a good story
and making sure the facts were all there.

In my own research on ageing, I have conducted many biographical interviews with older people. Such studies require the interviewer to gain the confidence of the life-story teller and to assure them that you are 'a safe listener' who will maintain absolute confidentiality, even if parts of what they say are used in reports, articles or books. In these circumstances the interviewer is an 'interested stranger'. The opportunity to tell your own story is a rare one for most people and as a result it produces recollections deeply buried and not infrequently elicits personal accounts which have never been told to anyone.

Even when the experience has unearthed difficult aspects of their past, people who are interviewed are almost always grateful for the experience. They see your careful non-judgemental listening as a rare gift. In the case of Stan Hazell, he gave a gift of immense magnitude to Teame. Not only was he an outstanding listener, who provoked him to dig up his past and talk about it, he translated it, shaped it and wove it into a coherent biography, week after week after week. With great respect for what he heard, Stan has produced an honest and highly readable book which honours the subject but does so as an intelligent reporter. A signal achievement.

As a reader of *Long Way from Adi Ghehad,* you will discover the life-story of a man of intellect, deeply held values and a believer that education can transform human institutions and societies. At the same time you are introduced to the troubled political situation in the Horn of Africa during the second half of the twentieth century, which led Teame to leave his beloved homeland and seek asylum in the United Kingdom.

There will be many in the widely dispersed Eritrean diaspora who will know of Teame Mebrahtu and want to read his story. They will also want to read themselves into the troubled career of their small, proud nation. Others will come to this book to understand the enduring principles and values of a leading international educator. Yet others will want to follow the life of a dedicated and principled asylum seeker who gave himself fully as a university teacher, but also as a model black person in Britain when racial tensions were high and he was one of few who were respected and trusted.

For myself, I am profoundly grateful to have had the opportunity to know Teame and to count him as a friend.

PROFESSOR MALCOLM JOHNSON

Introduction

I have known Dr Teame Mebrahtu for well over forty years – he a Bristol academic and me a local journalist – and in that time I heard intriguing snippets of his life. But I knew there was much more to discover. This is the result.

Teame is a modest man and took some persuading that his life was worthy of note. But I am glad I persisted because he has a remarkable story. It starts in the village of Adi Ghehad in the Highlands of Eritrea, where Teame was born – hence the title. Becoming the first of his family to receive an education, albeit with many difficulties along the way, he became one of his country's leading academics and teacher trainers.

But he lived in a period of political turmoil which saw him imprisoned as a teenage student demonstrator. He experienced the beginnings of the Eritrean liberation struggle which brought bloodshed to the streets of Asmara where he lived. And he was an eye witness to the moment Emperor Haile Selassie was overthrown by the *Dergue*, a military junta made up of many of the army's junior officers. During the regime which followed, led by Mengistu Hailemariam, a close friend and colleague was assassinated.

Granted permission to study for a PhD at Bristol he was then ordered to return by the Mengistu government. Realising his life was in danger he refused to go back. So he became an asylum seeker joining those of his countrymen and women who have become refugees, fearing for their lives from one or other of the political upheavals that have been a part of the region's recent history to this day.

Writing this account has seemed like describing a fictional adventure story, such have been some of the situations in which he found himself. But, as they say, life can be stranger than fiction.

His asylum in Britain granted, he declined state benefits saying he was not entitled to them. Instead he used his passion for education and his African background to give talks in local schools after first winning the confidence of the head teachers. Having gained his PhD he became a respected senior academic and Adviser to International Students at the Bristol Graduate School of Education. He helped hundreds of students on their academic journey. He would take a personal interest in their lives and well-being thereby implementing his firm belief that, if student welfare comes first, then academic success will surely follow.

But as I found out more about what he did in addition to his demanding role at the university his story became all the more remarkable. With his knowledge of the developing world and experience of being an asylum seeker, he has become an acknowledged expert on the problems faced by refugees, how the societies in which they end up can best integrate them, and how the refugees themselves can adapt their new lives to a different culture.

Multicultural education – improving opportunities for ethnic minorities and helping all children to understand the wider world outside their own borders – is something he has campaigned for and lectured about. He organised an international conference on the subject.

He served his new community in many different ways. It was partly out of conviction that it was his public duty to the country that had given him sanctuary. I think he was also influenced by an inherent humanitarianism and respect for the Eritrean tradition of caring for others which goes back to the ancient laws of *Adgina-te-Gheleba*, a creative piece of legislation laying down the behaviour expected from the population including how they should respect and help each other.

Whilst loyal to Britain, he has never forgotten his beloved Eritrea, working to create an education system as the country neared independence and, on a number of occasions, going into the war zone during the liberation struggle. Even now, amidst the travails the country faces which have multiplied the tide of refugees flooding into Europe, he has a vision of what he believes the country could still become.

I have found teasing out these, and many other facets of his life, a fascinating journey. There is much more to tell in the chapters that follow. It would be wrong to define him by his refugee status, or even by his passion for education and belief in its potential to bring about needed change, important as that has been in his life, because he has done so much more. He is a citizen of the world, a global educator as he would describe himself. And he demonstrates in this fast changing world qualities that bring richness to our increasingly multicultural society.

STAN HAZELL
December 2016

Eritrea

Eritrea, a country in the Horn of Africa, is bordered by the Red Sea which makes it strategically placed along one of the world's busiest shipping lanes. On its other borders are Sudan and Ethiopia. It is a country with a people proud of their heritage and with their own languages of which Tigrigna and Arabic are the official ones. The population is currently estimated to be between 3.6 million and 5.5 million, although there has never been a census, so precise figures are not available.

Eritrea was part of the first Ethiopian kingdom of Aksum until its decline in the 8th century. It came under control of the Ottoman Empire in the 16th century, and later the Egyptians. In 1885 the Italians captured the coastal areas and gained sovereignty over parts of the country. They ruled until World War Two when, in 1942, the British defeated the Italians and established a British Military Administration. From 1952 to 1961 a federation of a sort prevailed between Eritrea and Ethiopia until Emperor Haile Selassie annexed the country to Ethiopia – abrogating a UN resolution in the process.

At the time of the annexation Eritrea possessed a far more sophisticated urban and industrial infrastructure than Ethiopia. Ethiopia nationalised Eritrea's 42 largest factories and systematically dismantled the Eritrean industrial sector during a protracted civil war. They also suppressed the two official languages of the Eritrean population, ordering the burning of books – an act which fuelled the fires of liberation. Annexation had signalled the start of the bloody civil war between Ethiopian forces and Eritrean liberation fighters.

In 1974 the Emperor was overthrown by a Communist Military Junta later led by Colonel Mengistu Hailemariam. The Emperor died a year after being deposed. To this day the cause of his death is still shrouded in mystery. The Mengistu regime oversaw the Ethiopian Red Terror of 1977-78 – a campaign of repression against the Ethiopian People's Liberation Party and other groups opposed to the Dergue, the regime's secretive ruling body.

In 1991, after the Ethiopian People's Revolutionary Democratic Front, supported by the Eritrean People's Liberation Front, deposed Mengistu, the way was opened for fighters from the EPLF to gain control of Asmara and form a provisional government. Two years later, in 1993, a referendum on Eritrean independence was held, supported by the United Nations and the new Ethiopian government. There was an almost unanimous vote for an independent republic. Isias Afwerki, a leader of one of the liberation fronts, became Eritrea's first president. Liberation was hailed as a new dawn for the country with high hopes of a better future.

But the co-operation between the two new governments did not last long. Eritrea and Ethiopia disagreed about the exact demarcation lines of their borders. There were many clashes with both countries spending millions of dollars on warplanes and weapons. When it escalated to a full blown war between 1998 and 2000, it is estimated that 100,000 people were killed. A peace agreement was finally signed in December 2000 with an international Court of Arbitration ruling that Eritrea had violated international law by attacking Ethiopia in 1998.

The war, known as the Badme War after the disputed border territory, destroyed the country's economy. According to the World Bank, Eritrea lost US$225 million worth of livestock and 55,000 homes during the war. It is estimated a million Eritreans were displaced. Although a mainly agricultural economy, the presence of land mines in border areas has meant some of the country's most productive land has been unused. Recurrent drought in the Horn of Africa in recent years has hit food production.

Eritrea also has substantial mineral deposits – copper, gold, granite, marble and potash. As Reuters the international news agency reported, the country is looking to utilise them to kickstart the economy. The opening of the Bisha mine in 2011 – firstly to mine gold but latterly zinc and copper – has been part of that process. Other new mines are planned producing, gold, copper, zinc and potash.

But there are challenges for a country that has been described as one of the world's most secretive. The World Bank describes Eritrea as 'one of the least developed countries in the world'. Continuing tensions between Eritrea and Ethiopia have resulted in a 'no war, no peace' situation and the stalemate is considered 'a major impediment to the government's development efforts ...' Fighting broke out in the Tsorona border area in June 2016 with casualties reported on both sides.

Amnesty International in its 2015/16 Annual Report claimed that thousands of prisoners of conscience and political prisoners, including former politicians, journalists and practitioners of unauthorised religions, continued to be detained without trial. Many, says the report, have been detained for well over a decade. Amnesty also say that mandatory National Service is indefinite in a system they describe as 'forced labour' with thousands of people attempting to avoid conscription by fleeing the country.

A UN Commission of Inquiry on Human Rights in Eritrea reported in June 2016 that the country is an 'authoritarian State'. The report adds: 'There is no independent judiciary, no national assembly and there are no other democratic institutions in Eritrea. This has created a governance and rule of law vacuum, resulting in a climate of impunity for crimes against humanity to be perpetrated over a quarter of a century.'

Eritrea's government describes the UN report as 'unfounded accusations' and claims they are 'politically motivated and groundless'. They claim the report is 'entirely one-sided' because members of the Commission only spoke to Eritreans outside the country, many of whom have their own agendas.

The country has had a 'go it alone' culture which goes back to the thirty-year liberation war when they succeeded against seemingly impossible odds. The secretive nature of the Eritrean government means that they have never published a national budget making it difficult for the outside world to work out what is happening in the country's economy.

China has been providing aid of various kinds to Eritrea since 1992 and has been co-operating on health issues since 1997. Nine Chinese medical teams have since worked in the country. China has also been involved in the expansion of the Hirgigo power plant in Massawa and aided the setting up of the Eritrean Institute of Technology among other projects.

The EU has granted Eritrea an aid package amounting to €200 million, financed by the European Development Fund, aimed at supporting the country's energy sector and improving governance. The EU says they are insisting on the full respect of human rights as part of their ongoing political dialogue with Eritrea. The grant will run from 2016 to 2020.

The Africa Editor of BBC World Service News, Mary Harper, reported in July 2016 that despite the government's secretive behaviour and allegations of human rights abuses in the labour force there are signs of growing interest from foreign investors. Both Eritrean and foreign investors are also said to be looking towards the country's 1,200 kilometre (745 mile) Red Sea Coast, with its hundreds of unspoilt islands, rich fish stocks and ports, which all have significant economic potential.

The report adds: 'Whether any of this will be realised will depend on two main factors. Eritrea's willingness to adopt a more flexible attitude towards its economy, and foreign investors' readiness to engage with a country that has recently been accused of crimes against humanity and has spent years in international isolation.'

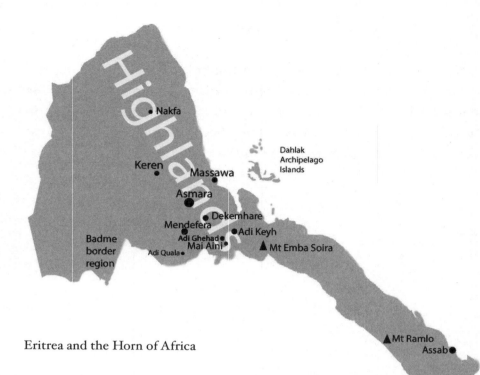

Eritrea and the Horn of Africa

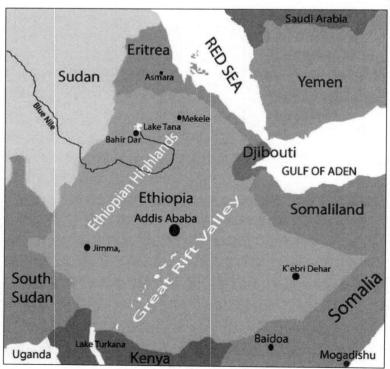

PART ONE

CHAPTER ONE

Early Life

Adi Ghehad is a village in the Eritrean Highlands, founded many centuries ago by the man after whom it is named – Ghehad. *Adi* means 'Place of'. The village, 150 kilometres from the capital city Asmara, is still inhabited by Ghehad's descendants.

The Mebrahtu family, whose name in one of the Eritrean mother tongues, Tigrigna, means 'God's Light', can trace their lineage back to the days of Ghehad. A father's name shows his antecedents. With no written records it was the only indicator of who they were descended from and was likely to be the first question one Eritrean would ask another on first meeting them.

Eritrea became an Italian colony in 1890. Following the second Italo-Ethiopian War in 1935, which lasted until May of the next year, there had been a large influx of Italians. Mebrahtu Beraky, a villager from Adi Ghehad, like many other Eritreans was enlisted into the Italian Army in the 1930s. He fought with them in their campaign in Libya. A self-educated man who had never had proper schooling he learnt fluent Italian and Arabic as well as some English in addition to his mother tongue Tigrigna. Following his service in Libya he became a carabinieri working with the Italian army and initially stationed at the town of Massawa on the Red Sea. He was now in his twenties, an age when it was customary for young men to marry.

The girl who was to be his bride was even younger, and was from Biet Semayti, a village about 40 kilometres from Adi Ghehad. Her name was Wagaye Berhe. *Wagaye* means 'My Worth'. She came from a family who were among the richest in the area in terms of the head of cattle they owned. Her father, Belamberas Berhe Gaffre, was one of the founding fathers of the traditional law, known as *Adgina-te-Gheleba*, practised in the Akeleguzay Province. Wagaye was fourteen years old, a not unusual age for a girl to marry in the local culture. As was the custom the marriage had been arranged by family members with Mebrahtu's mother Teblez Seghed playing a major part.

The young couple set up home at Metsalu, a suburb of Dekemhare – a large town in the Highlands about 40 kilometres south of the capital Asmara – after Mebrahtu Beraky was transferred to the police station there. He had been offered accommodation at the Palaso di Polisia, the police quarters in Dekemhare, but had to turn it down because he couldn't afford the rent. At that time he had a profligate lifestyle and was spending too much time drinking in local bars. Metsalu was a cheaper place to live.

Soon their first child was on the way. Wagaye was sent back to Adi Ghehad to have the birth at the home of the baby's grandmother, Teblez. The child was a boy. They named him Teame Mebrahtu. The year was 1939, although the exact date is uncertain as no records were kept at that time and the Eritrean traditional calendar is seven years behind its Western counterpart.

The house where Teame was born in Adi Ghehad was in one of four homesteads, each with about forty houses, where different branches of Ghehad descendants lived. The village had about two hundred households with a total population of about a thousand. The Mebrahtu house was in the homestead in the Western part of the village known as Tekleyes after one of Ghehad's sons.

When Teame was born the teenage Wagaye still wore her hair in the style for young girls. As he grew older Teame was allowed to call her by her first name and she used to tell him he was more like a brother to her than a son.

Some months later following the Christening ceremony – which according to the traditions of the Orthodox Church had to be on the 40th day after the birth for a boy (the 50th day for a girl) – Wagaye took the baby Teame back to Metsalu to join Mebrahtu Beraky. Two years later another son arrived – Anghesom. Over the next twenty-two years she had eight children, three sons and five daughters. Teame's youngest brother, Hagos, born in 1961, was later to join the Eritrean liberation fighters.

The time in Metsalu was a difficult one for the family who were living in relative poverty as Mebrahtu continued to struggle to make ends meet. Teame remembers his young brother once getting so hungry that he tore strips off a joint of raw meat to eat it.

Finally Teame's grandmother Teblez, unhappy to see the family living in such poverty, stepped in to help. She put up the money for Mebrahtu Beraky to join with a close friend and police colleague of his, Mesmer, to buy a pair of donkeys with licences to collect and sell firewood.

It was to prove a turning point for both men. Mebrahtu was regretting failing to manage his income properly and his drinking habit. He was determined now to care for his growing family more responsibly. The business proved lucrative and both families were able to afford to move to quarters in the police compound in Dekemhare. Soon afterwards Mesmer moved back to his home village in the Hamasien province. He sold his share in the donkeys to Mebrahtu Beraky.

The additional income from the donkey business, vegetables and butter from the family homestead in Adi Ghehad, along with Mebrahtu's better management of his finances, meant that the family fortunes had been transformed. They could afford a transistor radio for the first time. Meat was plentiful with Mebrahtu buying and slaughtering a goat every Saturday. The family could have new clothes.

When, in 1941 with World War Two engulfing North Africa and the British conquering the Italians in Eritrea, Mebrahtu Beraky was seconded into the British Army serving as a record keeper – a *diarista* – and was allowed to continue living at the police compound at Dekemhare. He considered himself lucky to have a job there. Many of his fellow Eritreans, who had served with the Italians, were sent back to their villages when the British took over. But, because of his self-taught skill in speaking and writing Italian, Mebrahtu Beraky was kept on.

Built in the Italian style, the compound had quarters for the staff comprising a main living room, sleeping areas and an outside kitchen. Under the British there were strict rules about cleanliness and hygiene in the compound buildings with regular inspections. With malaria a threat there were fears of infection. Teame still vividly remembers the smell of the disinfectant used to wash down the concrete floors every Saturday.

Teame quickly settled into life in the compound. He made friends with the children of other soldiers living there, played football and, helped by his parents, began to learn how to grow vegetables and flowers in the small plot allocated to them. When he was four his father decided to send him to a local church school. He was the first of his family to go to any sort of school.

It was run by an elderly retired priest at his home in Dekemhare. There were classes on six days a week, Monday to Saturday, with pupils attending just three morning or afternoon sessions to accommodate the number of children seeking places. Sometimes classes took place out in the garden because of the intense heat.

The priest was of the Orthodox faith. So only the children of Orthodox Christian families were accepted. Catholics, Protestants and Muslims had their own schools in the town.

Learning the Tigrigna alphabet formed a major part of the lessons. Unlike the English alphabets with twenty-two characters, this one has two hundred. Each letter has a number of different inflections, sometimes as many as seven or eight. The letter H for example has these different pronunciations: *Hae*, *Hu*, *Hi*, *Ha*, *Hiye*, *H'*, and *Ho*. They all had to be learnt by rote, repeating them out loud time after time until they knew them off by heart. The classroom was alive with the sound of the children's voices. The priest had a problem with one of his eyes so he relied on hearing the pupils at work. If he could not hear the sound of their voices reciting he knew they would be up to some mischief.

Religion, the Orthodox kind, was also important. The children were taught how to say the Lord's Prayer and other Biblical quotations and religious songs. But it was in Ge'ez, the liturgical language of the church which has common links with Tigrigna and also Amharic, the mother tongue of many Ethiopians. So his young pupils had to learn some Ge'ez as well.

There was a strong grounding in the Ten Commandments, also spoken in Ge'ez, with an emphasis on respect for elders, mothers and fathers. Respect for the teacher was also considered important. At the start of every class the pupils were expected to bow to the priest, say good morning, then kneel and kiss his knee before taking their seats. The tradition of respect in the classroom, and to one's elders, was to have a major influence on Teame.

Older pupils would be used as mentors, helping the priest keep the fifteen or so pupils in his charge under control and assisting with lessons. Discipline was strict. The priest used a length of ox hide to dispense punishment. Teame felt the weight of it when he arrived late for lessons one day. It was a painful experience and he was never late again.

Although learning to write was not part of the curriculum, the brighter pupils, Teame included, began to learn the basics as they recognised the characters in their lessons on the alphabet.

With only three half day sessions a week Teame had time on his hands. By now nearing seven years old, he became something of an expert tomato grower. His father had a small plot in the police compound, but little time to work on it. His job often meant night work when he would book in the criminals who had been arrested in the town, making notes of their offences and personal details.

So Teame had free range of the small garden. The family had a good crop during the growing season as well as a variety of flowers which he also cultivated. He made friends with another boy his own age who looked after his father's garden on an adjoining plot. His name was Zehaye Fessehaye and he was to become a life-long friend.

But gardening was not enough to keep a small boy active. Teame joined a gang of other boys, and a few girls, living in the compound. All of them were about same age, six or seven. Zehaye was one of them. Teame found himself the leader of the group. They got up to all sorts of mischief in the compound, sometimes stealing eggs from the kitchens. There were other gangs of children in the compound, some of them of older and bigger. There were often clashes between them. Teame found himself in conflict with the much bigger and stronger leader of another gang. He was four or five years older. There was a fight and Teame, not surprisingly, came off worst.

The gang used to venture around the town, sometimes playing football on open ground using rolled up old socks as a ball. One day the makeshift ball ran into a ditch on the side of the road. Searching for it they found a small bag full of money, probably dropped by thieves the night before.

The gang, especially Teame and Zehaye, had a long discussion about what to do with the money although they never actually counted it. Keeping it was a temptation. But the thought of being found out by their fathers, both policemen, along with an inherent sense of honesty finally took precedence. They decided to hand the bag of money into the police station. Having done so they had hoped they might get a reward. But their hopes were in vain.

One day, on the way to school, Teame and Zehaye came across a swarm of bees in a tree – a valuable and much prized commodity in the Eritrean villages. They marked the tree as a sign to others that the swarm was theirs.

Then they caught the swarm in the accepted manner by pouring water over the bees so they fell into a sheet, trying hard not to get stung in the process. Having got their bees, there was a long discussion about what to do with them. They discovered the value of the bees and Teame's father paid Zehaye's father for his share.

It was then decided that the swarm should be taken to Adi Ghehad, Teame's home village, and placed on the Mebrahtu homestead. The bees have since multiplied many times allowing the Mebrahtu family and some of the villagers to enjoy the honey. They are still known as 'Teame's Bees'.

Another time Teame and Zehaye, determined to impress a group of older boys who were taunting them, walked across water pipes – used to irrigate farmland – which straddled a 15-metres-wide ravine. It was a foolish and dangerous thing to do but they got safely to the other side with delighted shouts of: 'We've arrived.'

At that time Dekemhare had a large Italian quarter which was known locally as 'Little Bologna' as the homes and other buildings were so beautiful. The young Eritreans were discouraged from going there, but they would smell the cooking of the exotic Italian pastries, although they would never get to eat one. Many of the Italians, and those of mixed Italian/Eritrean blood, started to leave the country in the years following the British takeover of Eritrea.

Teame had now been at the church school for three years and was nearly seven. By this time he had two siblings. His brother Anghesom had been joined by a sister, Zighe. His mother, Wagaye, would go back to his grandmother's house, where he had been born, several times a year to help with the crops and looking after the animals. She would take her younger children with her. On her return she would bring several quintals of maize and *taff* flour which would keep the family fed for months.

The Mebrahtus considered themselves lucky to have this addition to their larder. Not every family on the compound were so fortunate. Wagaye would share the maize with other families living on the compound who would otherwise have been short of food. Policemen were not paid well.

At seven Teame became eligible to go to the government Elementary School in Dekemhare. His father was determined that he should go. He wanted his son to have the education he had missed. He told Teame he should improve his lot in life and the only way was through education. 'Do you want to end up like me?' he would say to him. Teame did not appreciate it at the time, but later came to realise just how great had been the sacrifices his father made to provide him with an education.

Teame had a sleepless night before his first day at the new school. He was anxious over who his new classmates would be. What his new teacher and the classroom would be like. In the morning he donned the new shorts and short sleeved shirt his father had bought him. His mother had ironed them so that the creases stood out just like those on the police uniforms. She had also made him a satchel made out of heavy cotton. For the first time in his life he had a handkerchief which his mother insisted he kept in his satchel. He had no shoes and walked to the school in bare feet accompanied by his father. Teame remembers feeling very proud to have his father at his side. It was not something he very often had time to do.

Despite his worries he was impressed by his new school which was within walking distance from the police compound. It was a modern glass fronted building built in the Italian style and surrounded on two sides by borders of flowers. Close by were the Catholic and Orthodox churches and the Mosque and a button making factory called Enda Sabbam. There was a bicycle repair shop run by two brothers known as Mussie and Aaron just across the road from the school.

There were thirty others in Teame's class, mostly boys. Few girls at that time went to school. The first thing he noticed was that some of the children were much better dressed than he was despite his new clothes. And they were wearing shoes. For the first time in his life he came up against inequality. He resented the looks and sneers from some of the better clothed whose parents, officers and businessmen, would have been wealthier than his father on his police pay.

He had a quarrel over the issue with one of the other pupils which ended in a fight. There was a severe reprimand from his teacher. But Teame had learned something about bullying in the classroom which would give him a better understanding of it in later life.

Once lessons started Teame settled down and began to enjoy life at the school. Such was the demand for places that pupils were limited to classes either in the morning or afternoon to provide more opportunities. The emphasis was on the Three Rs, Reading, Writing and Arithmetic along with General Science and Personal Health and Hygiene. Teame's time in the church school had given him a head start over some of the other pupils. He could already read and had begun to learn how to write. Exercise books and pencils were provided but had to be left at the school and not taken home.

Civic education was taught and included advice on how to treat others. It was not linked to a particular religion. The school had a mix of faith backgrounds among the pupils including Orthodox, Catholic and Muslim. The teacher would tell them of the need to have respect for others regardless of who they were and to think of those weaker and poorer than themselves. They were urged to be honest in their dealings and to share what they had with others who might need it more.

Teame was to get a chance to explore that last piece of advice during the half hour breaks in the middle of the school sessions. His mother always cooked him a snack of *kitcha* (bread) similar to a *chappati*. There were other children who had nothing to eat so Teame would share his meal with them. He wondered later if the teachers had known of the backgrounds of the pupils who had no food with them, and were encouraging others to share.

The teachers would give them songs to sing as part of the learning process. One of them struck a cord with Teame. It went:

> *Nab Temherti, Nab Temherti,*
> *Nsa eya Abay habti,*
> *Dleyuwa mealti mes leyti.*

It urged young people to go to school and get wisdom because that was the source of knowledge. It would open doors to the future. Education is the greatest wealth, not money. The words would always stay with Teame.

He successfully completed his first two years at the school and was doing well in his third year much helped by Memher (teacher) Haile-michael Ghebreyesus, a gentle and considerate man, who he remembers as being an excellent teacher who knew his subjects well.

But halfway through the year his father was transferred to another police post in Mai Aini, a town 60 kilometres away and had to leave

Dekemhare. Wagaye and the two younger children went back to Adi Ghehad. Teame had to be found somewhere else to live.

A police colleague of his, Sergeant Abraha Neguse, agreed to let Teame live with his family. It was difficult time for Teame. Although the Sergeant and his wife treated him well, they had five children of their own. Food was scarce and Teame was often hungry and angry. He was miserable and missed his mother to whom he was very close. He stayed there for about six months but then the Sergeant was given a new posting and had to move his family away from Dekemhare. Once more Teame's father had to find somewhere for his son to live and to ensure he continued with his education.

The only solution was a great uncle, Blata Kafil Seghed, in the town of Adi Keyh, 50 kilometres away. But that meant moving to the Elementary School there. It was an unhappy time. Although he was comfortable at the home of his relative, Teame found life at the new school difficult. In the strange surroundings with new teachers and classmates – some of whom were much older than him – Teame became shy and fearful. He had confronted his fears by saying a quick prayer and kissing the wall of the church of St Michael's on his way to school. He also threw a few pence over the wall of the church for the beggars in the hope that their prayers for him would help him cope with his anxieties.

He felt his prayers had been answered as despite his difficulties he managed to endure the last few months to the end of term and pass his Grade 3 exam. The next academic year, however, was to be an important one. He would get the chance to qualify to move up to the Middle School after a General School Examination. But, there were even more challenges to come. Teame was just ten years old.

CHAPTER TWO

Mule Journey

.

Teame's unhappiness at the Adi Keyh Elementary School was such that he did not want to return there. He pleaded with his father to be allowed to go back to Dekemhare. Reluctantly, his father agreed although it meant finding him somewhere to stay in the town. In the meantime Teame went back to Adi Ghehad where his mother was only too happy to welcome back her first born son.

Mebrahtu Beraky, still stationed at the police outpost in Mai Aini, was understanding of Teame's wish to return to Dekemhare Elementary School. But he worried that he would not be able to find anyone for him to live with. Eventually he came up with a solution. He found him a room in a house near the school and the agreement of a niece – Sanday Hagossa Berhe, the daughter of his sister – to cook for him. Mebrahtu Beraky would provide the food. But he knew he would have to find the money for Teame's upkeep and decided to apply for a permit to open a shop in Mai Aini to do so.

So everything was in place for Teame to continue his education. All that remained was to confirm a place at the school for the next academic year. Registration at the school was on a first come first served basis. Latecomers would be unlucky. Mebrahtu Beraky had every intention of getting in early and planned to get permission from his superiors to get away for the day and travel to Dekemhare for the school registration.

It should have been straightforward. But it was not to be. When he bet a colleague he could shoot a *zagra*, a guinea fowl, and did so – he was an excellent marksman – he could not have foreseen the consequences. Some local residents were alarmed by the shot thinking it could have come from the *shiftas*, the bandits operating in the area at the time, and alerted the authorities.

There was a police inquiry. Mebrahtu Beraky's colleagues were all questioned and denied they knew who had fired the shot. Realising the situation was becoming serious, and not wanting to make life difficult for the other policemen, Beraky owned up. He was arrested and hauled up before his superior officer, a British colonel. His plans to get to Dekemhare for the registration were in jeopardy.

Teame was not to learn the full story until many years later when, just before he died, his father gave him an account of what had happened. He was given the inevitable dressing down by the British colonel. Then, probably because of the shooting incident, he was asked to transfer to a new police post at Massawa on the Red Sea coast.

Mebrahtu Beraky refused. He said he could not possibly go to Massawa because, on his police pay, he could not afford to live there. The area was hot and humid and the cost of living much higher. He would not be able to take his family with him.

The officer was furious and insulted Mebrahtu Beraky using an obscene word. Mebrahtu Beraky knew some English and was in no doubt of the insult. Being a man who was not afraid to speak his mind, he shouted back at the officer using the same insulting word. Needless to say, however justified Beraky's reaction might have been, it did not go down well with the British officer who would not have been used to being answered back in that fashion – especially by an Eritrean police officer under his command.

The incident, and the fall out from it, delayed Mebrahtu Beraky's departure for Dekemhare for the school registration. He did finally get permission to go although he suspected the decision might have been deliberately delayed. When he finally got to the school it was ten days after registration started. He was too late. All the places were filled. The pressure for places was increasing at that time with more families living in the towns wanting to send their children to school.

Back in Adi Ghehad Teame heard the news with dismay. His father was intensely annoyed and frustrated and felt guilty that his son would have to wait another year before recommencing his education. By this time he had resigned from the police force and returned to the village. A combination of the problems he had encountered plus pressure from his mother to come back and look after the family smallholding had persuaded him to resign. His mother was finding it increasingly difficult to run the smallholding on her own and wanted him to return to claim his birthright. He became a traditional Eritrean farmer again like many others in the neighbourhood.

During his time with the police force he had never forgotten his responsibilities to the farm. Every pay day during his police service he had bought a goat for a few shillings and sent it back to the village. By the time he returned there was a large and productive herd of about seventy goats. With the cows and the crops they harvested there was ample bread, meat and milk for the family.

Teame, with his chances of schooling suspended, at least for the next year, had no option but to get on with life in the village. It seemed his only prospect was to become a shepherd looking after the family goats. (Shepherd is a generic term in Tigrigna for those who look after any sort of farm animal.)

But his father, never one to give up easily, had other plans. There was a well respected Elementary School at Mendefera, a town about 40 kilometres away across the mountains. He decided to make the journey to see if he could enrol his son there. It was a huge gamble. Firstly he did not know if there would be a place for Teame. Secondly where would his son stay if he did get a place?

The answer to the second question was, he hoped, a relative of his who lived in the town. With no way of contacting him he decided to take Teame to Mendefera and hope for the best. With no form of communications unexpected arrivals were not unusual.

On the morning they were due to set off there was a mood of unhappiness in the household. Teame's mother, Wagaye, was crying as she packed for the journey. She did not want him to go. Teame was not keen either. He was beginning to enjoy life in the village and the loving ministrations of his mother and grandmother. They were torn between wanting him to go to school and not wishing to lose him. When Teame saw his mother crying he started crying too. His father was angry, scolded his mother for spoiling him and gave Teame a slap on the face saying he was being a weakling.

It was an unhappy start to the journey. Their transport was the family mule, a sturdy beast with a reddish coat unlike the more normal grey coat of other mules in the village. The animal was used on the smallholding both for transport and carrying goods and crops. Had Mebrahtu Beraky still been a policeman he would have been eligible for a free ticket on the bus. Now he and Teame faced a difficult journey both sitting on the mule's back across rough mountain tracks to Mendefera.

This was early September and in that part of the Eritrean Highlands temperatures were high. Mebrahtu Beraky sat on the saddle with Teame behind him with just a cloth to sit on as they bumped over the mountain paths and through forests. The mule was also burdened with food for what Teame's father hoped would contribute to his son's stay with the relative. It included a 50-kilo bag of cereal and a tin of butter which was hanging beside Teame and banging against his side as the mule moved along the tracks. His backside and thighs were sore from the constant bumping up and down, especially when Beraky tried to make the mule go faster as he was keen to arrive at their destination before nightfall.

They travelled in silence. Teame was still annoyed at what he saw as his father's cruel treatment. He was also fearful of having to stay with relatives he didn't know and, remembering his unhappy experience at Adi Keyh, going to a new school with no friends.

By midday they had travelled about 20 kilometres and were tired and hot. They stopped by the Mereb River, one of the main waterways in that part of Eritrea, sitting down by the river bank to cool off and to have a meal.

Mebrahtu Beraky was known for always giving priority to his animals. He would let the cattle wander off to graze and not shackle them as many of his fellow farmers would. So the mule was allowed to wander down the river bank to find the best grass and drink unhindered from the river.

Teame, still angry with his father, remained silent and refused to eat his lunch. But Mebrahtu Beraky began to break the silence. He talked to his son and helped him wash his feet and dry his face. He explained why he had been hard on him because he felt he had to be tough to ensure he got another chance of continuing his education. It was a question of being cruel to be kind. For the first time Teame began to see a different, softer, side to his father. Despite his tender years he began to understand his father's motives and to accept his decision to make the journey to Mendefera. He told him: 'I understand, father.' It was to be the beginning of a new and trusting relationship with him.

It was time to continue their journey. But where was the mule? Leaving Teame to mind the baggage Beraky went off to look for it. An hour later he eventually found the animal grazing happily by the river bank two kilometres away. Leading it back he loaded their baggage and continued their journey, now running late and with little chance of getting to the town before sunset.

Setting off, they first had to find a safe crossing over the river. Some stretches were dangerous with treacherous currents and deep gullies. Eventually they found a ford to cross to the other side. The water was fast running and was up to Teame's chest as he struggled through it holding desperately on to the mule's tail as his father pulled the animal to the other bank. Eventually they got safely to the other side and carried on over the mountain tracks with the heavily laden mule being urged on at every step. It was an uncomfortable journey for Teame, sitting on the thin piece of cloth behind his father as the mule negotiated the rough terrain.

At about 7.00 pm they finally arrived in Mendefera. It was a sizeable town and Beraky had no idea where his relatives lived. Leaving Teame and the mule in the town square he went off in search of their house. Having found out where they lived he and Teame arrived long after sunset when traditionally guests would not be expected.

Their knock on the door was greeted with surprise by Mebrahtu Beraky's relative and his family. Not only was he not expected, he had his son with him and it was pretty clear there was the hope he could stay there. Despite the surprise, the family welcomed them as is the Eritrean custom of hospitality. Teame, by this time, was very tired and sore from the journey. After a meal he was sent off to bed while his father sat down with his relative to explain the reason for their unexpected arrival.

Mebrahtu Beraky told them of Teame's failure to get into the school at Dekemhare because of the late registration. He expressed the hope that his relative could use his influence to get Teame into the Elementary School. Eritreans have a saying, *Aya Beya*, or elder brother, which means that one relative will look after another.

The following morning Teame was told to stay in the house while his father went to register him at the Elementary school. The morning passed slowly. At 2.00 pm his father returned. He was looking downcast. The answer had been no. There was no place this time either because he was, once again, too late. Their journey was wasted.

The second rejection hit Teame's father hard. He probably regretted giving up his police job and the confrontation with his superior officer which, had he handled it differently, might not have resulted in a delayed departure for Dekemhare.

He was frustrated and angry and cursed his bad luck. 'Why does it have to happen to me?' he shouted. He was not one to hide his feelings and could also have vented his annoyance at the Mendefera school authorities at the latest rejection which would not have done him any favours.

There was nothing more to be done but return to Adi Ghehad. Mebrahtu Beraky was in despondent mood and little was said between father and son as they set off back over the mountain tracks with the hot afternoon sun in their faces.

The journey was even harder than the outward one. There were more uphill sections for the poor overloaded mule to negotiate. In the middle of the day it was very hot and Teame was taking regular swigs from his flask of water. His father, anxious to get home, was urging the mule forward with Teame clinging on as they advanced over the rough terrain. At times he almost fell off as he bumped painfully along the mountain tracks.

When the sun went down and it got dark it was very cold. Beraky's mood had lightened and he gave Teame his shawl, known as a *netsela*, to cover his head and shoulders. Teame grew fearful as they went, in pitch black conditions, through the forests and up more mountain trails. The *shiftas* were known to operate in the mountains, and he could hear the cries of jackals and hyenas following them. But his father urged him not to be afraid.

Years later, when he studied English Literature, he recalled the experience and was reminded of the words of John Milton in his poem Samson Agonistes:

> O dark, dark, dark, amid the blaze of noon
> Irrevocably dark, total eclipse.

It may not have been a successful trip. But, on the positive side, Teame was discovering more about his father. He had seen that he was a man with no fear or inhibitions. And that he would always do his best for him even if it meant treating him harshly as he had done at the start of the journey. He was very keen to see Teame improve his lot in life. Tough love, he would say, was necessary. He told Teame an old proverb-like story of a father asking his daughter if she would marry a farmer. The daughter replied: 'Why would I marry a man who tills the soil and follows a pair of oxen behind a plough?' It was Beraky's way of telling his son to improve his life by education.

The days together on the journey had created a stronger bond between father and son – although Teame would not understand the full extent of it until he was older. But he had begun to see that behind his father's hard exterior was a kind and loving heart.

It was 11.00 in the evening before the two of them, on a now exhausted mule, arrived back at the family homestead in Adi Ghehad. The barking of the dogs announced their arrival and they were greeted by Teame's delighted mother and grandmother.

The homestead was now to be where Teame would live for the next year. With no more opportunities to get a school place, he would have to suspend his education until a new academic year the following September. It would be a very different life from the one he had been used to.

CHAPTER THREE

The Village

Teame settled into life in the village. There were compensations. After the emotional turmoil of his difficult time at Adi Keyh School and the failed attempts to gain a place at Dekemhare and Mendefera, he found the comforts of home and his mother's cooking to be a blessing. He could eat well. There was plenty of meat, milk, yoghurt and bread in the home. Both his mother, and his grandmother, felt the first born son had suffered enough and needed their love and care.

It was to be a time when his knowledge and experience of the culture and values of his Eritrean heritage was to be broadened as he observed and experienced the traditions of his forebears which were still part of village life.

The village was in the province of Akele Guzay, one of nine Eritrean provinces, which were governed by traditional rules and regulations known as the Laws of *Adgina-te-Gheleba*. It was a creative piece of law-making which laid down the behaviour expected from the population from birth to death. The rules, which included how the members of the community should respect and help each other, were administered by a panel of Elders, one of whom was Teame's grandfather on his mother's side, Belamberas Berhe Gaffre. The laws preceded colonial rule by the Italians and the British, but both colonial powers recognised their value and described them as 'fair and useful'.

Teame's father expected him to pull his weight on the family small-holding so he was given the task of looking after the goats. But having lived most of his life in towns he had no experience of farm work or handling animals. He was not trusted to work on his own. Two girl cousins, Berhanu Hagos and Menet Dumtsu, both three or four years older, were delegated to work with him.

They were bigger and stronger than Teame and a match for any of the other shepherds in the village. The two girls, toughened by life on the farm, looked after him well becoming both friends and mentors. As well as looking after the goats they would collect and carry huge bundles of firewood on their backs for the homestead fires.

Teame's day started after the cows and goats had been milked. He was not allowed to do that, unlike his younger brother Anghesom who didn't go to school but had become an experienced farm worker. Teame did build a small shelter for the kids and one of his responsibilities was to clean it daily. He, like the other shepherds, also ran errands for the village Elders and helped to erect makeshift tents for weddings and funerals. So his days were busy ones.

When the daily milking was completed the kids and calves would be separated from the adult animals who would be allowed to roam off into the hills to find the best grazing spots. They would roam freely with the shepherds keeping an eye on them. Teame, after his years in the town, was not initially as fit as the other young shepherds. But walking up to 10 kilometres every day following the goats soon toughened him up. They had dogs to scare off the many hyenas and jackals who threatened the animals but he also had to summon up the courage to shoo the prowlers away when they got too close to the flock.

He underwent part of the then 'right of passage' of a young boy in the village, having a silver ring on his right ear lobe and a smaller copper ring on the upper part of the same ear along with the traditional 'Mohican' type hairstyle with a strand of hair running front to back of his head.

He began to learn his social responsibilities and a degree of cultural sensitivity. Caring for the less fortunate, especially orphans, was an important tenet of village life. So was respect for the elderly who were perceived as wise and valued members of the community. They were not dismissed as infirm but considered to be people who had risen to a higher status in life.

One specific responsibility that Teame took on was that of 'Neeshto Hamut', a role at weddings of close relatives on his father's side which involved wearing a traditional costume with a spear and a shield and performing a war like dance in front of the in-laws. It was an ancient custom which was meant to protect the bride from verbal and physical attack from the local girls when she returned to her new husband's village on the back of a mule. When he performed this task for the wedding of his cousin, Berhane Dumtsu, in the bride's home village Teame was rewarded with a shilling and one of the twelve pieces of chicken given to special guests at the wedding feast as tradition demanded.

One day Teame found himself reluctantly involved in one of the initiations new young shepherds in Adi Ghehad and the surrounding villages were subjected to. It took place at a water hole where the shepherds would take their animals to drink. The initiation involved a form of wrestling, the newcomer taking on one of the more experienced village boys. Teame found himself up against a boy much older and stronger than he was. Inevitably it resulted in him ending up on his face in the sand. Humiliation seemed to be part of the ceremony.

He could have suffered an even worse beating but for an intervention from Berhanu and Menet, his cousins, who shouted at the older boys ordering them to leave Teame alone. They told the boys that they might be stronger, but Teame had been to school and could read and write – something they could not do. After that Teame was left alone.

Life was hard. It rained a great deal, often with thunder and lightning. Berhanu and Menet showed Teame the best trees to shelter under during the storms. These were the stronger ones, where branches were less likely to fall. They told him one young shepherd had been killed by a lightning strike.

He learnt to recognise and collect the many edible fruits and berries in the area and to ignore the poisonous ones. How to extract gum from certain types of trees and to detect a bee-like tiny insect called 'tsidenay' that produced a medicinal honey hidden in cracks in the rock or under the ground. He learnt to respect the sense of fair play which was required when someone found and marked a bee's nest – a valuable commodity – so that others would leave it alone. That would have brought back memories of the time he and his friend Zehaye had found the bees nest a few years earlier.

There were forests around the village which were a happy hunting ground. The Eritrean highlands at that time were thickly forested although the country has suffered considerable deforestation in recent times.

Teame, his father, mother and siblings had all been living in their grandmother's house. Each branch of the family had their own part. But with his growing family Mebrahtu Beraky was given a plot of land on the homestead to build his own house.

Houses in Adi Ghehad had stone walls one storey high and roofs made of wooden planks or tree branches cemented together with mud. Windows had slats of wood placed across them but were otherwise open to the elements. They would have verandahs providing shade from the hot Eritrean sun and where the family would often eat and sometimes sleep. There were also silos attached to the back or side of the houses for safe keeping of crops like maize, linseed, and *taff*.

Opposite the verandah there would be a dedicated area for the cattle to rest. The compound would also have covered shelters for either sheep or goats.

All the villagers, men and women, would help with building a new house. The process, from putting up the stone walls, to erecting the roof, was accomplished in just two days. A group of twenty villagers arrived to help build Mebrahtu Beraky's new family home. It was the responsibility of the family to provide them food and drink, including *Suwa*, the local home made beer.

The family settled into their new home. Teame's mother, Wagaye, would use the fire in the middle of the main room to cook sauce for the *injera*, a flat pancake made out of the flour of cereals like millet or *taff*. The fire would also be used to boil coffee as well as keeping the home warm. The pungent aromas from the cooking would permeate through the evening air as supper was prepared. Behind the silos at the back of the house was the area where Wagaye baked the *injera*.

In August-September when the first corns on the cob were harvested the young Teame would love to sit around the fire with the fresh cobs roasting in the embers waiting to snatch and eat one. It is something he has never forgotten.

Every Wednesday and Friday were fasting days for adults and children above the age of ten. No dairy products were consumed. But *injera* and *shiro*, a favourite meal made with minced onions and garlic, were allowed.

Communal meals were considered important. Families ate together in the evening. There would be a blessing of the food, by a priest or an elder in the family, followed by the Lord's Prayer spoken in the liturgical language of the Orthodox Church, Ge'ez, which although not taught would be picked up by word of mouth.

Chicken had a special significance in these communal meals. First the elder or the priest would take a piece of *injera*, break off a piece and hand it to the person on his right who would do the same until the injera had gone all the way round the table. The chicken had to be carved into twelve separate, but not equal, portions by the woman of the house who would have prepared and cooked it in a special sauce. She would garnish the meal with hard boiled eggs and then had the tricky task of distributing the chicken portions to the assembled guests in order of their importance and hoping not to offend anyone if she got it wrong. For instance, there would be a special piece known as '*gide zakunay*' for a deacon, or '*feresegna*' for a cavalier – an experienced horseman.

The Orthodox religion was an important part of life in the village. Teame's early exposure to the Coptic faith had come at the church school in Dekemhare where he had learnt prayers, hymns and passages from the Scriptures – all recited in Ge'ez, the liturgical language of his Tigrigna mother tongue. He did not fully understand the mysteries of God's existence, but his experience under the elderly priest at the church school had left him with belief in a Supreme Being which encompassed the power to change one's life for the better. He believed that God could solve daily problems and keep him out of harm's way.

His view would mature as he grew older to the belief that a world without God would be one without tenderness and generosity and where goals for our lives would revolve around self interest. The faith of his childhood was to remain with him. Even as a philosophy student several years later he did not subscribe to the view of some of his fellow students, that faith was the desperate view of a blind man in the dark looking for a black cat.

An important influence in his life, both spiritually and practically, was his grandmother. Although he was no longer living in her house, he was very close to her and spent many hours there, sometimes staying the night. He would sleep at the opposite end of his grandmother's bed. The beds in the houses were made of smoothed stone raised from the ground and covered with an animal pelt. Heavy cotton would be used for blankets. In many houses the beds would be large enough to accommodate all the children in the family.

Teame's grandmother, Teblez Seghed, was a widow. Her husband had died before Teame was born. As was customary for a widow she had her head shaved and wore a small band made from cowhide around her temple and tied at the back. She was a striking looking woman standing over six feet tall. Teame remembers her towering over him as he stood before her.

Every night before bed she would say prayers and recite scripture for over an hour whilst standing up. The prayers would all be recited in Ge'ez.

Teblez was the matriarch of the Mebrahtu household. But she was also an important person in the local community. The priests of the Orthodox Church in the village entrusted her with the church valuables which were kept in her home. That was an unusual honour, especially for a woman in a very male dominated society.

So supplies of cereals collected for distribution by the church to the needy would be stored in her house awaiting collection by the priests. There were also important church documents, many written on sheets of cow hide known as 'brana'. Some of them were centuries old.

Teame once incurred his grandmother's displeasure when his curiosity got the better of him and he went into the small room where the documents were kept and she caught him fingering and looking at them. He was struck by the deep red used to highlight key words in the text. But his grandmother was very angry and told him never to go near them again.

From February to April when the cereals – such as *taff* and *dagussa*, both varieties of grain – were gathered in, Teame would help his father with the harvest. It was a time when the animals would be sent off to grazing land alongside the Red Sea over a 100 kilometres away. The climate there at that time of year was wetter and the grass more plentiful. Rain was likely to be once a week rather than every day but it was still better for the animals than the dry conditions in Adi Ghehad at that time of year.

Teame's father had formed a life-long friendship with a Muslim nomad, Aboy Saliho, who would take the animals to the Red Sea, driving them all the way, a journey which would take up to three weeks.

The arrangement was mutually beneficial. For Mebrahtu Beraky it meant he did not have the responsibility of looking after his animals when he was concentrating on harvesting. Aboy Saliho would milk the animals and sell the butter he produced as well as feeding his own family. He would return the animals to Mebrahtu Beraky at the end of the harvest season well fattened up with Red Sea grass. There had to be trust. The animals were like currency. They were a farmer's most important possession. A cow was always part of a wedding dowry.

Mebrahtu Beraky, meanwhile, had allocated a plot of land for Saliho to grow crops which Mebrahtu would tend in his absence and hand over the harvest of cereals on his return to the homestead. Saliho would set up a tented encampment for his family, not far away from the village. Teame was allowed to visit him there and would be given as much milk as he could drink.

Being a nomad by occupation Saliho travelled about the area and would be aware when bands of *shiftas* were in the locality. He would warn Mebrahtu Beraky so he could avoid them on his own travels and keep his animals safe.

The close friendship between an Orthodox Christian and a Muslim was not unusual in the country. But in the case of Mebrahtu Beraky and Saliho it was also a symbiotic relationship with each of them dependent on the other. They were good friends regardless of their religious differences. The friendship continued for many more years and was a fine example of the nature of trust between Christians and Muslims in the country.

Teame's stay in Adi Ghehad was coming to an end. With a new academic year approaching it was time for him to resume his schooling. He had experienced a different sort of education in the village. One that had brought him closer to the culture and traditions of his forbears which would always stay with him. Although he did not regret the year away from his schooling he was now looking forward to getting back to the classroom. Mebrahtu Beraky, too, was keen for his first born son to improve himself through education. He would have to make sure that he did not miss out again on registering Teame at Dekemhare Elementary School. This time he was determined not to make a mistake.

CHAPTER FOUR

Back to School

Registration did indeed go smoothly and Teame was safely enrolled. On arrival on the first day of term, now eleven years old, he found himself in a mixed ability class of forty-five pupils. Some of them were over seventeen and already married. There were about a dozen girls.

But he relished the thought of getting back to his lessons. Although the class was unusually large there was spirit of camaraderie among the pupils. It was largely thanks to their teacher Memher Hailemichael Ghebreyesus, who had so impressed Teame twelve months earlier. He was delighted that Memher Hailemichael was back teaching the Grade 4 pupils and continued to treat them with care and great empathy. For Teame, and others like him who were separated from their families, his approach was greatly appreciated.

Teame was by now living on his own in a room in Dekemhare and being cooked for by the aunt, Sanday Hagossa Berhe, who had already agreed to do so a year earlier before the debacle over the failure to register for the school in time. She was married to Aya Mohamed Nur Hagos, a Moslem – an unusual partnership at the time but a happy one. Meanwhile, as part of the earlier arrangements, Teame's father was paying for his room and food.

Memher Hailemichael was a wonderful teacher. Teame was to consider him one of the most outstanding educators to teach him during his school days. He taught all subjects at his class, Grade 4A, including Physical Education. And he had the skill, which not every teacher has, of getting onto the same wave length as his pupils despite their great numbers. They looked up to him and took heed of his advice. Lessons were challenging but fun.

Classroom rules, however, were strict. Memher Hailemichael had a reputation for being fair but firm and had a list of classroom rules on the wall behind his desk. That included keeping the room neat and tidy. Students guilty of lateness, or failing to submit homework on time, had to kneel in a corner of the classroom. But there was a democratic flavour to the rules. Pupils were first asked to consent to them before they were implemented – an interesting piece of psychology. It worked because there was little of the normal classroom misbehaviour.

Other teachers might need classroom survival strategies to cope with their boisterous students. But Memher Hailemichael managed to create a will to study among his pupils which meant he did not have to waste time maintaining order. Teame remembers they were all keen to study. It was a happy place for him and he felt privileged to be there among teachers like Hailemichael who he looked up to as role models, purveyors of knowledge and truth.

The school was not well resourced by Western standards. There were no purpose built laboratories, library or gymnasium. Educational outings and field trips were unheard of. But the students regarded the school and what they were learning as the key to new employment opportunities. A chance to better themselves and, as in Teame's case, rise higher in life. It was exactly what his father wanted and why he was making sacrifices for him to be there.

Their aspirations and the conviction that knowledge was wealth contributed to keeping the Grade 4A students concentrating on their studies and, on the advice of their teacher, staying away from the bars and tea shops in the town playing Sudanese music from across the border.

Life out of school in his rented room was going well. Teame's aunt cooked him delicious food – from the supplies provided by his father – and also washed the few clothes he had every week. He had a small electric lamp in his room when doing his homework and he also made himself tea.

Teame was working very hard and making rapid progress, achieving high marks. One of his happiest moments at the school was when, as a reward for his academic performance, Memher Hailemichael made him a class monitor. It gave him the status of a leader among his classmates.

At the Christmas break Teame went back to Adi Ghehad to spend it with his family. He hitched a lift in a lorry owned by an Italian transport contractor, Signor Borini who passed through the village on his way to the market at Quoatit where he made regular deliveries. Signor Borini had been befriended by Teame's father who spoke Italian. To make sure he did not miss the lorry leaving for Adi Ghehad in the early hours, Teame had spent part of the night sleeping on top of the lorry.

So, much to his family's surprise, he arrived at 5.00 am. He proudly told them of his new monitor status, awarded for his educational success. His hope was that the achievement would bring a reward from his father of a new pair of Bata shoes. To his disappointment, his father told him he did not have the money for new shoes. But he promised to find it if Teame continued to be top in his class. It was an incentive for Teame to work even harder next term.

Back at school, and in confident and relaxed mood, Teame, when he wasn't studying, started playing football and enjoyed reading old copies of Tigrigna newspapers. He found time to help some of his more educationally challenged classmates, coaching those who had to help their parents at home and lagged behind with their homework. It is worth noting that he was still only twelve years old. And although he could not have known it at the time his first attempt at tutoring was to become a lifetime passion.

One of those he felt sorry for was among the oldest and biggest in the class, a boy called Ghebrehiwet Ghebray. He came from one of the remotest villages in Eritrea – an area inhabited by the Irob tribe. He had a hair style different to the rest of the boys. His auntie, with whom he lived in Dekemhare, insisted he wore his hair in the style of their local area. Most other boys had a thin tuft of hair from front to back – similar to the Mohican style. But this boy had also had a tuft going the other way, from ear to ear. He became a figure of fun and was teased by his classmates who were all young urbanites.

Two other boys Teame sympathised with were Asta and Hageray both teenagers in forced marriages, a not uncommon practice. They called each other '*Arkay*', meaning 'my best man' or 'friend'. The two boys walked 8 kilometres each way from their home village to get to school and carried sticks for protection. They had chores at home and got behind with their homework. Teame empathised with their position but they, too, were both feared and ridiculed by other members of the class – mainly because they were married at such a young age.

One of them, though, went on to run a transport business owning several trucks, and Teame was to meet one of his sons many years later when he came to London to study as a private student paid for by his family. It proved a point to Teame that there is always hope for those who struggle at school, for whatever reason, and no-one is a lost cause.

At the end of the academic year in Grade 4 the pupils sat a General Examination, held throughout Eritrea, to qualify for the Middle School. It was a tough and competitive exam which thirty of the class passed. Teame was among them. To his delight their inspirational teacher Hailemichael Ghebreyesus was also promoted with them and would be teaching them at their new school.

The Middle School in Dekemhare was about half a kilometre away from the Elementary school. It had a wider curriculum which included Algebra, Geometry and Amharic – the major language in Ethiopia – although other lessons were in English. Eritrea, at that time, was considered by the Ethiopians to be a foreign country and an inferior one at that. The Amharic teacher, Ato Efrem Bekelle, who was an Ethiopian, was given an allowance in addition to his regular salary which was 250 Ethiopian dollars, compared to the 94 dollars a month paid to most of the Eritrean teachers. Inevitably this created some resentment among the Eritrean staff and even the pupils. The Ethiopian teachers wore suits and expensive shirts. The Eritrean staff could only afford the traditional khakis.

The headmaster of the Middle School, Memher Kinfe Tesfagaber, was another highly respected teacher. Teame remembered him as an exemplary and inspiring educator. He taught Algebra as well as carrying out his duties as headmaster. He helped the newcomers to the school to settle in quickly, and was an effective motivator of his students.

He could be firm when necessary, but had a great sense of humour. He did not take himself too seriously and was always prepared to admit a mistake if he made one. Most importantly he made his students feel valued. Later in life he invented Tigrigna shorthand which was adapted to be used in the rest of Ethiopia. He went on to work for a Catholic charity in Rome helping Eritrean and other refugees.

(Many years later when Teame gave the eulogy at the funeral of his wife Teblez's niece, Alem Berhane, in Norway, Memher Kinfe's daughter congratulated him for keeping up the Eritrean tradition in Europe. Teame, who had never met her before, was surprised and delighted to see her.)

Teame was still a class monitor, but now was sharing the responsibility with one of his closest competitors for classroom honours, an eighteen-year-old boy called Arefaine Berhane. Although they were rivals Arefaine became a supportive friend and protected him from some of his classmates – jealous of his success – who would call him 'The Teacher's Pet' and 'The Sick One' because at that time he suffered from bouts of malaria and a skin disease.

The jealousy largely arose after Teame was entrusted with the task of taking his teacher's bicycle back to his home in the evenings after school. He was proud to have the trust of the teacher and would wheel the bike through Dekemhare to the teacher's residence avoiding the temptation to ride it.

Teame's father, Beraky, had now opened a shop in Mai Aini to help with his son's living expenses. It meant that he could finally afford to buy Teame the much prized Bata shoes. There was a change of accommodation too. A good friend of Teame's, Mohamed Omer joined him in a new rented room in a better part of Dekemhare.

Mebrahtu Beraky would regularly travel on a bus from Mai Aini to Dekemhare to buy produce for his new shop. Every day he would also use the bus to send both Teame and Mohamed baskets of food prepared by their respective mothers. Sometimes the bus, which was old and unreliable, would break down. When that happened Teame and Mohamed had to go without their food, as the man who loaded the baggage on the bus would eat it. But they did not complain for fear he might refuse to take further food packages.

Teame had further support from his younger brother, Anghesom, who helped their father in the shop. With his father's approval Anghesom would send Teame a few coins, probably some pocket money or even taken from the shop till with tacit approval from his father. Teame would use the money to buy himself and Mohamed a cup of tea in one of the less fashionable tea shops in the town run by a Yemeni from Hadramouth and known as Ami Ali. Besides selling tea, Ami Ali sold stray hunting dogs formerly owned by Italians. One market day, he was bargaining to sell a dog to a group of villagers who asked how successful a hunter the dog was. He told them it caught so many wild animals like a hyena, fox or even a lion. Suspicious that such a small creature could kill a lion, the buyers all responded, 'Nefeset' – meaning 'impossible'. But, keeping a straight face, Ami Ali replied, 'Walahi nefeset keman tehayz,' meaning that the dog could even do the impossible. Not surprisingly his protestations proved to no avail.

It was a good life although not without its problems. Teame was struck by a strange rash on his thigh. It made walking difficult. A cream supplied by the local hospital had not proved effective. One day he was helping his father to take some merchandise from one of the Yemeni shops to the bus for Mai Aini. The owner of the shop noticed Teame's discomfort. He called out to Beraky that he had something important to say to him. He claimed that Teame was possessed by evil spirits – known as Akhezahu in Arabic. Shocked, Mebrahtu Beraky had a long conversation in Arabic with the Yemeni shop owner and missed his bus as a result. He sought the Yemini's advice on a cure.

The Yemeni urged him not to take Teame to hospital again but to buy a piece of pork and force him to eat it. Mebrahtu Beraky was sufficiently impressed to postpone his journey and take Teame to Bar Centrale, in the Italian shopping area in Dekemhare where pork products were on sale. He bought Teame a ham sandwich. This was despite the fact that he would have been well aware that it is forbidden for Coptic Christians to eat pork – although he did not tell Teame this.

Teame, who had never eaten pork, enjoyed the sandwich so much that he asked for, and was given, a second one. It might have been a coincidence, but Teame's rash mysteriously disappeared a few weeks later. He would never know if the pork had done the trick. But his father felt sufficiently guilty about forcing Teame to eat it that he confessed his sin to his priest.

His rash gone – with or without the help of the pork – life began to get better again for Teame. Along with his competitive friend Arefaine, he had done well enough in his end of term exams to be awarded a double promotion from Grade 5 to Grade 7 at the end of the first term. By the end of the third term Teame and Arefaine ended up among the top three students in Grade 7 and were awarded books as prizes.

Around June all those who successfully finished Grade 7 throughout Eritrea had to sit for a national exam to move up to Grade 8. Teame was again successful and to his delight was now eligible to continue his studies at the Scuola Vittorio Secondary School in Asmara, the capital city. It was a joyful and proud moment both for him and the family. The results were published in the Eritrean weekly newspaper.

His success in gaining a place at Scuola Vittorio brought a new challenge. His father was faced with finding him somewhere to stay. The only option was to ask another relative, an uncle of Teame's, to help. He was a head gardener in charge of a team of others working for an Italian in Asmara. He offered to let Teame stay with him and his family. Mebrahtu Beraky accepted gratefully, happy that his son could continue his education.

Scuola Vittorio secondary school had been established by the Italians in 1926 mainly to train the indigenous population as interpreters and administrators – although in the days of Mussolini it was run on Fascist principles.

When Teame joined the school in the mid 1950s things had changed. It was now accommodating students, who had successfully passed their Grade 7 and 8 exams, from all of the nine Eritrean provinces. It was a mix of different regional cultures and included

Christians and Muslims. Lessons were in English which provided a common denominator for the different mother tongues present among the students.

It was an impressive building by Eritrean standards. Walls of the school were covered in art deco paintings and there were still signs of the Italian influence. The front entrance bore the name 'Duco Da'osta', one of the titles of the original founder of the school, Vittorio Emanuele III.

For students like Teame, who had never travelled far from their home towns, sitting in their assigned desks alongside other students with different ethnic and cultural backgrounds as well as mother tongues, was an eye opener.

The school was about 4 kilometres from his uncle's house. Teame would walk there every day leaving at 6.40 am and not getting there until 8.30 am. Then he would make the two hour journey back in the evening. His auntie Sanday Hiwet, a kind and soft spoken lady, provided him with a packed lunch which he would eat in the school compound. Other children living nearer to the school would go home for lunch. But Teame would sit under the shade of a eucalyptus tree to eat his lunch. He said it gave him time to revise as well.

His mind was being stretched at his new school. Lessons included World and European history, geometry and algebra, and social and natural sciences. The curriculum was designed to prepare pupils for higher education or university.

The teachers were all Eritreans, both Christian and Muslim. One who Teame grew to respect, was Memher Amanuel Ghebrehiwet a tall man with an insatiable quest for knowledge who was largely self-educated. He was a caring and far-sighted teacher who encouraged his students to take their studies seriously. A much older man than the other teachers he was often refered to as an '*Abboy*' which means 'father', because of his age and wisdom. Another was Memher Abdu

Karar, who Teame remembers as gentle, caring and also far-sighted.

Teame was an able pupil and was appointed a class monitor by his class master, Memher Berhe Araya, a teacher with great artistic talent. His studies continued to do well and he ended up winning the top academic prize in his class.

After a year at the Scuola Vittorio, Teame, and all the other pupils who had successfully completed Grade 8 throughout Eritrea, took another exam to gain admission to a brand new secondary school in Asmara. It had just been built on the instructions of the Emperor and named after him – the Haile Selassie Secondary School. The striking looking modern building far outshone the Scuola Vittorio which perhaps was what the Emperor intended. Critics argued that it was a propaganda exercise designed to win hearts and minds in a region where he was not popular.

Glass fronted, it was built on a hill and could be seen from all over the city. The Emperor was rumoured to have paid for the building himself as a gift to the people of Eritrea. It had attractive dormitories, shiny toilets and shower rooms and the student boarders were given three course meals – far in excess of what Eritreans would normally eat. There had never been a school like it in the country. Just fifty-six out of two hundred and fifty students passed the exam to go there. Teame was one of them. The results were published in the government newspaper with Teame taking great pride in seeing his name among the other successful candidates.

He was overjoyed. It was an opportunity to complete his school studies, gain his School Certificate, and win a place at university. The future looked good. It was a boarding school which would solve Teame's problems over accommodation and those long walks to and from school.

So it was with a sense of pride and expectancy that Teame arrived at his new school accompanied by his Uncle Rezene Michael, the gardener, at the start of the new academic year in September. Along with the other 56 new students he was wearing a pair of newly tailored khaki long trousers and long sleeved coat. On his feet he wore a pair of locally crafted solid sandals. Other students wore the coveted Bata shoes which would have been too expensive for Teame's family to afford.

There was an impressive opening ceremony with bands playing and many guests including the student's families and local dignitaries. Teame was registered in Grade 9. He discovered a few days later that some students from Grades 10, 11 and 12 at Scuola Vittorio who had also gained places without having to pass an examination, had been put in Grade 10 at Haile Selassie Secondary School – much to their concern as they saw it as a 'demotion'. Teame never discovered why but suspected the authorities wanted to send out a signal that the Ethiopian curriculum was of a higher standard than the Eritrean version.

The school headmaster was a Canadian with an Ethiopian adminis-trator and the teaching staff made up of British, Indian, American and Ethiopian academics. Lessons each day started with an Ethiopian flag hoisting ceremony – something the Eritrean students disliked.

For his first year at the school Teame, and others who were hopeful of getting a place as boarders, attended as day students as the kitchen and dormitory facilities were still being completed. Teame was still living with his Uncle Rezene, who now owned a grocery store in the covered market – *Mercato Coperto* – in Asmara. He had asked Teame to run the store for him until he found a permanent employee. Anxious to help, although mindful of the extra pressures, Teame agreed.

So every morning, before going to school, Teame would get up at 5.00 am, open the shop, go to the market to buy vegetables, then leave some cash and the key with another employee at the shop before getting to school by 8.30 am. It was hard work and the only way he could get to school on time was by borrowing his uncle's shiny new Italian bike called a '*Torpado*'.

But at least he had the expectancy of a boarding place to look forward to. However, towards the end of the year, as they completed Grade 9, rumours began to circulate that the school authorities were assessing the economic background of students before accepting them as boarders. But there was an assurance that priority would be given to those who came from poor backgrounds.

Believing that with his background of coming from a family of poor farmers he was sure to qualify Teame completed his Grade 9. After the summer break he returned as a Grade 10 student the following September fully expecting to become a boarder.

But he was shocked to discover his dreams were to be shattered. To his dismay he was told that because he rode an expensive bike to school the admission committee had decided he must come from a rich family. This despite the evidence of Teame's shabby clothing that clearly signified his humble background.

Suddenly his joy and pride at winning a place at Haile Selassie Secondary School was replaced by sorrow and despair. The future that had looked so bright a year before was now ruined. And it was all because of a bicycle.

CHAPTER FIVE

Prison

Teame was distraught at being told he could not attend the new Haile Selassie Secondary School as a boarder. It had shattered his dreams of getting a university place. He was disillusioned by the injustice and felt deeply unhappy.

To him it seemed like his world had come to an end. Education was the most important thing in his life. Thanks largely to the encouragement from his father he had grown up believing that he would be liberated through education.

He continued at the school for another few months as a day pupil, but having to work in his uncle's shop – and getting up early to go to the market – was making it difficult to also get to school and do his studying. Lack of money was also an issue. On occasions some of the boarders took pity on Teame and others who had failed to gain boarding places, and gave them bread to eat. But finally, the strain became too much. He gave up his place.

It was a sad end to his hopes for the future. There were times when he even contemplated suicide. He could see no way out. He could not understand the degree of injustice. He was obviously from a poor background. His father was a traditional farmer who lived miles away. But he was being described, without any justification, as coming from a rich background simply because he had been seen riding a bike from his uncle's shop to the school.

He was convinced that corruption had been at play in the decision to turn him down. Although about 75% of boarders were from poor families, children of influential families did get places. Teame was convinced that some supporters of the Emperor were being granted favours for services rendered – as there were three or four students who came from Addis Ababa, the Ethiopian capital, who were accepted as boarders. One of them was the son of a high ranking Ethiopian official.

It was a time during the mid to late 1950s when the student protest movement in Eritrea was gaining momentum. Embittered by what had happened to him, Teame joined their ranks. The students were not just campaigning on educational issues, like the inequality of the boarding places, but also on the issue of Eritrean independence and the Federation with Ethiopia. There were demonstrations in the main street, Haile Selassie Avenue, with placards complaining about corruption. (The Avenue was re-named Queen Elizabeth II Avenue after Eritrean Liberation in 1991.)

The police arrested some students perceived as potential leaders, although Teame was not among them. But he joined others in demanding that the student leaders be released. They attacked some of the boarders at the Haile Selassie Secondary School during their lessons because they refused to join the demonstrators. Stones were thrown at the windows. It developed into a full blooded riot.

Teame, his anger rising, saw one boarder, a brilliant student, who he used to compete with for honours in the classroom. He hit him but cut his arm on glass as he jumped through a window to escape. The police, some of them mounted on horses were carrying sticks with which they whipped the students. Teame got a whipping but managed to evade capture – although others were caught and carted off to prison. Those who managed to run away made for the surrounding countryside where there were forests to hide. Some hid in the branches of the trees.

Teame and another student, a year younger, Eyob Ghebreyesus, (who much later in life became one of Eritrea's first naval captains) ran off into the countryside not wanting to go to their homes where the police could find them.

Searching for somewhere to hide away at night they came upon a menagerie owned by an Italian who would send exotic animals to zoos in Europe. There were pythons, hyenas, tigers and parrots all contained in cages. Teame and his friend settled down by the hyena cage. The nights were bitterly cold and they were frightened to be in such close proximity to some dangerous wild animals.

They spent two nights there, going into the outskirts of the city to hide away and catch up on sleep which had been difficult in the menagerie. Then they decided it was time to get in touch with other students who had been in the demonstration and hold another protest at the arrest of their leaders. They felt they could not let them down.

The next day they joined a large group of students in the city congregating outside the police station where the student leaders were held and demanding their release. But the police again moved in. This time Teame could not escape. He was arrested along with many others.

They were taken to a former Italian prison camp, The Carcelli on the road to Edaga Arbi. There they spent the night. Cold and hungry, many of the students cried out saying they were starving. Local residents, many of them supportive of the students, threw bread over the fence for them under the cover of darkness to avoid being seen by the guards.

The students, who had no blankets, broke down doors in the prison and burnt them to keep warm. But their action only antagonised the guards. They were kept there for another night.

Teame's uncle and other relatives of the imprisoned students were told that if the students apologised for their actions, confessed that they had committed crimes and promised not to repeat them, they would be released. If not they would be subject to more penalties. The relatives apologised on the students behalf and gave the undertakings being requested. The students, Teame among them refused to apologise. But they were released following pressure from locals who sympathised with their cause.

Two weeks later the student leaders had still not been released. There was another demonstration. They were arrested again. Teame and the others found themselves in the Caserma Mussolini jail right next door to the Ministry of Education in Asmara. It was full of blood sucking creatures and the walls were running with water. They were held in cells deep underground and their shouts could not be heard outside.

The next afternoon, after a sleepless and cold night, the imprisoned students were herded into lorries, stumbling out into the sunlight. The lorries set off. The students had no idea where they were going. They seemed to be driving towards the Ethiopian Army camp in Gejeret on the outskirts of Asmara. The lorries were travelling through the Settanta Otto area of the city with many people on the streets. The students, fearing for their lives if they got into the hands of the army, started shouting for help, some of them writing notes encouraging all students to boycott their schools and throwing them out at the passers-by.

The lorries suddenly changed direction. Instead of arriving at the Ethiopian Army barracks, the students found themselves at another prison – Adi Quala, 70 kilometres from Asmara. There appeared to have been a change of heart perhaps brought about by pressure from local residents who sympathised with the students. Whatever the reason, Teame was sure that if they had ended up in the Army camp none of them would have survived. The Ethiopian soldiers were angry at the damage to the Emperor's new school. They had a chilling motto, '*Embi yale besanja*,' which means, 'Whoever says no to Ethiopia put a bayonet in his stomach.'

The next day the students heard that all the secondary schools in Eritrea had stopped working in support of their plight. It was probably another reason why they were not handed over to the army.

Adi Quala was a high security prison with barbed wire topping the walls. It had been notorious during the British Military Administration for harbouring dangerous criminals. Many were still there. Murderers, thieves and gangsters some of them serving life sentences.

The students found themselves sleeping on the floor in a huge room with high walls. They were put under the charge of another prisoner, a man named Dundaz. He had been sentenced to life for killing an Eritrean. Dundaz was a seasoned criminal who had also once tried to kill the Colonel in charge of the prison during an escape attempt. He was fearsome looking with cross eyes and a scar on his face.

But the British Colonel, looking beyond the attempt on his life, must have been an astute judge of people. He realised that if Dundaz was given responsibility he could be useful in the prison. So he became a 'trusty' – a trusted prisoner – with the role of looking after other prisoners and keeping them in line. He lost no time in stamping his authority on the students. Armed with a large stick he would not hesitate to use it. Any infringement of the prison rules – quiet after lights out for instance – would bring him running. The prisoners had trouble working out who he was heading for because of his cross eyes.

Word of their imprisonment reached the surrounding population. They had been arrested without charge. Articles began to appear in the newspapers. Questions were being asked. The prison food was hardly edible but the students had to eat it or starve. But as word spread about their plight local residents and relatives of the students – mostly from Asmara – began to send them food. Teame's uncle was among them.

For Teame being incarcerated was better than spending the bitterly cold nights hiding in a menagerie with the smell of the hyenas in his nostrils and unable to sleep. Life in prison was, ironically, much safer. There was a structure to life. He and his fellow student prisoners went to bed at 9.00 pm and were woken up at 6.00 am to the sound of Dundaz making his rounds and calling anyone who got in his way a 'spoilt brat'.

On getting up they swept and tidied up the floor of the area where they slept, emptied and cleaned the containers used as toilets during the night, and washed themselves in time for breakfast which was a cup of tea and piece of bread. Then they would have to clean the entire compound. There were two 'aria' periods at 11.00 am and 4.00 pm when they were allowed out into the fresh air for exercise.

During the night, when they were supposed to be sleeping, they would talk to each other, keeping their voices down so as not to alert the guards. The political situation was a constant topic of conversation and Teame found himself becoming more politicised as he heard the experiences and views of others.

But, teenage boys being what they are, there were some rather more childish pranks going on too. Among them 'passing wind' competitions between four or more of the students, each demonstrating their prowess one after the other accompanied by laughter from the other prisoners and bringing Dundaz charging down the corridor brandishing his long whip and demanding, '*Silenzio*.'

Supplies of food for the prisoners was only allowed on Saturdays. Huge piles of it began to arrive, bread, pieces of chicken, *injera*, the traditional Eritrean food. The students would look forward to visiting times on a Saturday afternoon when their relatives and friends would arrive with food supplies all the way from Asmara. They would dream of those Saturday afternoons.

Much of it came in containers which had to be returned. There was so much of it that it was piled high to the ceiling. The students realised they would have to organise such a huge amount. They separated it into different types of food such as bread, chicken and sauce. The pile of food was so high that only the tallest students could reach up to put supplies on the top.

The food was enough to last them through the week. The imprisoned students, or 'rebels' as the Ethiopian government described them, were a mixture of Christians from various denominations as well as Muslims. They all ate the food provided despite their different dietary requirements under normal conditions.

The students set up a committee to organise distribution and included other prisoners and the warders in the food hand outs. It made the students' plight palatable in more ways than one. They organised their own entertainment with food as prizes for the best performers. An entertainment committee was established. Groups sang – they had no instruments – there were dance groups and plays. The winners got a *Panetone*, a type of Italian sweet bread, or a *himbasha*, a sweet-savoury flatbread.

Teame discovered a namesake among the prisoners, Teame Ghebreyohanes, the son of an adviser to the Emperor, Dejasmatch Ghebreyohanes Tesfamariam, an Eritrean who despite his closeness to the Emperor had the courage to speak out for Eritrean independence on several occasions.

The two Teames, supported by others, gave a demonstration of how 'street crooks' duped villagers with a card game called *jalamala* showing how they cheated them out of their money. They got a piece of *himbasha* for their efforts. But the best prize, chicken pieces and eggs, went to the winners of the 'passing wind' competition.

The students were in prison for three weeks. The authorities told them they would be released if they confessed that they had done wrong. They said they shouldn't have broken windows and attacked the boarders at the school. They had to promise to abide by the law in future. If they did so, they were told they would be able to go back to school at the beginning of the next academic year. Reluctantly they agreed to the conditions although most of them, Teame included, had no intention of carrying them out.

They went back to their homes. The Haile Selassie Secondary School had closed for the winter holidays. Teame held on to the hope that he could return there as a boarder despite being turned down unfairly. But when the school re-opened in September there was more disappointment. He was told once again that he could not become a boarder.

CHAPTER SIX

Tutoring – Teacher Training

The latest rebuff from the school authorities had left Teame in a quandary. He was desperate to continue his education and tried once more to persuade the authorities at Haile Selassie Secondary School to change their minds. But to no avail.

All the odds seemed stacked against him. He was still convinced that he had lost out to favouritism by the Ethiopian authorities towards their own supporters. He was desperate to continue his schooling and continued as a day boy in Grade 10. But it was becoming increasingly difficult to carry out his duties at his uncle's shop and still get to school and keep up his studies. He began to think of other options.

Along with his annoyance and frustration he felt guilty that if he could not get an education he was letting down his family who had invested so much in him. He was feeling very low. But alongside his feelings of despair was a steely determination to overcome the situation. He told himself he would not let this latest setback dictate his life.

If his attempts at continuing his schooling failed, he had to survive somehow. He thought about going back to his home village of Adi Ghehad to live with his parents. But that would have been an admission of defeat. If he was to leave school and stay in Asmara he would have to find some way of earning enough to live on. It was frightening predicament for a sixteen-year-old.

He could have got a job of some sort to earn enough to live on. But his aim was to continue his education in whatever way he could. He did not want to be beaten by those lucky students who had got boarding places and all that went with it. There were meals, dormitories and sports facilities plus good tutoring which would get them through their Matriculation and on to university.

Fate, though, was about to take a hand in the shape of an American serviceman and some careless driving. It so happened that the main entrance to the huge American base in the city, Kagnew Station, was a few hundred yards from the backyard of the Haile Sellasie School. One day, riding his Uncle's Italian bicycle – the one that had first caused his problem with the school authorities – he was hit by a car being driven by the American serviceman. The American, who had a local girl with him in the car, drove off without stopping.

Teame was left lying in the roadway with a seriously broken arm. The bike was badly damaged too. The injury would put Teame out of commission for weeks and there was also the question of his Uncle's expensive bike. Things looked bleak.

An Italian woman was his saviour. Her flat overlooked the junction where the accident had happened. Looking out of her window she saw the accident and called an ambulance which took Teame to hospital. But, in addition, she also testified to the police that the accident had been the American's fault. Most importantly she had taken the registration number of the American jeep.

She made a statement that the driver of the car had seemed drunk and was singing and laughing with the girl. They may have been playing music on a tape.

The Americans still had a large base in Asmara at that time. At first the officers in charge of the base denied that their GI was responsible for the accident. Teame's father and his uncles were angry and the family hired a lawyer. The GI at first denied being responsible then finally admitted he had caused the accident.

There was an out of court settlement. Some of it went on paying the legal fees. But Teame was left with about 200 dollars. It was a stroke of good luck, Teame called it God's Blessing. And it enabled him to start on a new adventure.

Backed by the compensation money he decided the answer to his search for the next move – having given up hope of continuing his schooling – was to become a tutor. He would teach English, Tigrigna and mathematics. It was a bold move for one so young – especially as he was likely to be teaching people much older than him. In fact he was still in short trousers at the time.

His first student was Mohamed, his old school friend from Dekemhare. He was now a police clerk but if he wanted to improve himself and become an officer he had to improve his English. Teame got hold of some Essential English books printed in Nairobi and began his first lessons as a tutor. His tuition proved fruitful and four of Mohamed's colleagues also joined Teame's tutorials.

(Mohamed's career blossomed and he eventually went on to become a Colonel. Teame kept in touch with Mohamed for many years. He died in Ethiopia in January 2016 and Teame, according to the local custom, gave money for feeding the poor which was distributed at the funeral.)

Word quickly got round about Teame's tutoring and, despite his lack of years, there was no shortage of people wanting help with their English. He did his tutoring in people's homes or in a quiet corner of a tea shop. Another of his pupils, Aregay Ghebresellasie, ten years older than Teame, was a cleaner in a bank. His boss encouraged him to study. He told him if he learnt to read and write he could be a postman within the bank. It would represent a big jump for him in the Eritrean workplace. Teame taught him to read and write in both English and Tigrigna. He got his promotion and a scooter to go with it.

Teame realised he enjoyed teaching. It would not have been his first choice career. He had aspirations of becoming a doctor like many of those more fortunate students who had been able to continue their education. But he found he had an aptitude for imparting knowledge to others and helping them to learn. He was turning out to be a natural teacher. Although he did not realise it at the time his actions, which started out merely to provide himself with a living, were to prove life-affirming.

The level of his tutoring would depend on what was required. Some needed basic English lessons, others more advanced English. Teame also taught mathematics – a favourite subject of his – to a few of his charges including Mohamed.

There was little money to be made. Those he tutored would often pay him by buying him a delicious Shehan Ful which was an Arab breakfast popular in Eritrea comprising of a plate of groundnuts with butter and yoghurt. Other times there would be a sandwich and a cup of tea. But one man he tutored, who worked in a bank, would give him the loose change in his pocket. Later he moved out of the tea shop and hired a small room when his tutoring customers would pay him five Ethiopian birr (the equivalent of a few pence) to cover the rent and electricity. So Teame's costs were covered but he made little money for himself.

He was managing to survive through living with relatives – he had by this time moved from the home of the uncle with the shop. So he was getting a bed for the night, and enough to eat by living with another uncle in Asmara, Ghebremichael Besserat a highly respected journalist, who was editor of the government newspaper. In spare moments he would help his uncle's children with their homework.

Then he found another way of making a living using his growing skills as a tutor. He started teaching English classes in the evening at a small school in the compound of St Mary's church in the city. This represented a major increase in his income. For the first time in his life he had money to spend.

He took the opportunity very seriously. For his evening class students, again men much older than him, he wore long trousers and shoes. Young men like him would often wear just sandals or, in some cases, no shoes at all.

His new role came with its challenges. One of them was his height. He was so lacking in inches that he could not reach the top of the blackboard and had to stand on a stool. But it did not stop him doing an effective job. He would get to the classroom early and write up his lessons on the blackboard. The school did not have sufficient text-books or duplicators to be able to ensure everyone had hard copies of the lessons. So Teame's efforts in placing it all on the blackboard in advance was much appreciated by the class participants. His classes became very popular.

As a result of the work in evening classes, and because of the support and encouragement of his uncle Ghebremichael and his auntie Azieb, Teame was able to start paying back his family for the sacrifices they had made for him.

This financial help for his family was especially useful when Eritrea was hit by a severe plague of locusts. Farmers lost their harvest and there was famine in the villages including the area where his family now lived. His father was so desperate to feed the family that he took the decision to go to another part of Eritrea near the Red Sea to cultivate crops, especially maize, during the rainy season in that part of the country. He walked for four days to get there. Teame's mother went to stay with a brother taking the rest of the family, and a few goats and cows for milking, with her.

Teame got news of their plight from another uncle, his father's eldest brother, Uncle Dumtsu Ghide. He sent a message via a villager who came to Asmara. The family were facing starvation and Teame's father had not been heard of for weeks. When he finally did come back, his attempts to find food for the family had not been a great success. Distressed at the news, as the eldest in the family Teame knew he had an obligation to do something.

He bought two quintals (200 kilograms) of millet and maize, a staple diet in Eritrea, and asked a bus driver – the same driver of the old bus on the route to Mai Aini and an old friend of his father – to take it back to the family. The man, who hadn't seen Teame for some months, expressed surprise at how grown up he had become. Teame explained the desperate situation his family were in and the driver agreed to take the food to them. Right through the summer he continued the food supplies sending enough to feed the whole family which included his parents, eight of his siblings and other relatives.

Tutoring and evening classes was not, however, Teame's only commitment. Determined to gain the Certificate of Education, which he had been denied by the refusal to grant him a place at the Haile Sellasie School, he had also started to study for that exam in his spare time. The Oxford School Leaving Certificate was an essential qualification to proceed to higher education. So he started buying or borrowing the textbooks he needed from the students of Comboni College in Asmara who were studying for the same exam, and crammed in the extra studies in spare moments during the day.

As the time for the exam approached he realised that he did not have enough money for the fee which had to be paid before he would be allowed to sit. He went to another one of his uncles, Fesehazion Ghebremedhin, who had a good job with a French company working in Asmara and, with some embarrassment, explained his predicament. He felt ashamed that he had to ask for help but had no other option.

His uncle, a much taller man than Teame although not that much older, was surprised that he was taking the exam because, as he explained, he was also taking it. But he said that he would be happy to help Teame with the exam fee. Teame thanked him but made it clear did not expect a gift and would only accept if it was a loan.

So Teame got the money he needed and sat the exam shortly afterwards. And, to his delight, he heard a few months later that he had passed. It was a triumph for his determination not to be beaten.

And life for Teame was about to take another new and career-changing turn. He spotted an advertisement in the Asmara weekly newspaper for applications to study at a Teacher Training College in the city. The college, set up by the British, was tiny. Not much bigger than a medium sized house with a small playground at the back.

Despite his success at tutoring and as an evening class teacher he had still seen this as a stop-gap to earn enough to survive. His ambition had been to become a doctor like those from more fortunate backgrounds would surely become.

But now Teame came to the conclusion that teaching really was his great passion. He had finally given up his ambition to become a doctor. So he took the plunge and applied to join the ranks of trainee teachers. However, there was strong competition for places. He was one of over three hundred people who applied and he had little confidence that he would be successful. There would be just twenty-four places available.

First he sat a stiff examination. Having completed it he waited anxiously for results. As he sat in a tea shop an excited friend of his rushed in waving a copy of the government newspaper which had published the names of the lucky candidates who had won places. He was shouting that Teame's name was on the list. A delighted Teame leapt into the air with joy. It was a wonderful moment for him. And to his further delight he was not only among the twenty-four successful candidates but also had the fourth highest grades. Teame felt that at last he was getting some good fortune after all the bad luck he had experienced.

It was not quite the end of the story because there was still a rigorous medical examination at the government hospital in the city. But that, to his relief, proved a formality and all twenty-four of the successful candidates – which included just one woman – were accepted. Teame's new life as a teacher was about to begin.

In the autumn of 1959 he started his teacher training. He found his fellow students a highly competitive bunch. They were all high achievers. Teame and his co-trainees were introduced to subjects like pedagogy – the art of teaching – psychology, classroom management, assessing and preparing questions for exams. He relished every minute of it. There was also teaching practice which took up a third of the course and took the students in to local schools for first hand experience. Teame found himself assigned to one of Eritrea's largest elementary schools for girls, situated between Gheza Kenisha and Enda Mariam. He also found himself appointed leader of the nine or so trainees assigned there. He was charged with ensuring their attendance, appearance and behaviour was up to scratch and also to liaise between the college and the school when issues that needed dealing with arose.

There was another feather in his cap too. He became class monitor – getting the position over the heads of some of his most competitive colleagues much to his delight.

It was meant to be a two-year course but the College, under the wise leadership of Memher Ghebrelul Woldetsion, condensed it to a year and half. At the end of the course there was another accolade for Teame. He graduated as the best Student-Teacher of the year.

It meant he had to make a valedictory speech at the graduation ceremony attended by the head of the Eritrean government at the time, Dej Asfaha Woldemichael. Although an Eritrean he was a trusted right hand man of the Emperor who publicly supported annexation. A big man, well over 6 foot with a huge neck, he was much feared because of his links with the Emperor but also respected for his eloquence and erudition.

The Graduation Ceremony, which took place inside the auditorium of the Teacher Training College, was a great and unique occasion in several ways. It was unique in that the graduands chose to wear their respective regional costumes instead of the more usual suit and tie. The wearing of the traditional costume required some skill in keeping the 'netsela' shawl in place. Teame was aided by his aunt Woizero Azieb Ghebrehiwet, who attended the ceremony as a guest. She helped him and some of the other male students, to pin the netsela correctly.

In his speech Teame likened the role of a teacher as being like a farmer, preparing the land and the crops then harvesting the results. His words must have resonated with the great man because he repeated them when he gave his own address.

The then Secretary of Education in Eritrea, Ato Asfaha Kahsay had promised, by way of motivation, that the first three trainees in the final examination would be offered teaching posts in Asmara. Teame had come second so would be eligible for one of the much sought after jobs in the capital. Others lower down the list would be sent out to less popular posting in towns elsewhere in the country.

So Teame was looking forward to staying in Asmara. There were many more opportunities there. But despite the Minister's promise it was not to be. He was told he was going back to Dekemhare where he had been a pupil at elementary and Middle School. It was a big disappointment but he had no option but to comply.

CHAPTER SEVEN

Teaching

Teame quickly came to terms with not getting a promised teaching post in Asmara with all the opportunities it presented. Unlike his experience of losing out on a place at a boarding school, he did not think there was corruption or favouritism involved.

The promise might have been a cynical way of encouraging them to work hard at their studies. But the fact was there were already plenty of teachers in Asmara whilst in the provinces there was a shortage. He considered he had a duty to go outside the capital city for his first teaching job.

So Teame found himself at his old school in Dekemhare – a place of which he had many fond memories. He was in a positive frame of mind believing then – and still believes fifty years later – that education is the cornerstone upon which a nation develops. As requested, he reported to the office of Grazmach Kidane Woldeselassie, the Provincial Education Officer of Akeleguzay, one of the nine provinces of Eritrea. He was told that appointments for the newly graduated teachers were still being finalised. In the meantime he was asked to take a class at the elementary school in the town which he had attended himself as a schoolboy twelve years earlier.

So he was full of enthusiasm and eager to teach as he returned to the school this time as a teacher. He was given Grade 2 pupils to teach,

most of them aged 7 or 8. There were fifty pupils in his class and
Teame taught them all the subjects – arithmetic, basic science, English,
general knowledge and health and cleanliness. He taught in one of the
Eritrean mother tongues, Tigrigna.

Initially Teame wanted to set up home in the town with Zehaye, his
childhood friend from his days at Dekemhare, who had also trained
to be a teacher at the same college. At the teacher training college
Teame had always acted like an older brother to his friend, who liked
the good life, was a good dancer and enjoyed the social round. Teame
did his best to keep him away from bad influences. But, the idea of
sharing a home with Zehaye did not work out as his parents still
lived in Dekemhare and he was living with them. So Teame found
temporary lodgings elsewhere.

But their time in Dekemhare was about to end prematurely. After
four weeks Teame was called by Graz Kidane to be told that he was
being posted to another school at Adi Keyh, a town 110 kilometres
from Asmara. Teame was annoyed, not only that he was being
transferred so soon after settling in at Dekemhare, but he had also
just set up the flat, paid a deposit and obtained furniture.

Graz Kidane was polite and understanding. He said he understood
Teame's feelings and was proud to have him working in the province.
But he had a difficulty. Sending newly graduated teachers to the large
towns caused problems with older, more experienced teachers who
had served their time in the villages. Although he could not change
the decision to send Teame to Adi Keyh he promised that he would
be given a free bus ticket and that his furniture would be transported
in a government vehicle to his new base.

But Zehaye's position was also under scrutiny. Zehaye was a
Catholic and so was the Provincial Education Officer. He was worried
that if he allowed Zehaye to stay in Dekemhare it would look like
favouritism to a fellow Catholic. There were rumours circulating that

he might be allowed to stay in Dekemhare with his parents. The outcome was that Zehaye was posted to Adi Keyh as well.

Zehaye was furious and it coloured his relationship with Teame for a while. But they sorted out their differences, accepted the inevitable, and moved together to their new posting where they again set up home together.

They found a house with a compound. Zehaye found a maid, a girl from Asmara, who cleaned the house, cooked and did their washing. She was a good cook, having cooked for an Italian family in Asmara. The two friends paid her well to encourage her to come so far from Asmara to work for them.

So life at the Adi Keyh Elementary School began. Teame was given responsibility for Grade 2 and Grade 4 pupils with a minimum of sixty to sixty-five pupils in each class. He taught the young pupils, aged seven or eight, in the mornings, and the older Grade 4 pupils in the afternoons.

The two new teachers were well paid by Eritrean standards getting 94 Ethiopian dollars a month. It was much more than the 74 dollars a month some other teachers were getting because of the higher qualifications Teame and Zehaye had. But Teame recognised that there was an element of unfairness in the pay difference. The situation was later remedied.

The director of the school was a much older man, in his sixties, Memher Eyob Zewde. He had been in education for many years and was waiting for his retirement. So to have an enthusiastic Teame, with all his fresh ideas, constantly knocking on his door must have been a shock to the system.

But Teame, in his first teaching job, was developing the ideas and the principles which would shape his thinking in the years ahead. He was beginning to see the importance of the school environment on the children and the need to involve them in the learning process.

His teaching was developing as he started utilising different approaches. He would not just teach his pupils by talking to them to pass on knowledge – important as this was – he would also help them to learn by getting them to sing what they were learning which helped it to stick in their minds. He would organise field trips so that they could learn by discovering for themselves what they saw and found.

Teame recognised the importance of a clean and well organised learning environment and made sure his classroom fulfilled his own high standards. Sometimes the children would be enlisted in cleaning duties which he considered was part of their education.

It quickly became clear to him that there was a need to involve parents in the education of their children – keeping them informed on their children's progress and encouraging them to ensure their offsprings did their homework.

He also began to understand what he considered an important lesson about the teaching-learning process. Learning, he realised, was not just about knowing. It was also about the learner discovering about themselves, who they were and what they wanted to be. It was, for Teame, the beginning of a conviction that was to become a tenet of his teaching career – that the welfare of the student is the precursor of good learning.

It was also becoming clear to him that pupils learn better when they are actively engaged and motivated which, he believed gave them self-esteem. He was learning that developing a positive relationship between the teacher and their pupils, as well as between the pupils themselves, enhanced their learning.

And he also accepted that he was not infallible. He knew he could make mistakes and was determined to learn from them. But knowing that he had a passion for teaching he wanted to improve both his knowledge and his ability to help his pupils achieve their full potential. There was no doubt in his mind now that teaching was his life calling.

As he considered his life as a teacher he would sometimes go to a church hidden away in the countryside to quietly reflect and seek inspiration for his future. Such solitude, particularly during the weekends, gave him the opportunity to avoid the temptations of the bars and billiard halls in the town where he could easily have wasted his time. So, he would instead sit quietly in the small church of Abune Teklehaimanot. It would clear his mind and ensure he could keep his vow to himself that he would not be left behind by those lucky students who got boarding places at the Haile Selassie Secondary School and were assured of university places.

Teame had not failed to notice that the floors in the classrooms were very dusty. With sixty children running around it was hardly surprising. But he started a regime to keep the dust at bay. On a rota basis children would drop water on the dust and sweep it up. Inevitably, though, the brushes would wear out. Teame persuaded the director to provide new brooms which quickly wore out resulting in another request.

Chalk for the blackboards was also strictly rationed, so were dusters. Teachers were asked to make them last as long as they could. There were few textbooks – if pupils were lucky they would share one book between four of them. Few would have books to read at home either. So everything they learned had to be written on the blackboard and copied into the exercise books. Some of the keener pupils would come into the classroom at breaks and continue copying from the blackboard.

The director was not pleased with Teame's constant demands for new school resources. There was also a feeling among some of the other staff members that Teame was playing the role of 'the new broom that sweeps clean'. But irrespective of the negative atmosphere Teame continued with his planned operation to keep the children engaged and active. Just telling them what to do was not enough.

Memher Eyob continued to be suspicious of Teame's ideas and did not subscribe to his philosophy of child centred education. Teame understood his point of view. The Director, by virtue of his age and training, belonged to the old school of thought. His was a philosophy that put the focus not on the learner but on the subject matter. It was a philosophy which emphasised the role of the teacher as the fountain of knowledge and one where discipline, including corporal punishment, was deemed necessary.

Teame took a different view, one which he considered more enlightened, which prioritised student welfare, and encouraged them to be part of the learning process by helping themselves rather than being empty vessels waiting to be filled.

But the two respected each other. The director began to see the results of Teame's work with the children. Their behaviour changed for the better. Attendance and cleanliness improved. Teame had a pair of scissors and regularly checked that finger nails were not too long or dirty. He encouraged clean clothes, too, however old they were or how many holes they had in them. Homework had to be done on time. He was firm but rarely used corporal punishment.

The director became convinced of the effectiveness of Teame's methods when, one Saturday morning, he found Teame in the school garden cultivating flowers and vegetables. He had encouraged some of the children to help. They were singing a song in Tigrigna about learning. It was one of Teame's favourite songs which began:

> *Nab temherti nab temherti*
> *Nsa eya Abay habti*
> *Dleyuwa Ntemherti mealti mis leiti.*

Translated into English it would be:

> Let us march forward towards education
> Let us search for it day and night
> As it is the greatest wealth on earth.

Teame and the director became good friends. He told him: 'Young man, you are full of energy and we are happy to have you in our school.' He added: 'You can take as many brooms and coloured chalks as you need.'

It was coming up to the national examinations when Teame's Grade 4 pupils would sit to win a place in the Middle School. The director was keen to see them do well. The school had not done so in the past. So Teame felt a heavy responsibility to get his sixty pupils through the exam.

But one of them was a particular problem. His name was Beyene. He disrupted other pupils in the classroom, rarely turned up when on the cleaning rota and was often given ten minute penalties kneeling in the corner for not doing his homework. Although uncomfortable with the practice, it was common in schools at that time and Teame did not want to challenge it in only his first year as a teacher.

Eventually Teame discovered something about his home background. The boy was hyperactive, slightly dyslexic and out of control as there was little peace with his parents. He was very unhappy. But gradually Teame was able to win his confidence. He wondered whether some responsibility would bring out the best in him and made him captain of the football team. His attitude changed. He became a less disruptive scholar. Teame was delighted to meet him thirty years later to discover he had become a policeman.

Keen to give his pupils every chance of getting through the Middle School exam Teame would sometimes give them extra lessons at weekends. And as part of his desire to provide the children with other interests Teame arranged a field trip to a local archeological site at Quohaito about 11 kilometres from the school. He had to get the parents permission and the headmaster also gave his blessing. They took their lunch with them and the forty children, with Teame the only teacher supervising them, set off to walk to the site.

The children made drawings and scrambled around the ruins. Teame considered expeditions like this were instructive, allowing the children to make their own investigations and write about them. But it was a hot day. Some of the children cut their feet on the rocky ground. There were both girls and boys on the expedition who needed constant supervision. Teame began to realise that taking a party that large under the supervision of just one teacher, was not a good idea.

His fears were proved well founded when some of the children on their way home began jumping into the small lake to cool themselves down on such a hot day. There could easily have been an accident, perhaps even a drowning. It was with some relief that Teame managed to get them all safely home.

It was a valuable lesson. He knew he had been lucky that nothing untoward had happened. His decision to go on his own was foolish. There were no repercussions. But he vowed to be more sensitive to the safety of those in his charge in future.

CHAPTER EIGHT

Teaching Teachers

As his first year of teaching neared its end a new opportunity emerged for Teame. The Ministry of Education had been granted support from a US aid project to improve the academic level of teachers in middle schools. It was to include the schools in the province where Teame was teaching.

Teame was an elementary school teacher with little experience. But when he saw an advertisement in a local newspaper seeking candidates for the scheme, he was interested. The Americans, to cut costs, had decided to use local teachers rather than bring in others from outside the area. Teame, not without some trepidation, decided to apply. He felt he had nothing to lose.

Along with many others he was given a test designed by the US Aid Office and supervised by some officials at the Ministry in Asmara. Soon afterwards he heard that he had been selected. He was instructed to help middle school teachers improve their algebra, a subject he had excelled at and always enjoyed. So, despite his comparative youth – he was in his early twenties – he was well qualified to teach the subject.

But he was still an elementary school teacher who was being asked to teach middle school teachers most of whom would be both older and more experienced in the classroom than him. It was a big challenge.

He arrived at his first evening class at Adi Keyh Middle School to be met by a disgruntled group of teachers. They did not like the idea of being taught by someone they considered their inferior. Some shouted: 'He is only an elementary school teacher. What is he doing teaching us?'

Teame was hurt by their attitude. His ability to teach them was being questioned. But he understood their feelings and anxieties. They were his senior in age and had more experience in the classroom.

The headmaster of the school, Memher Araya Woldeghebriel, called the staff together and told them their salaries would not rise unless they upgraded their qualifications. This year it was algebra, next year it could be another subject. They had to take the Ministry instructions seriously, he told them.

There were heated discussions among the teachers. Pride may have been at play at the thought of being taught by one so young, a teacher at the elementary school in the town. But others said: 'Give him a chance.' In the end a majority put their hands up and said, yes, they would join the evening class.

So Teame started teaching them. The lessons were held at the Middle School. It would have been an affront to dignity if the teachers had been asked to attend classes at Teame's elementary school.

At first only about twelve turned up. Soon others, who had initially opposed the idea, changed their minds and joined them. The sessions went well. Teame tried to make his teaching style lively and interesting. The teachers, many of them in their fifties and sixties, began to enjoy the sessions. It was hard work for Teame who had already spent the day teaching at the elementary school.

His charges knew their algebra but were rusty since their college days many years previously. They worked hard though. Teame set them homework, collected and marked it. There were not enough text-books so Teame asked the US aid office in Asmara to lend some. They

also duplicated books in their office. It meant the teachers had
something to study at home.

He became friends with some of the teachers. One in particular was
Ustaz Taher Mohamed Nur. He had been one of the group who had
been supportive of Teame and had helped change the minds of the
doubters. The two of them would go for walks together and he invited
Teame to his home for tea. He produced a spiced tea, traditional in
Muslim homes, which Teame found delicious. Their friendship was
to continue long after they both left the town.

The lessons proved a success. Teame felt he had been helped because
the teachers, educators themselves, had quickly grasped what he was
trying to convey. He didn't have to spend time explaining things in
detail as he would for younger pupils. All the teachers, apart from one
who withdrew through illness, were upgraded and received higher
salaries. Many of them privately thanked Teame for helping them.

Teame was to take further classes with the Middle school teachers
in the next academic year as well as continuing to teach at the
Elementary school in Adi Keyh. But he had seen another opportunity
– this time to fulfil his dream to go to university. Spending the
Christmas vacation in Asmara with his uncle, Ghebremicael Besserat
and his family – who had embraced him as their own – he spotted a
notice in the weekly newspaper requesting applications for candidates
with the right qualifications to win places at the American University
in Beirut.

It was a chance to achieve his long held ambition. He had held it
ever since losing the opportunity to advance his education at the Haile
Sellasie boarding school in Asmara. The bitterness and disappointment of that experience was still with him. But he had his Oxford
School Leaving Certificate, an essential qualification for university
entrance which he had gained in Asmara whilst also doing his tutoring.
He could now make use of it and knew he must apply.

There was immense interest and therefore strong competition. Four hundred others had applied. Teame was surprised to see so many when he arrived to take the first examination in Asmara. Many of them were civil servants as well as teachers like him. About a hundred of them passed the first hurdle. Teame was relieved to be among them. But the tests continued. The applicants were never told how many places were available at Beirut – a strategy which allowed the powers-that-be to cut the numbers down as and when necessary.

The one hundred candidates still in the running had to go through another examination to whittle the numbers down still further. They were questioned on their general knowledge, their life history, as well as academic subjects. Teame got the impression they wanted to know about the person as well as their abilities. In all the written exams and tests the papers arrived in sealed envelopes from either the American University in Beirut or the US Aid Office. Other tests were to follow.

Teame was back teaching in the Elementary school by this time and would get regular phone calls requesting him go to Asmara for yet another test. The process went on for months. It was very disruptive of Teame's teaching with so many enforced absences. Fortunately the calls usually came towards the end of the week so that the children's lessons did not suffer too much. He had to travel by bus the 110 kilometres to Asmara for each test.

Receiving the calls was quite a drama. There was no phone in the school so the calls went through to the Senior District Officer in the town, Kegnazmatch Hailemariam Debenna. A messenger would arrive at the school on his bicycle. Teame would hear a knock on the classroom door and be told about the latest call. The SDO had got used to them by now and called Teame 'that young teacher'. The school was half a mile away from the SDO's office so he would have to run there while the line was kept open for him to arrive. The only way he would know if he had passed the latest test was when he was called in for another one. It was torture.

Eventually Teame got yet another phone call. To his delight and relief, he was told he had been selected. He was just one of four candidates. One of them dropped out because he was ill – Teame suspected he had succumbed to the pressures of all the testing.

But then the number of places was reduced to two without explanation, although all the remaining three were encouraged to apply for their passports. To his immense relief Teame was told he was one of the lucky two. The other turned out to be a young man called Kidane-mariam Tesfay who Teame had met in Asmara. He had attended the Comboni Catholic School, one of the best secondary schools in Eritrea. Teame had bought textbooks from him while studying for his Oxford Certificate as a private candidate. At that time Kidane had just finished his secondary education and did not have a job. But Teame recognised him as a brilliant scholar with a sharp and intelligent mind.

Reflecting on the numbers being drastically reduced to just two, Teame thought that the pressure on places, and the constant cutting down of numbers, had been political. The Ethiopian authorities, he felt, had wanted to restrict the number of scholarship winning students from Eritrea in order to offer more places to Amharic speaking Ethiopians.

Eritrea was still part of the UN-backed Ethiopian Federation at the time but the way the selection process had been handled seemed to illustrate the growing animosity between the two. The following year the Emperor was to annex Eritrea sparking off the long and bloody struggle for Eritrean liberation.

Things now happened very quickly. Teame resigned from his job at the Elementary School. He was able to finish preparing his pupils for the examination to the Middle School and was later delighted to hear that 90% of them passed. It was a record performance at the school.

He and Kidane had to go through health checks and then they were given passports. They received generous government grants of 100 dollars a month for their four year degree course at the American University.

The two arrived at Asmara Airport for the flight to Beirut. Teame was excited but also a little apprehensive. He had never flown before and wasn't even sure where Beirut was. His parents, uncle and other relatives came to see him off. No-one from their village had ever been on a plane. News had spread fast of his success in gaining the place at the American University which, to many Eritreans, would have been seen as somewhere at the end of the earth. It was a source of great pride to the family.

Teame's mother was terrified for him. She had never been near an aeroplane before or to an airport. She worried that she would never see her oldest son again. Teame's father had to restrain her from holding on to her oldest son. Kidane's parents were there too. He, like Teame, had never been abroad before. Kidane's mother asked Teame, who was older than her son, to look after him. This request dismayed Teame's aunt, Azieb, whose home he had lived in. She was like a second mother to him. Azieb thought it was putting too much responsibility on him. But Teame agreed to keep an eye on Kidane.

Tearful farewells completed, the plane took off. The next day, after an overnight stop in Cairo, they landed at Beirut. It was a new land and a new experience. For Teame his dream had come true. He was finally going to University.

CHAPTER NINE

Beirut

Disembarking at Beirut was a revelation for the two Eritreans. The airport was huge, one of the biggest in the Middle East at that time. Terminal buildings were many storeys high, there were shops selling expensive goods. Travellers were arriving from all over the world. They had never seen anything like it.

Negotiating their way through the huge arrival hall with their luggage they were, to their relief, met by a member of the university staff. Driving through the streets of Beirut for the first time they marvelled at the expensive cars and the displays of wealth in the shops and restaurants.

They were dropped off at the gates of the University in Hamra Street, one of the main thoroughfares in Beirut and an area inhabited mostly by rich Lebanese and the international community. The ravages of the Lebanese civil war, which destroyed much of the city, was still some years away.

But now they were on their own. There were security gates with buttons to press for entry. The two new arrivals had never seen anything like it and were baffled as to what to do next. A security guard came to their aid. Noticing their uncertainty, and realising they were new students, he opened the door for them. Carrying their luggage they entered the large entrance hall.

To them it was an awe inspiring sight. The compound was beautifully maintained. There was a huge Cyprus tree in the middle and well maintained flower beds. It was yet another new sight for them to take in.

They had been told to report to the admissions office but it was closed. Standing uncertainly in the hall they were spotted by a fellow Eritrean studying at the university. To their delight he addressed them in their native Tigrigna and offered to buy them breakfast. Their new friend was Yemanu Tesfayohannes, the son of Dejasmach Tesfayohannes Berhe, a Minister who later on became Deputy Governor of Eritrea.

He took them to the cafeteria which was another eye opener for the newcomers. They were astonished to see the array of food, some of it unheard of in their native Eritrea. There was bacon – the food that Teame's father had to confess his sins for after making his son eat it – eggs, yoghurts, all kinds of fruits and croissants as well as cereals including corn flakes, all new to them. A feast for the eyes as well as the stomach.

They were also surprised at the many nationalities among the students eating in the cafeteria. There were Americans, British, French, Greeks, Latin Americans and many Iranians – this was when America had friendly relations with the Shah of Iran. It was a huge mix of nationalities, both men and women. There were many different languages being spoken.

Seeing men and women happily socialising together was also new to Teame. Back in Eritrea it would not be part of the culture. He found himself having to turn his gaze away from the mini skirts the girls were wearing. He was having his first exposure to Western culture.

They were taken up to the rooms they had been allocated, in Penrose House, named after one of the founding fathers of the university. It was another revelation. He had an individual room, with a study and bathroom. Well furnished, beautiful lampshades, a comfortable mattress on the bed and a desk and shelves for books and paperwork. The building, six storeys high, had lifts which only the finest building in Eritrea would have had installed. Teame still remembered it vividly years later.

Everything was a new experience. But Teame was determined to embrace it and learn everything he could. One thing that counted in his favour was his good command of English which, being an American University, was the language used for lectures. Some of the other foreign students, particularly the Iranians, struggled with their English and had to have extra classes.

As he settled into his new surroundings Teame's life at the university began in earnest. In those days there was no Education degree course. It was a much broader curriculum that included education as well as modules on psychology, sociology, linguistics and philosophy.

His Professor in Philosophy of Education was Habib Kurani, a Lebanese. Teame found him a quiet and humble man but he was very influential in his field. He enjoyed the professor's lectures which covered every major philosopher from Socrates, Maria Montesorri, the great Italian educational philosopher, French philosopher Jean-Jacques Rousseau to Bertrand Russell.

Professor Kurani explored the idea, brought out by many educational philosophers, that children could participate in the learning process rather than be just passive receptacles of information. This resonated with Teame. He had already began to realise from his experience involving his elementary school pupils in activities, that participation was an important part of the learning and teaching process.

Encouraged by Professor Kurani, Teame began to understand how education was an ongoing process for both teachers and learners. Learning never stops. But it can be vicarious too. You learn from personal experience. He was absorbing all these ideas like a sponge.

He looked upon Professor Kurani as his philosopher father. His teaching, he thought, was philosophy with legs. He considered it was putting ideas into practice in terms of modern life. Throughout his academic career he continued to develop the practice of encouraging students to be pro-active in the learning process and to learn through experience. He stayed in touch with Professor Kurani after leaving the University only to lose contact after the Lebanese crisis and the civil war in 1967-68.

Education psychology was the other core subject. He studied the theories of Jean Piaget, the Swiss developmental psychologist who declared that 'only education is capable of saving our societies from possible collapse, whether violent, or gradual.'

As an elective he chose General Knowledge and was introduced to *The Magic Mountain*, a book by the German novelist and Nobel Prize laureate, Thomas Mann. A complex book, it explores the destructiveness in civilised society and questions attitudes to life, health, illness and sexuality. The story revolves around the lives of people living in hideouts in the mountains – hence the name. Teame, although finding it a tortuous read, discovered it stimulated his mind.

He identified with Mann's criticism of human society and his concern for people, although he found the author's cynicism rather annoying. But it made him think about the society he knew. There were the poor students he had taught who walked many miles to school, often after milking the cows. Sometimes they would go without lunch because their parents could not afford to provide it. Mann's writing magnified Teame's own views and helped him become more aware of the deeper problems of society.

He studied English literature under Professor Curnow who also introduced him to linguistics, the study of languages. An idiosyncratic character, he had a twirly moustache and often lectured with a pipe sticking out of his mouth. But he was an able man much loved and respected by his students. He taught them the origin of words. How many in the English language came from other European languages. He made his lessons very lively. He introduced his students to Geoffrey Chaucer's *The Wife of Bath* and *The Waste Land* by T.S. Eliot. Unlike some professors he didn't mind interruptions and welcomed questions.

Teame would have long discussion with his fellow students late into the night. He would question some of the theories he was being taught. But his mind was being stretched. There were moments of enlightenment. He had, for the first time in his educational journey, begun to write essays. Being partly self-educated, because of losing his secondary school place, he had never been asked to write one until he got to university. But he became used to writing essays of fifteen or twenty pages. Writing by hand, a mistake meant rewriting the whole page. Correction fluids, like Tipp-Ex, were not then available. It was laborious work with three or four essays for each semester. Teame, like the rest of the students, spent an entire Christmas vacation completing his essays.

They all had to make presentations in front of their fellow students – another new experience for Teame. Classmates were encouraged to criticise each other's work. Teame enjoyed the cut and thrust of the discussions and had no problem with those who took issue with any of his arguments. He didn't take it personally. But most of the other students were not comfortable with the idea and didn't like being criticised before their peers.

Physical education was given a prominent place in the curriculum. It was compulsory and reflected the University founder's belief in producing well rounded individuals along the Spartan-Greek tradition of: 'A healthy mind, in a healthy body.'

Teame took up swimming in his first Semester. It did not come naturally to him. He remembered how he struggled to cross the

Mereb River during the mule journey with his father as a ten-year-old. His first swimming test resulted in failure. He had to take extra lessons and his supervisor was his friend Yemanu who was an excellent swimmer. With Yemanu's help and encouragement Teame mastered the art of staying afloat and was soon enjoying his swimming. He improved his skills and became good enough to get a life-saving certificate and badge. He also played in one of the second level university football teams.

It was a far cry from the situation back home where there were rumblings that annexation of Eritrea was on the way. The first shots in a long and bloody liberation battle had already been fired. Beirut was a different world but Teame's thoughts would often turn back to the unfolding events in Eritrea and the increasing likelihood that Eritrea would be annexed and become part of Ethiopia.

CHAPTER TEN

Annexation

On November 14, 1962, the year after Teame's arrival in Beirut, Emperor Haile Sellasie did indeed annex Eritrea. The Eritrean parliament was dissolved and Amharic became the official language. News of the Emperor's annexation of Eritrea had not come as a surprise. The probability of it happening had been rumbling on for years. But it was still a bitter blow. The Eritreans felt they had become second class citizens in their own country. Their sense of identity was fragile.

Officially they were Ethiopians. They had Ethiopian passports. But if Teame had been asked his nationality he would have said Eritrean. The only exception would be if he was asked by an Ethiopian. Then he would have felt obliged to say Ethiopian. He felt a conflict of identity. Although he was a proud Eritrean he had to embrace, at least publicly, the idea of being an Ethiopian.

So it was with a sense of horror that Teame and his friends at the university in Beirut got news of the situation as it unravelled. The dissolution of the Eritrean Assembly, where the nine Ethnic groups in Eritrea all had representatives, was seen as a loss of democracy and freedom of speech. Infrastructures were destroyed. Their mother tongues were abandoned as their official languages and replaced by Amharic. There was deeply held resentment at what was seen as the superior attitude of Ethiopians to Eritreans. Privately Eritreans, like Teame, never accepted annexation whatever they felt impelled to say in public.

When Eritrea became part of a federation with Ethiopia under a UN mandate in 1952 – giving them a degree of independence – they were given their own flag adorned with the UN emblem. It flew over the Parliament buildings. Under annexation it was replaced by the green, yellow and red flag of Ethiopia. That was a symbolic gesture which, to Teame and his fellow Eritrean students watching events from 1,300 miles away, was another sign of their loss of independence.

Teame was reminded of his time as a student revolutionary in 1957 when he was imprisoned for taking part in demonstrations against the regime and was furious at, what he believed, was the corruption which stopped him getting a boarding school place. The student revolt had even then been in protest at the growing inequalities of the Emperor's regime. His feelings were personal as well as political.

Partly because of their different mother tongues the Ethiopian and Eritrean students did not congregate together in the university. There was a hidden tension between the two groups. When they did meet, which inevitably they must, both groups avoided talking about the issues of annexation directly, keeping to the generalities of the political situation, or avoiding it altogether. The Eritreans steered clear of airing their views on what to them were the iniquities of annexation.

It was generally believed that among the Ethiopian students were some who were government informers. It would have been dangerous to be heard criticising the Emperor. Any Eritrean heard saying anything against the actions of the Haile Sellasie regime was likely to be reported to the government who were paying for the students to be there. They could lose their place at the university if they had spoken out of turn. It was a strong incentive to remain silent.

But Teame did make friends with some of the Ethiopians in his accommodation hall. They had things in common. Although they kept clear of politics they were all students with ambitions. Some of them were on Teame's course. They discussed their studies. There were social occasions when they met. Teame always made a point of treating everyone with friendliness and courtesy. He was unlikely to have been seen as a threat by the Ethiopians. Later in his career, back in Eritrea, he was to discover there were many Ethiopians who acted professionally without regard to ethnic origin. One was even to play a part in saving his life.

But, despite the concerns at what was going on at home, he knew he also had to knuckle down to his studies, and did so. By the end of his second year, in 1963, he had gained an Advanced Diploma in Teaching. His course had included practical teaching experience in the International School attached to the University attended by children of the international community as well as some of the University staff. It meant he could continue his studies for another two years to get his degree.

He had the summer off and decided to go home to see his parents. He flew back to Asmara and was keen to find out how things had changed since annexation. When he arrived home he was welcomed joyfully by his parents – especially his mother – and his Uncle Ghebremichael and Auntie Azieb. He met old friends too. They hardly recognised him. Despite his regular visits to the gym he had put on a lot of weight thanks to the good and plentiful supplies of food at the University.

His mother Wagaye's joy at seeing him had been coloured by her feelings at losing her first-born son when he first flew off to Beirut. Ever since, when she saw a plane fly overhead, she had waved her hands and sang in Tigrigna: '*Orobnaleye, tanika leyleye, ntumay selam belileye,*' which, loosely translated into English, means 'You beautifully crafted flying tin, please convey my heartfelt greetings to my son.' It was a sign of how much she missed him.

There was not much noticeable difference in the country that he could see in the parts he visited during the vacation. In the rural areas farmers seemed too busy planting their crops and taking advantage of the plentiful rain in that summer of 1963. Although a few of the Eritrean supporters of the Emperor and of annexation attributed the rain to his 'saintliness' and took it as a good omen.

Teame, needless to say, did not hold that view. In fact, as the country's residents were soon to discover, the Emperor's administration had hatched plans to transfer numerous industries and factories based in Eritrea to Ethiopia.

After spending a few days with his family he decided to go to Addis Ababa, the capital city of Ethiopia. He had never been there before. He had always considered Addis to be the enemy fortress. But it was time to find out what the capital city was like. He went by bus, a three day journey. It was not what he had expected. The Imperial Palace, home of the Emperor, was very grand. But he thought the rest of the city much less beautiful than the Eritrean capital, Asmara, with its many fine Italian buildings.

The few Ethiopians that Teame managed to talk to – practising his rather shaky Amharic – seemed little phased about annexation other than delighted that they now had access to Eritrea's coast by the Red Sea. On the other hand, he did meet several Ethiopian students at the University of Addis Ababa who expressed sorrow – genuine or not Teame was unsure – over the annexation of Eritrea. One of them used an expression that resonated with him. 'Soon you will discover that you will be thrown back like the urine of a camel!' It was implying that a democracy annexed by an autocracy can only travel backwards. The sentiment would stay with Teame and history would prove the truth of the remark.

But his time in the country soon came to an end. A few days later he was on his way back to Beirut to complete his studies at the American University.

He had another two years of hard work ahead of him to obtain his degree. Having obtained the required grades to be upgraded to a bachelor degree level from the Advanced Diploma, Teame's studies were going well. He gained in confidence and began enjoying English poetry and Philosophy of Education modules led by Professors Curnow and Kurani who he respected as being masters of their respective subjects. Many years later he could still bring to mind Professor Curnow's seminars on 'The Waste Land' by T.S. Eliot and Professor Kurani's lectures on the contribution of John Dewey and John Brubacher on the interactions between philosophy and democracy and education. He also particularly enjoyed the stiff competition from Lebanese classmates who were better educated, well travelled and multilingual.

He was still wary of the Ethiopian students and avoided confrontation with them over the vexed issue of annexation. But, to his surprise, he discovered that they actually had great respect for him. A vacancy came up for President of the Ethiopian Students Association in the Middle East (ESAME) within the university campus, as the incumbent, Nebiat Tefferi, a medical student, had served his term. ESAME included students in Greece, Cyprus, Jordan, and Egypt as well as Beirut. Teame was asked by some of the Ethiopian student leaders to be a candidate. Although taken aback by this support from an unexpected quarter Teame decided he would let his name go forward despite having a few reservations.

There were about ninety Ethiopians at the American University and only twenty Eritreans. A substantial number of the ninety were attending short courses like Agriculture Extension at Zahle, in the Bekaa Valley in Lebanon. Among Teame's reservations was that he was

a member of the minority group which had serious political differences with the majority – albeit largely unsaid. But, more importantly
his knowledge of Amharic, the Ethiopian official language, was sketchy.

There were two other candidates, both of them Ethiopian who were
keen to get elected. Teame, along with the other two candidates, addressed the Association at the election meeting. He explained that his
Amharic was not good and that could be a drawback. But the mostly
Ethiopian audience seemed largely unphased. Some of them laughed.
It did not seem to be the issue that Teame feared it would. Privately
he regarded Amharic as the language of the oppressor. In reality,
though, it was not a major obstacle because the language of the
University was English and everybody spoke it. There was a vote and,
much to Teame's amazement, he was elected. There was even applause.

Why did they appoint him? He was a friendly and popular character
in the University. But he still had some resentment towards Ethiopia
and some of its leaders. This though did not apply to all Ethiopians.
He had got to know many of them in classes and socially despite the
difficulties between the two groups. He discovered that they were
human beings like him. In fact he considered some of them were as
exploited as Eritreans. They were among the ethnic groups in
Ethiopia who had also been forced to embrace Amharic. He wondered
if they had seen him as a fellow victim of the Emperor's regime. It
was quite possible that they swung the vote his way. Teame would
never know. But he took up the Presidency enthusiastically determined to bring new ideas to the role.

Shortly afterwards, during the next university break, his new
responsibilities took him to Bologna in Italy. The Ethiopian Students
Association representing the country's students around the world had
called a conference there. It had been sponsored by Emperor Haile
Sellasie. Teame went representing the Ethiopian students in the
Middle East.

He discovered that many of the other Ethiopian student presidents from the different groups around the world were also Eritrean despite, as in Teame's case, being in the minority. There was no shortage of Ethiopians at the conference either. But Teame had the opportunity to meet and talk to his Eritrean colleagues.

During the day, when the conference was chaired by the Student President Teklemariam Zeghu, the delegates discussed a range of professional matters as well as hearing about the history of Bologna, the beautiful Italian city they were in. The delegates kept away from discussing the political situation from the podium. It would not have gone down well at a conference that had been sponsored by the Emperor and highly advertised. There would almost certainly have been agents of the Ethiopian government present. But on the lighter side there were cultural activities with dance troops brought in to entertain the conference guests.

For some of the Eritreans it was a different story in the evening. They would meet secretly together in quiet corners. Inevitably the talk was about the situation at home. Like Teame the other Eritreans were furious at the annexation of their country. Some took the dangerous step of distributing leaflets critical of the Emperor's action. Teame joined them. They would gather in the basement of the conference hall and prepare the anti-annexation propaganda.

The pamphlets would be duplicated and the students would take them around the city and the conference hall during the hours of darkness. They managed to avoid detection. Had they been seen there would have been serious consequences.

Their actions caused shock waves in the conference hall. The Ethiopians were alarmed and tried to find out who was responsible. They must have realised it was the Eritreans. But they were not able to discover the culprits. Teame, although not a prime mover in the distribution of the anti-annexation propaganda, had taken a big risk.

He and the others would certainly have been arrested, perhaps worse, if they had been caught. But, despite the activities of the student activists, the conference was seen as a great success.

As for Teame, having survived the experience he went back to Beirut to complete his degree course. But he would also be meeting one of the world's most controversial figures in racial politics.

CHAPTER ELEVEN

Malcolm X

There were over seventy nationalities studying at the American University. Many were from African countries. Ghana, Nigeria, Kenya, Sudan and Egypt, as well as Ethiopia, were all represented. Each had their own student associations. For the first time Teame began to see himself not just as Eritrean, or even Ethiopian – as he now was following annexation – but as an African and a global citizen as well.

As President of the Ethiopian students at the American University of Beirut he would meet mostly the leaders of the other African student associations. He had never before had the chance to share experiences with the other Africans. It was a revelation to be able to talk to them about their experiences of their countries and hopes for the future.

Teame suggested they set up an African Students Union to give them a united voice. He, and several others, said they needed to think as Africans not just as members of their individual countries. As a result the African Association was set up. Perhaps because it was his idea, Teame was nominated to be the first President if and when the Association was accepted by the University authorities.

It was 1963, a time when there were race riots in America. The budding African Students Association wanted to show support for black Americans. They watched in dismay as the TV news relayed pictures of what was going on. There had been bombings on the homes of civil rights leaders triggering riots and mass protests for racial justice.

One of the most controversial black activists in America at the time was Malcolm X. Imprisoned for theft at the age of twenty in 1946, he had become a member of the group Nation of Islam known as Black Muslims. The group were opposed to racial integration and instead campaigned for their own schools, churches/mosques, and support networks.

The still unapproved, African Association at the University heard that Malcolm X was making a pilgrimage (one of the five major tenets of Islam) to Mecca and, on his way back, was staying in Beirut. They decided it was an ideal opportunity to invite him to address them on the plight of black Americans.

It was argued by the African students that although they were in an American University – some of them on American scholarships – they wanted to know how democracy in the United States allowed the lack of human rights of black Americans.

Along with four other members of the Association, Teame approached the Dean of the University requesting permission to invite Malcolm X to address one of their meetings. The Dean refused. He was unhappy with the idea of an African Association, saying that if any Africans had problems they could take it up with him through their individual national associations.

It looked like the plan was doomed. But the president of the Sudanese Students Association came to the rescue. The Sudanese Embassy was just down the road from the University. He managed to persuade them to host the controversial American. Teame thought it was a brave decision.

There was an outcry from the University authorities. The student leaders, Teame among them, were threatened with deportation. The fact that Malcolm X was a controversial American and this was the American University of Beirut, and therefore the sponsors, may have had something to do with the fierce opposition.

The students said they were only attempting to put into practice what they had learnt at university in their philosophy classes on the rights of the individual. They said they had never been to America, didn't know what life was like there but were opposed to all the violence that was going on. They just wanted to hear what Malcolm X had to say. Faced with so much argument in support of the idea, the university authorities finally backed down and declared that they had no objection, if the meeting took place off campus.

When Malcolm X arrived at the Sudanese Embassy to address the meeting, the hall was packed. To the students'surprise and amusement the front row was full of professors from the university. So many people wanted to hear Malcolm X that they had to erect loud speakers outside the hall for the overflow.

A big man, over six feet tall, Malcolm X gave his version of events in America. He talked of the treatment of his fellow black Americans and his own beliefs since his conversion to Islam whilst in prison. Facing questions he was asked what was his solution to the problems he had described. He talked about his faith as a Muslim being the answer he had found. Forbidding alcohol and womanising. He said Christianity had been watered down. He wanted to see the black man defend himself and called for a Free State within America. He also went on to explain why he dropped the family name of his former slave owners. Hence the 'X'.

There was a mixed reaction from the audience. Many of the students came from Christian backgrounds and would not have been comfortable with the views they had heard which were critical of their faith and propagating Islam.

1 The Haile Selassie Secondary School in Asmara, where a 16-year-old Teame was refused a boarding place.

2 Graduation ceremony at the Asmara Teacher Training College, 1960. In the presence of the then head of the Eritrean government, Dej Asfaha Woldemichael (seated left) Teame gives the valedictory address after graduating as best student teacher of the year.

3 Beirut. Eritrean students with maids they taught to read.

4 Teame supervising teaching practice in Asmara.

5 A lorry is commandeered to take students from the TTI to the Red Sea coast at Massawa as a break from their lessons and allowing them to relate to the environment as part of their studies.

6 Teame at his desk at the Asmara Teacher Training Institute.

7 Teame addressing an international conference in Caux, Switzerland.

8 Interpreting for Madam Irene Laure from France at a public meeting at the Cicero Stadium in Asmara.

9 Pupils leave their school in Asmara during the time of the student unrest in Eritrea.
Photograph: John Bond

10 September, 12, 1974. Emperor Haile Selassie is marched down the steps of the Imperial Palace and put into an ancient VW Beetle, as he is deposed in a Marxist coup. Teame witnessed him being driven away as he watched the scene from nearby offices.
By Officer of the Provincial Military Administrative Council

11 Cultural activities, including regional dances, were introduced at the TTI during Teame's time there as Co-ordinator of Teaching Practice and later as Director.

12 Teame with his close friend Mohamed Omer, the first student he tutored and who went on to become a police colonel, with his wife and family.

13 Teame and Teblez
shortly after their
marriage in 1968.

14 Teame's
father-in-law,
Medhane Sahle.

15 Teame with members of staff at the Teacher Training Institute in Asmara.

16 Teame presented with a ceremonial shield on leaving the
Asmara Teacher Training Institute as Director in 1975.

But the overwhelming majority of the audience, including the professors, applauded his words. Teame was fascinated by him. Even mesmerised. He was struck by his wittiness, his clarity of analysis and his bravery and honesty. But he felt he was wasting his talents. He was disappointed that such an articulate and able man was not serving a wider circle of humanity, not just black Americans. If only, he thought, Malcolm X could liberate himself from his bitterness and temper his confrontational attitude towards white Americans.

But despite his reservations he was glad to have met such a controversial figure and felt his knowledge of America and its people, and the problems they faced, had been broadened. He felt the visit by Malcolm X had been a success and was well worth all the effort to make it happen.

Meanwhile Yemanu, the Eritrean student who had welcomed Teame and Kidane on their arrival at the university two years earlier, had finished his course and was flying back to Asmara. Teame and some of Yemanu's other friends went to Beirut International airport to see him off.

On their way out of the airport after saying their farewell they came across a group of obviously Eritrean young women being shepherded through the arrivals terminal by an arrogant Lebanese man. Teame approached the frightened women and spoke to them in their native Tigrigna. They expressed delight at meeting a fellow Eritrean. They had all (about 90% of them illiterates) been brought over to work as maids for rich Lebanese families.

But the Lebanese man was furious. Teame, in his broken Arabic, asked what he was doing with the women. The man insulted him and said it was nothing to do with him. Tempted to hit him, but keeping his temper under control, Teame told him they would follow him and make sure the Eritrean women were properly looked after.

Carrying out their threat they saw that one of the women was staying at a house near the university and they made a note of the gate number. Over the next few weeks they found out where others of the maids were staying and kept in touch by leaving notes at the house gates and sometimes even ringing the house phones. They discovered the women were treated very badly and worked long hours. Some of them had no decent accommodation and were beaten by their employers.

Teame, in his capacity as President of the Ethiopian Students Association, was acquainted with the Ethiopian Honorary Consul in Beirut, Bisharat Saig, a Lebanese. He raised the plight of the maids with Mr Saig and was invited out to his luxurious home in the jebel — the mountains — on the outskirts of Beirut to discuss it.

The Consul was keen to help. Teame gave a detailed description of the conditions the maids worked under. He said they should be given their basic human rights, have regular time off on Sundays, and get the chance to meet each other.

His plea on the maids' behalf proved effective. With the Consul's support the maids were granted better conditions by their employers. They were given more freedom and shorter hours. Teame found himself something of a hero much to his embarrassment. News of the victory also got back to the women's relatives in Eritrea.

But most of the women could not read or write. Teame and his friends — one of whom was Tukue Woldeamlak — would read their letters for them and write replies. But he found it uncomfortable dealing with their private correspondence. Before his course ended and he returned home he was determined to teach them to read and write so that they could handle their own letters.

Every Sunday afternoon Teame, and some of his Eritrean friends, would go to one of the homes where the maids worked and give them reading and writing lessons. The maids, who often stood outside their homes waiting for Teame and his friends to arrive, offered to pay for the service rendered. But Teame and the other Eritrean students categorically refused to accept payment. They compromised and allowed the maids to pay their taxi fares and gladly accepted the delicious Eritrean meals they cooked for them.

Teame was delighted to have helped. The maids learnt to read and write and some even learnt English. He considered this educational venture was part and parcel of his role as an educator. But there was a downside. Teame's studies had suffered he had spent so much time with the maids. He had to work hard to catch up.

But the free time – one of the concessions that Teame had won for the maids – meant that they could travel. They were Christians in the main and one place in the Middle East that they wanted to go to was the Holy sites of Jerusalem. For them, it was like going to Mecca for a Muslim.

Teame felt he wanted to help. As an Orthodox Christian he was also keen to visit Jerusalem. So did some of the fellow Eritrean and Ethiopian students. Jerusalem was a two-day bus journey away. But Teame had no idea how to organise such a trip.

Booking two buses for the sixty people, students – Ethiopians and Eritreans – and the maids, who all booked up for the trip was the easy part. But where would they stay? They were planning to go during the Easter break when the maids, as well as the students, had time off. But being Easter – the busiest time of the year – finding accommodation in Jerusalem was proving near impossible. Even if they had found a hotel the cost would have been well above what they could afford.

Publicity about the trip had already gone out and he knew he had to find a solution. He contacted the Head Priest of the Ethiopian Orthodox Church monastery in Jerusalem asking for help. With no mobile phones it had to be done by a series of letters which went back and forth for weeks. The priest didn't think the monastery, which was small, could possibly put up sixty people, which included fifteen of the maids. Teame tried to put his mind at rest, saying they would bring blankets and sleeping bags and sleep on the floor. It was a very tenuous arrangement but he hoped things would work out.

The party set off passing through Syria into Jordan where they broke their journey at a small residence close to the border which was owned by King Hussein of Jordan. Bisharat Saig, the Ethiopian Consul who had helped Teame with the maids, paved the way for them to be given hospitality there. They were treated as guests of honour and offered Arabic coffee, very thick and drunk with salt – not what they were used to. Out of respect they drunk it and, with speeches of thanks, they continued on their way.

The next day they reached Jerusalem having slept as best they could on the buses as they drove through the hot desert country. Reaching the monastery Teame discovered the place where he had hoped they could stay was very small indeed.

The party were hungry and tired. All their provisions had been eaten on the bus journey. The few monks and nuns in the monastery, now overwhelmed by this large group, provided bread and tea. There were few rooms in the monastery so the only place to sleep was on the hard floor of the main hall. The floor was uneven and sloping, some of the students found themselves sliding into each other as they tried to sleep. The ladies were given their own area cordoned off with blankets.

Over the next few days they visited the Holy sites in Jerusalem, went to Bethlehem, walked along the Station of the Cross where Jesus had walked on the way to his crucifixion, and swam in the Dead Sea.

Some of the students, Teame included, had tattoos with the Christ symbol and the date of the Ethiopian calendar. It was 1964. But because the Ge'ez/Ethiopian calendar is eight or nine years later than the Gregorian calendar their tattoo shows 1955. Teame still bears his tattoo on his forearm.

The maids brought prayer beads and Holy Water which they sent back to their families in Eritrea. It was a special time for them all. Teame felt that for him it had been a spiritual experience. But he was also relieved that it had gone off successfully after all the worry of organising it and the fear of losing face.

There was, though, one last drama on the way home. The buses stopped by the River Jordan. It was a hot day and one of the students jumped into the river for a swim. The water which was muddy was deceptively slow-moving and peaceful. The student got into difficulties and was in danger of being swept away. There were prickly thorns along the bank which made it difficult to get out.

Teame, as the leader of the group, decided it was his job to do something about it. Remembering his life saving skills learnt the year before, he dived in, and, with some difficulty as he was swimming against the current, managed to get the student to the side and on to the bank. His hands were torn by the thorns as he struggled to rescue the man. He thanked God there had not been a tragedy as the party returned to Beirut.

The experience of organising the trip and leading it, taught Teame that human beings in general, and Ethiopians and Eritreans in particular, could live together, irrespective of religion or the different shades of the colours of their skin, if they decided to discard their divisive ultra-nationalistic tendencies.

His return to academic life, though, meant he had once more to catch up on his studies. His final exams were rapidly approaching.

CHAPTER TWELVE

Teacher Training Institute

Teame was awarded his BA in Arts and Sciences at the end of his four years at Beirut. It was a proud moment for him. He had enjoyed the eclectic approach of the broader curriculum that included education as well as modules on psychology, sociology, linguistics and philosophy. It had worked well. He now felt fully qualified for the next stage in his career as he returned to Asmara in the summer of 1965.

He had to wait to be told by the Ministry where his next assignment was to be. He could have been sent as a teacher to any part of the country. In fact they wanted him to be a teacher trainer and had arranged a post for him at the Asmara Teacher Training Institute. Three others from Beirut, all senior to him in age and experience, were also assigned there. It was a decision which would define the rest of his career.

The Institute was highly regarded as one of the best teacher training centres in the whole of Ethiopia. The catchment area for trainees covered the five northern provinces of Ethiopia of which Eritrea was, after annexation, now one. The other provinces were Tigray, Gojjam, Begemeder and Wollo.

The majority of the students were Ethiopian, far outnumbering the Eritreans. There was an uneasiness between the two. Amharic was now the official language. The Ethiopians considered themselves superior to the Eritreans. Books in Tigrigna had been burnt after annexation much to the dismay of Teame and his fellow Eritreans.

Life was difficult for the Eritrean students because the Ethiopians expected them to speak in Amharic which many of them could not speak well. They had no option but to learn to speak what was now the official language. One salvation for them was that lessons at the Institute were in English.

There was a huge Ethiopian Army barracks right next to the Institute and the Eritreans saw themselves as living under occupation. At weekends many of the Ethiopian students would visit the soldiers there, some of them were relations. The liberation fight had already begun and liberation fighters were operating in the hills surrounding Asmara.

The director was an Ethiopian, Ato Matewos Gessesse, who had a Master's degree from an American university. Since annexation in 1962 it had been the policy to put Ethiopians in positions of authority throughout Eritrea. Under the Eritrean Parliament they had their own Ministers. Now Ethiopians were in all the top posts. It caused resentment among Eritrean professionals like Teame, who considered themselves well able to run things themselves. Schools were given Ethiopian head teachers which meant students had seen the policy at work in their own schools. Teame considered it disastrous.

He was to teach Psychology of Education, Philosophy of Education and Pedagogy, the art of teaching. All of them were subjects he had specialised in at Beirut and enjoyed. He was glad to be able to put politics aside and concentrate on teaching. It gave him great happiness to be back in Asmara where he stayed with his uncle Ghebremichael and his aunt Azieb once more. They warmly welcomed him back into what had become his second family.

Teame guarded his own thoughts on the situation with care, especially in the presence of the Ethiopian student teachers. He would not go out of his way to praise the Emperor – whose photograph was on the cover of every school textbook – as the Ethiopian teachers would do.

There was nothing political in his lectures. He was determined to maintain his neutrality and be completely professional. He would tell his students all he was interested in was producing reliable, mature, caring and knowledgeable teachers wherever they came from or subsequently taught.

In his heart he felt that a revolution was on the way. There were already rumblings of dissatisfaction among the Ethiopian soldiers who had seen many of their comrades die in conflicts with the Eritrean liberation fighters. The soaring cost of living and their low pay was another cause of discontent.

But he felt his job was to prepare teachers to do their job properly and serve the needs of their pupils to learn. He was keen to put into practice what he had learnt in his philosophy classes at Beirut that everyone should have equal rights and educational opportunities should be available to all.

His philosophy, developed over his early teaching experience at Adi Keyh and advanced by his time at Beirut, told him that he was not filling student's brains like an empty pot. He was there to encourage them to reflect and question, and participate in the knowledge process. But he needed to win them first. He knew that if his students did not have confidence in him as a professional teacher and as someone of integrity, he would have lost them.

He had a good salary as a teacher trainer, 450 Ethiopian dollars a month, which was a lot more than the 94 dollars a month he received as a teacher in Adi Keyh. It meant he could begin to support his parents, siblings and other relations again. They were all enormously proud of him. He was the first person from their area of Eritrea to be educated at university and to acquire higher education abroad.

Teame worked with an international group of other teacher trainers. There were members of the American Peace Corps, British, Filipinos, and Indians as well as Ethiopians and Eritreans. Teame was a popular lecturer. He was elected best teacher of the year by his scholars.

He got on well with his colleagues and developed good links with the deputy director, an Indian. He found himself with the responsibility of liaising with the other teacher trainers to plan their teaching practice schedules. He was democratic and gave the teachers a chance to have a say in what was planned as each one of them had to supervise trainees after carrying out their teaching roles. If there were problems with resources he would chase them up. Taking responsibility came naturally to him. Perhaps it had been developed by his days as a monitor at each of the schools he attended.

Teame was among many of the staff who perceived the Director to be a slightly autocratic man in his dealings with others. He was in the habit of issuing orders without explanation and expecting them to be obeyed. He seemed to play little part in the academic side of the Institute as the teaching timetable and other administrative activities were ably handled by his deputy. Teame considered him a political appointee of the Ethiopian government and his main job appeared to be keeping the status quo.

The two would sometimes clash but Teame would not hesitate always to speak his mind. In time Ato Matewos seemed to recognise that Teame was acting professionally and honestly. He had begun to trust him. Teame's success in helping his fellow teacher trainers organise their day probably had something to do with it too. In return Teame recognised that behind his austere exterior Ato Matewos had sound qualities.

Part of the courses at the Institute included the student teachers being sent out to local schools for practical teaching experience. In his second year came a sign of the Director's growing confidence in him. He was asked to co-ordinate the teaching practice. It was a promotion with a slight increase in salary – although he would still have his full load of lectures.

The appointment did not go down well with some Eritrean and Ethiopian lecturers who were older and more experienced than Teame who was now twenty-seven. As these individuals coveted the job Teame felt uncomfortable about the situation. But he had not asked for the job or lobbied for it as his colleagues seemed to suspect. As some of these colleagues did not get on very well with the Director they soon found themselves transferred to other secondary schools as Directors.

Teame began his new responsibility as Co-ordinator with great enthusiasm. He soon began introducing new ideas in his co-ordinating role for teaching practice, an essential part of any teacher's training. He set up collaborations with fifteen local primary schools, choosing them carefully after assessing the ethos and the qualities of the heads and their staff.

There were meetings with the school staff explaining the modus operandi of the teaching practice programme – trainees watching regular teachers in action in the classroom and then conducting classes themselves.

Teame's co-ordinator role also included facilitating the development, both professional and personal, of the trainees and monitoring their progress. He would be acting as a link between them and the Institute, and in some cases, the Ministry of Education. In addition he was also developing cross-fertilisation of educational ideas and theories between the school and the Institute. He found this one of the most rewarding parts of his work.

As well as organising the teaching experience of the trainers and trainees, he also introduced music and dance clubs. The Institute had no music class so he set one up. Instruments were in short supply but he managed to get enough funds to buy a flute. Otherwise the music had to be limited to singing.

Some of the students came from far flung parts of Ethiopia, in some cases up to 500 miles away. Many of them felt isolated so far away from home and were frightened. Asmara was a dangerous place. There were killings in the city with liberation fighters in the vicinity and the Ethiopian army, in barracks next door to the Institute, patrolling the streets.

In an effort to make them more at home and secure, Teame encouraged the students, who came from different ethnic groups in the country, to demonstrate their own traditional music and dances. The students were divided into their various cultural groups. One of them was the Oromo tribe from Ethiopia who had their own language and traditions.

They performed for the student population one week and another group would perform the next week. All the five hundred student teachers and their trainers at the Institute would turn up to watch.

The Amharic and Tigrigna speaking students also took their turn performing songs and dances from their own cultures. These dance and music sessions, which took place mostly during the weekends, proved extremely popular on several fronts. It gave them respite from the constantly tense situation in Asmara. It also gave those from the different provinces – Wollo, Gojjam, Begemeder, Tigray and Eritrea – a sense of pride in their identity and culture. Finally such an opportunity gave the groups, and their trainers, a first exposure to traditions outside their own provinces.

Teame knew that what he had introduced could be risky politically. Questions were being raised by some Ministry of Education officials. But the activities were allowed to continue, in the belief of the strength of unity in diversity which is the policy upon which present day Ethiopia is governed.

The Institute had a number of specialised practical courses in addition to the more academic classes. Gardening and domestic science were among them. Teame felt that the courses were not tailored to the local environment and considered the teacher trainers were sticking to textbooks which took no account of the way lives were lived in Eritrea and Ethiopia. He wanted to change that tradition.

He didn't blame the teacher trainers, mainly from the Indian sub continent, who were only doing what they had been trained to do in their own countries. But he wanted to change the culture to one where the teacher did not rely just on textbooks (which in many cases weren't available in Eritrea) but to put something of their own experience into their teaching.

One example of how he changed the thinking was in the gardening classes and teaching biology. Using compost for fertiliser was not a common practice in Asmara at the time. But Teame had learnt about it in his time working for his uncle's shop as a schoolboy when he had regularly been to the vegetable market and seen the rotting vegetables which turned into compost.

One day he took some of the lecturers and trainees to the local rubbish tip on the outskirts of Asmara on the road to Massawa. The Italian gardeners in the city had introduced composting during the colonial days. Collecting some of the compost produced from the garden waste at the tip, Teame took it back to the Institute to use it in the garden plots there.

Not all the students appreciated having to sift through the rubbish. Teame was furious when he saw some of them – who had already angered him for not getting their homework in on time – holding back from the task saying they hated the smell. He shouted at them: 'Do you think you are above those poor people who come here to find something to eat in order to survive?'

There was another member of staff accompanying Teame, a lecturer from the Philippines who was much older than Teame, a quiet and respectful man, he called him Mr 'Ato' Teame. Witnessing Teame's outburst he called him aside and told him an old Japanese proverb which goes: 'He who smiles rather than rages, ends up a winner.'

Teame realised that his anger would not have helped the situation and was grateful to his colleague for teaching him a valuable lesson. He would remember the advice from his elderly colleague and vowed to curb his anger in future.

He had also been instrumental in establishing vegetable growing as part of the gardening courses. The students put up fences to keep the local goats away from the plants. There were vegetable growing competitions and the students would give up part of their weekends to tend the plots. Teame had made his point that the students and teachers could cultivate and harvest their own crops. It was part of the learning process and they could also eat the proceeds.

Teame had become something of a father figure to Ethiopian students who he went out of his way to help. They were aware of the resentment towards them not only from the Eritrean students, but also from the local residents. They would hear about the killings and kidnappings by the Eritrean liberation movement. Hundreds of miles away from their homes they often felt isolated and fearful. He was mindful of the things his father had taught him as a boy about treating all people with respect, caring for visitors to the home by washing their feet.

Sometimes he would organise trips out to the countryside to give the students a break from their studies. On one occasion he and a colleague, Abraha Ghermazion (better known by his nickname 'ChegaE') organised a trip to Massawa and a lorry was commandeered to take them to the coast. There they got their first sight of the Red Sea and enjoyed swimming in it. Teame took the opportunity of a dip too. Although the trips were opportunities for fun and relaxation there was a serious side. Teame wanted to also inspire them to link their teaching with the geography, history and climate of the country.

Teame became a confidante of the students if they had problems on their minds. He would be the person to break the news to them if a relative had died and would encourage the Eritrean students to show their sympathy. Teame would make sure that the proper traditions of mourning were followed. He would buy food for the ceremonies because the students sometimes didn't have enough money to buy their own. Then he would sit with them until 10.00 pm at night. As he left the students would all stand and say, '*Gashie, enameseginalen*' – 'thank you' in Amharic.

He wanted to treat them with respect as human beings. They were not the Ethiopian government. In fact back in their home villages many of them were worse off than many Eritreans. He did not want to hate them just because they were Ethiopians. Don't hate them, hate the policy, he told himself.

But his feelings were to get the better of him during a very different scenario. It was an altercation with an American Peace Corp volunteer. The incident was to cause Teame considerable heartache and resulted in him having to explain himself to no less a person than the Governor General of Eritrea.

The American's wife was working at the Teacher Training Institute. She had approached Teame wanting to discuss some issues over adopting an Eritrean child. Teame explained it was not a subject he knew much about. But he felt, as the Co-ordinator who liaised with staff, he should at least listen to her problems. They chatted several times during coffee breaks in the Institute's crowded staff room.

One evening Teame went to Bar Centrale, in the centre of Asmara, for a coffee. The woman's husband frequented the same coffee bar. He was there on this occasion sitting with a group of four others. As soon as he spotted Teame, sitting quietly on his own at another table, he rose to his feet with an angry expression on his face and advanced towards him shouting as he did so. The American, who was much bigger and taller than Teame, was issuing a torrent of abuse. Although Teame did not catch every word, he was quite sure of one expression. He had been called a n*****.

He had, up until this point, remained in his seat hoping to calm the American down and find out why he was so angry. But on hearing the insult he stood up, his temper rising, and called out to others in the café to bear witness that he was being provoked. He spoke in English so that everyone, including the man's acquaintances, could understand him.

But the American then rolled up his sleeves and took a swing at Teame who managed to deflect the blow with his arm before aiming a punch of his own which knocked the American's glasses to the floor.

Now furious, Teame told the American: 'If you have something to say to me come outside and we will settle it man to man.' But by this time the man's friends had separated the two of them. He stormed off and Teame did not see him again.

Teame thought it possible that the American might have got the wrong impression about his talks with his wife and wrongly suspected there was more to it than an innocent conversation. But he was never able to get to the bottom of the abusive outburst.

His angry reaction was not just because of the man's behaviour in the café. It was also fuelled by dislike of Americans who, he felt, treated Eritreans like second class citizens in their own country. And he still remembered with some bitterness the American GI who had knocked him off his bicycle some years earlier.

His fears that the matter would go further were proved right. A summons arrived from the then Director General at the Ministry of Education, Ato Ghebrehiwet Neberay, who Teame was already acquainted with as he had been a fellow student at the American University in Beirut. Teame never discovered how he had heard about the incident but suspected the American might have made a report to the Eritrean authorities claiming that he had attacked him.

The Director General interviewed Teame several times about the incident. Teame was annoyed that he seemed to be taking the side of the American and was accusing him of misbehaving. He told Teame his career could be ended. This infuriated Teame even further. He asked the Director General: 'Why do you condemn me before even knowing my story?'

He was also annoyed that he was not shown any reports of the allegations against him. He told the Director General he was prepared to be judged by a court. If he was guilty he would accept the punishment, but concluded: 'Don't pre-judge me.'

The matter was to go higher still. This time Teame was ordered to meet with the Governor General of Eritrea, Ras Asrate Kassa. The meeting was in the Imperial Office, an imposing building in Asmara.

The Governor General was a big man, educated in Britain and with excellent English. He smoked a pipe as they talked. At first Teame spoke in his rather poor Amharic but asked permission to speak in English. The Governor General agreed which gave Teame confidence that he would be given a fair hearing. At first the mood was tense but later became more relaxed and Teame found he was being asked about himself. The Governor General seemed more interested in his life than the unfortunate incident with the American although Teame did outline his version of events.

He was surprised that this highly important and influential man in the Ethiopian administration seemed to know a great deal about him and his work at the Teacher Training Institute. He wondered whether the Ethiopian students at the Institute, who he had gone out of his way to help, had given positive reports about him.

Teame felt sufficiently at ease to begin expressing his views on the Eritrea-Ethiopia situation. First he asked if the Governor General wanted to hear him talk about things as they truly were. After an assurance that he could say what he honestly felt – not what senior Ethiopian administrators might want to hear – Teame felt free to express his views as an Eritrean. What started as a meeting about a minor scuffle with the American had become a much wider discussion about the situation in the country following annexation.

Teame expressed concerns about the corruption in the country especially among government officials and those in positions of power. He said there was a problem of good leadership. The bloodshed and anger in the country, he said, could be attributed to the basic injustices which followed Eritrea's annexation. He said he did not deny his Ethiopian identity but did not want to be treated as a second class citizen in his own country.

The Governor General listened closely as he continued. Teame told him that he knew he could do something about the situation if he chose to. He raised the much despised issue of Tigrigna books being burnt and Eritrean students forced to use Amharic text on the orders of the Haile Selassie regime.

He outlined his vision for the country saying he wanted to serve his people by sharing what little knowledge he had. He wanted to see justice done everywhere regardless of who you were. His aim was to share knowledge, destroy ignorance and illiteracy and to see people provided with their basic rights of food and shelter.

It was unlikely the Governor General would have heard an Eritrean speak so openly and passionately about his hopes for the country. Teame ended by saying that he was happy for the case over the American's claims to go to court. He just wanted a fair trial.

He had left the meeting wondering whether he had been too outspoken. Had he been foolish and fallen into a trap? The Governor

General could easily have had him arrested, but Teame decided that he must have recognised the truth of his words.

He was to hear no more about the allegations against him. The matter was quietly dropped. He never discovered why. But he thought it likely that it was decided there was no case to answer. Witnesses had corroborated his account that he was attacked by the American, not the other way round. In fact over forty years later by pure chance he was to meet a man in Britain – a stranger to him – who said he had seen what happened and had gone to the police station to give a statement in his favour. Although at the time Teame was fully prepared to fight the case in court he was hugely relieved that the matter was not taken further. He felt justice had been done.

(Things did not turn out well for the Governor General. Seven years later when the Emperor was overthrown and the Dergue took power, he was imprisoned and later executed along with sixty other Imperial officials on 23 November 1974.)

CHAPTER THIRTEEN

Student Strike

The grievances Teame had outlined to the Governor General were at the heart of the Eritrean liberation struggle. A further sign of the tensions bubbling away amongst the Eritrean population came shortly after his meeting with the Governor General. Students at the secondary schools in Asmara went on strike, refusing to continue their studies and to take the Ethiopian school leaving exams. They were protesting at lack of resources.

But the underlying grievances were more wide ranging. Like many of the Eritrean population the students were angry at the treatment of Eritreans by the Ethiopian administration. And, above all, they were supporting the campaign for independence. Feelings were running high.

With thousands of soldiers of the Ethiopian army stationed in Eritrea there was every chance that the situation could deteriorate and end in bloodshed. Criticism of the regime could provoke arrests or worse. Senior army officers wanted to take action against the students. It was a dangerous time.

The strike and the issues behind it created considerable concern among some of the Elders, the leading figures in the city, including a former member of the Eritrean Assembly, Dejazmatch Gebreyohanes, Sheikh Mohamed Ahmed Surur, Ato Mesfun Hailu and Kegnazmatch

Ghebremedhin Tessema, the Auditor General of the Eritrean Administration under Ethiopia.

Some in the Elders group had been inspired by seeing the all-African film, *Freedom*, which highlighted the moral and spiritual struggles of independence. Produced by Moral Re-Armament (MRA, now Initiatives of Change) the film had been widely shown around Africa and, in the run-up to Kenyan independence in 1963, had been seen by 70,000 Kenyans. The film was later said to have helped provide the stability needed in Kenya after independence.

Members of the MRA group, who had brought the film to Eritrea and had been invited to show it in the port city of Massawa on the Red Sea, worked with the Elders as they pondered what to do about the increasingly dangerous situation in Eritrea.

It was at this time that Teame was introduced to one of the MRA group, Englishman Jim Baynard-Smith, by a mutual acquaintance.

Teame found himself impressed by MRA's commitment to upholding the need for absolute moral standards in society along with a belief in the value of people of all faiths or none, to listen to their 'Inner Voice' to seek direction in their lives.

He recognised that these were values which were part of his upbringing and which he shared. Although he considered the idea of absolute moral standards was an impossible target to reach he acknowledged that it provided valuable guidelines in life and was something to at least try to live up to. The idea that changes in society could come about if people started by looking at what needed to change in themselves, was also a thought that intrigued him.

At first he had been concerned that the group might be interfering in the delicate and dangerous political situation in the country. But he became satisfied that they were non-political and were not pushing a Federalist agenda which neither he nor any of his Eritrean colleagues – all strong liberationists – would have supported.

Soon after meeting up with Jim Baynard-Smith he had been invited to a leadership training programme at the MRA international conference at Caux, Switzerland.

He discovered the conference was very open-ended with no pre-determined objectives and the subject matter not overtly religious. It concentrated on universal human issues such as justice, the search for self-worth and ethics.

With many ideas being expressed in music and song on the conference stage, Teame was struck by verses like: 'When I point my finger at my neighbour, there are three more pointing back at me.'

Among the trainers was Professor Theophil Spoerri, formerly of the University of Zurich, the son of a Methodist preacher whose upbringing gave him a powerful religious, social and political commitment. In 1940 he joined with others to form an anti-Nazi organisation called the Gotthardbund, becoming its first president.

Teame was interested to see that the trainers, Professor Spoerri among them, volunteered to join the other delegates on the washing up and service teams which kept the conference going. Teame joined in too. A new experience for him. He learnt how to make a bed, using sheets and blankets with the ends firmly tucked down with hospital corners – not a style he was used to in Eritrea. And much to his great delight he won a competition as the best bed maker. He also found his tie dipping into someone's soup when endeavouring to play his part on the service shift in the dining room.

But he discovered joining in with the conference chores had other benefits than learning how to safely dispense soup or make a bed. He enjoyed his discussions with the many other conference delegates who came from every continent in the world.

Among those Teame met was West Indies cricketer Conrad Hunte with whom he had long discussions. Hunte had been one of the world's greatest opening batsmen and a member of an all-conquering

West Indies side. He and Teame went for lengthy walks together. Teame told him of some of his experiences, including the altercation with the American, as well as his heartache at the situation over Eritrea's annexation.

Hunte was a good listener and a man renowned for his ever present smile. He told Teame of some of his own heartaches such as when he was passed over for the captaincy of the West Indies team when the job became vacant – despite the fact he was the vice-captain. But he told Teame of how he had been able to overcome his bitter feelings helped by his Christian faith and a wider vision.

Teame also met a former member of the French Resistance from World War Two, Madame Irène Laure who, after losing her bitterness against the Germans, had contributed to the reconciliation between Germany and France after the war. He met, too, Rajmohan Gandhi, grandson of Mahatma Gandhi, who had been instrumental in setting up a centre for conflict resolution in India.

Teame found listening to such stories both stimulating and challenging. He realised that he too, with memories of his feelings towards the Ethiopian rulers as well as the American he had tussled with, was not without bitterness. He struggled to come to terms with what he should do about it and spent much time in prayer and reflection.

He came to the painful conclusion that a change of heart was needed as well as an acceptance of the power of forgiveness. It went against his Coptic faith, he decided, to harbour ill-feelings against individuals or groups. He found forgiving those he harboured bitterness towards was liberating. It was an experience which was to colour his relationships with others in the future.

His time at the conference had also given Teame fresh insight into the world's problems outside his own country. It had reinforced his conviction that humanity, despite its immense advances technologically, needed to 'grow up morally and spiritually'.

As he later reflected on the experience he would acknowledge he had learnt that leadership is about who you are not what you know. It had also reaffirmed his belief that high moral conduct is required for anyone in a position of power and influence – such as heads of state but also teachers.

Back in Asmara the Elders decided to do whatever they could to resolve the dangerous situation created by the student unrest. They were anxious to avoid a conflict with the Army and inevitable blood-shed. Teame, who was then aged twenty-eight, joined the group of Elders as by far their youngest member. He took part in their regular meetings to discuss the situation and what to do about it.

It was decided to ask the students, through their leaders, to attend a meeting in the local stadium when the Elders would address them. Thousands of students turned up. The Elders, with the most senior ones speaking first as was the custom, urged the students to allow them to be a bridge with the Ethiopian government. They said tell us your problems and we can discuss them with the authorities.

Some of the students barracked the Elders shouting that they had been sent by the Ethiopian government – an accusation which angered Teame as he knew it was entirely unfounded. Outside the stadium were hundreds of soldiers ready to move in if the situation got out of hand. There were fears that they were waiting for an opportunity to act. If they had, bloodshed would almost certainly have been the result.

With the atmosphere in the stadium very tense the Elders continued their attempts to pacify the students. They tried to calm the situation and advised the students to finish their studies and not waste time by having to take their exams a year later.

As the most junior member of the Elders, Teame was the last to speak. He began by saying he was addressing them as an Eritrean not as an employee of the Ethiopian Government (which, as a staff member at the Teacher Training Institute, he was). His short speech was unprepared. He said he and the other Elders wanted to help solve their problems. He also took them to task for not giving the Elders the respect they deserved.

Then he used the analogy of an airliner running out of fuel but not being able to land because there were boulders on the runway. He asked the students: 'What do you think is going to happen to that plane?' Sooner or later, he said, it would crash with loss of life.

He told the students that if they continued their protests they would eventually run out of steam – as the airliner would run out of fuel. The analogy was Teame's way of warning the students of what awaited them if they fell foul of the Ethiopian soldiers. He knew the result would be the army moving in with their guns and bayonets. His words and those of the Elders seemed to have a salutary effect on the students who quietened down.

The meeting ended peacefully, although with no resolution. But in the succeeding weeks some of the Elders met with some of the student leaders informally. The students had begun to realise the Elders had their best interests at heart. Most of the students called off their strike and went back to school. They took their examinations. The issues over liberation would continue. But bloodshed had been avoided.

Teame was glad to have played his small part along with the other Elders. His words to the students stayed with some of them. Years later he was to meet a group of Eritrean People's Liberation Front (EPLF) fighters who had been among the crowd at the stadium. They told him how struck they had been by his question: 'What would happen to that plane?' They had no answer. But it had made them think and pulled them back from the brink of disaster.

After the student strike threat had died down Teame continued his involvement with the Elders Group. There were public meetings with keynote speakers continuing the theme of reconciliation rather than conflict and encouraging civic responsibility. Among the meetings was one addressed by Madame Irène Laure whom Teame had met in Switzerland. The meeting in the Cicero Stadium in Asmara had been widely publicised and the stadium was full.

Teame used his linguistic skills to translate her French into Tigrigna. Madame Laure, who after the war became Secretary General of the Socialist Women of France, told the crowd of her experience in the French Resistance in Marseilles when she had 'wanted every German dead and the country wiped off the map of Europe'. But, she told her audience, she had a change of heart after she was asked: 'How do you hope to rebuild Europe without the Germans?'

Rajmohan Gandhi, who Teame had also met in Switzerland, spoke at another packed meeting in the Cicero Stadium with Teame once again translating into Tigrigna. Gandhi told the crowd that his grandfather, the Mahatma, had been a man of peace. He had campaigned for the rights of the 'Untouchables' and renamed them 'Harijan' – The Children of God.

And he described how his grandfather also devoted his life to heal the divisions between Hindus and Muslims. Gandhi's grandson told the crowd that, despite the assassination of his grandfather, he was still continuing to tackle prejudice and build trust not only between Hindus and Muslims but also between Hindus and Sikhs. He told the crowd that divisions between ethnic groups often arose because they were too quick to judge others rather than first judging themselves. As Teame translated his words he was hoping the message would strike home.

Teame was also instrumental, along with Hugh Elliott a former British Colonial administrator, in producing a play entitled *Ane Salisay Eye* (*I am the Third*), which challenged people to think of others before themselves. Elliot's wife, Bridget, a talented artist, designed and produced the scenery backdrop.

A group of younger Eritreans helped Teame and Hugh Elliott to produce the play. Volunteers from other countries played a role too providing ideas, energy and extra enthusiasm. The play, translated into Tigrigna by Teame, was performed first in Asmara and later in major towns.

What effect did it all have on the delicate and dangerous situation in Eritrea at that time? Teame did not know then and does not know now more than fifty years later. But his hope then, and now, is that some seeds were planted to strengthen the traditional Eritrean moral and spiritual code which, he firmly believes, can be the country's salvation.

The experience of working both with his fellow Eritreans and an international group, who all had shared values, had reinforced Teame's faith in the God he worshipped and his desire to serve others. It had strengthened his belief in sowing those seeds of understanding between different peoples and upholding moral and spiritual values.

CHAPTER FOURTEEN

Marriage and Family

Marriage was not high on Teame's agenda as he immersed himself in his work. He had taken on an even greater workload, in addition to his demanding role at the Institute, by teaching English to adults who wanted to complete their secondary education in the evening school attached to the Institute from 6.00 to 9.00 pm.

It was a busy life with no time for socialising. Although now twenty-nine, well past the age most men got married in Eritrea, he had thought he should first further his career. Although keen to get married at some point he didn't think it was important to him at this stage in his life. His relatives had almost given up trying to persuade him to be more receptive to the idea.

Eventually one of his relatives, Berhe Asbaha, who lived in his home village many miles away, came all the way to Asmara to see Teame saying he had something he wanted to discuss with him. Intrigued, Teame agreed to meet him.

When they met a few days later he told Teame that what he wanted to discuss was very important. He wanted to tell him about a young lady whom he thought would make Teame an ideal wife. Families making introductions for marriages were part of the Eritrean tradition.

The lady's name was Teblez Medhane and her family came from

Mebred, a village just 15 kilometres from Teame's home, Adi Ghehad. One of her ancestors had moved the family to the Keren region of Western Eritrea, a largely Muslim area, several generations earlier and her father set up a business there. It was where Teblez had been born.

Teame was told that this young lady was highly educated and was working at the Locust Control Office in Asmara. He passed the building every day on his way to work although he had never met her. Berhe Asbaha urged him to explore the possibilities. He told him it was too good an opportunity to miss.

When Teame questioned him further he was told that Teblez had come back from Addis Ababa to Asmara after her mother died, to look after her father. But what equally interested him most was the family were from his area and, despite being away for generations, had kept up their links with their village. Her sister Solomie Medhane even had a house built there in the same compound where her great grandfather had lived.

Teame decided, yes perhaps it was time he settled down and got married. He would like to take things further. First, though, a meeting was arranged with other members of Teblez's family including her sister Solomie. Feeling in need of some moral support Teame took along his best friend Mohamed, who was his first tutoring pupil and had remained in close touch.

They met at the home of Teblez's father, Fitewrari Medhane Sahle, which was only a few streets away from where Teame lived with his uncle. Neither Teblez or her father were there. Teame liked Solomie, finding her a wise and caring woman. She told him about her family. Her father was an important businessman as well as influential in politics. He was a unionist – not something Teame would have agreed with but his own father, as a former police officer, had at times been a unionist too. Their views in the days of colonial rule would have been that it was better to have a united black country than one ruled by Italians or British.

Teame and Solomie talked about their respective backgrounds. The meeting went well and another one was arranged. This time Teblez would be there.

Two weeks later Teame, a little more nervously this time, arrived to meet Teblez and they were formally introduced. There were glances and nervous smiles between them. But conversation at this stage would not have been part of the strict protocol. First the negotiations had to begin. Teame though was instantly struck by Teblez's quiet serenity and beauty. Berhe Asbaha, he decided, had chosen well. He had already begun to think that perhaps he had found his life partner.

Mohamed was again with him providing moral support. Teblez remained silent as Teame and her relatives talked. Teame was impressed to hear that she had given up a good job in Addis Ababa to come to Asmara and look after her distraught father following her mother's death. Such a move demonstrated the presence of qualities Teame upheld. Moreover, the more they talked, the more her qualities and virtues as a long term partner and mother were making their mark.

Teblez answered questions with yes and no answers. Despite her reticence Teame got the impression that although Solomie was in favour of the marriage, Teblez was unsure, believing that she was not ready. Her mother's death had been a big loss and she would have wanted her to be at her wedding. But she was polite and, perhaps urged on by her sister, agreed to meet Teame to discuss things further.

They went to a quiet lakeside resort in Teame's ancient Volkswagen. Talking alone for the first time they began to find out more about each other. Teame told her that he had not wanted to get married earlier because he had been working so hard and had wanted to help members of his family financially. He had helped with dowries for two of his sisters to get married. He told her there had been an opportunity to marry a Lebanese woman in Beirut, a fellow student, whose intellect and beauty he had admired, but he had walked away remembering his roots and responsibilities and realising it was the wrong match for him.

But he was keen to develop the relationship. He would call Teblez in her workplace and could never understand why her replies to him were so abrupt until he discovered that she worked in an open plan office and felt too inhibited to speak openly.

They had more meetings, sometimes over meals, and would go for long walks at weekends exploring the local countryside sometimes on their own, at other times, accompanied by Mohamed. Solomie would also create occasions for them to meet. The affection between them grew and Teame felt that he and Teblez shared many important values. He was beginning to think she might agree to marry him. At least she hadn't shown any signs of turning him down.

There was by now no doubt in Teame's mind that he was falling in love with this beautiful and intelligent young woman. He was determined to win her hand and even went to the lengths of arriving outside her home and serenading her below her bedroom window. Teblez might have been impressed but the neighbours whose sleep had been disturbed were not.

Later on, Teame heard on the family grapevine that Teblez's uncle, Ato Abbay Haileselassie, had been making enquiries about him and had given positive reports to her father. Ato Abbay also assured Teame that Teblez's reluctance was because of her mother's death.

Finally Teblez made her feelings clear. Teame's enthusiastic wooing of her had not been in vain. She acknowledged that she had feelings for him too. They had fallen in love with each other.

But first he had to have the blessing of her father whom he had yet to meet. According to custom the father would never agree to meeting a potential husband for his daughter unless he knew she was in agreement with the match. A refusal would be too much of a humiliation.

Teame took a delegation of his own family, including his father, and Uncles Dumtsu, Ghebremichael and Menghis to meet Teblez's father and other relatives and set the seal on the marriage. The uncles formally asked Teblez's father for his daughter's hand. The father gave his permission – the final act in this journey of traditional Eritrean courtship. His agreement might have been a formality but Teame still felt a great sense of relief mixed with joy. He liked Teblez's father. Although he was an important businessman and Teame's father was a traditional farmer, he treated him with respect and friendliness.

A date was set for the wedding. Tradition dictated that the groom's family donated a cow for slaughter. The wedding was held at the St Medhane Alem (Saviour of the World) church in Asmara. It was a joyful occasion attended by relatives, friends and work colleagues. The best man was Teame's close friend Mohamed. As a Muslim he would not normally be allowed into an Orthodox Church. Mohamed was not sure about it either. At Teame's insistence the Orthodox priest eventually gave his consent and Mohamed agreed to be best man as long as they didn't try to convert him.

Teame and Teblez decided to hold a joint wedding reception at the Caravel Hotel. Their primary motive was to save their respective families having to organise two cumbersome and time consuming traditional wedding ceremonies, as was customary.

Teame had hired an Eritrean band, Mahber Teatre Asmara, who played Tigrigna and English songs for the many international guests. Years later Teame and Teblez could still fondly remember the band playing the song '*Selel abiliyom deki adiki eyom*', which, translated into English, goes, 'Let them float around with joy as this is their mother land.'

The song reassured them in some symbolic way that they had not yet lost the culture of their country. Another fond memory was that of Peter, the four-year-old son of their British friends Jim and Sally Baynard-Smith, wearing a traditional Eritrean costume.

Towards the end of the evening the band were asked to play traditional Tigrigna music and songs for the benefit, in particular, of Teame's many relatives who had come down from the village to attend the wedding. Many of them had been angry that there had not been traditional dances at the ceremony and that it was held in a smart hotel in which they felt ill at ease. They felt it should have taken place in Teame's uncle's house where he had been living. Little did they know that Uncle Ghebremichael and Aunt Azieb anticipated this ill-feeling and wisely organised another celebration for them the next day when they uninhibitedly enjoyed themselves beating their drums and dancing to their hearts content.

But Teame and Teblez had felt they had to compromise in order to accommodate the large number of international staff at the Training Institute who were invited – Indians, British, Americans, Pakistanis and Filipinos as well as Eritreans and Ethiopians. The Locust Control Office, where Teblez worked, also had international staff who were there. In the end it proved less time consuming and expensive to use a hotel.

For the young couple it was the start of a new life together where the growing love between them – along with the strong Christian faith they shared – was to provide the bedrock of their marriage. It was to be a union which lasted the many tests that were to come and Teame would never cease to be grateful for Teblez's unwavering support.

The newly-weds set up home in a new block of flats behind the Municipal Hall in Asmara. A relative of Mohamed's, Ibrahim Khalilo who was a carpenter, built them some beautiful wooden cupboards in which many of their wedding presents – and the treasured photo album of the ceremony – were kept. Teame felt gratitude to the relative who had been instrumental in bringing them together. But he also felt guilty that he had not done more for him at the time. Years later, when the man became ill, Teame paid for him to go to hospital.

Teblez gave birth to their first daughter, who was named Aida Mebrahtu, the following year. Teame was overjoyed at becoming a father and was immensely proud of his new daughter. Despite his long days at the Institute he would take his turn looking after her. Many a time he would drive her round the town in his ancient Volkswagen to put her to sleep when she cried incessantly in the middle of the night.

By this time, as well as being a new father, Teame had found himself being asked to help villagers from his home area with legal problems which often involved court hearings in Asmara. It was usually disputes with neighbours over land rights or crops. They saw Teame as someone who would stand up for them and knew he understood and recognised the authority of the Elders in the villages.

They said they looked upon him as an Elder. Groups of them, usually about three or four, would descend on his home seeking help and a bed for up to a week. Teblez and Teame would feed them although it was not always easy with a small baby in the house. The villagers would often arrive with a present of a huge can of butter produced from the cows on their farm.

Often it seemed like the village elders expected Teame to solve disputes in their favour regardless of the rights and wrongs. They thought Teame would just go to the judge and persuade him to rule in their favour.

He would speak to the court clerks on their behalf although he would not bend the truth. He didn't want to be the cause of injustice to the other party if the villagers were in the wrong. The villagers didn't always win the case. But they felt they were being looked after and that Teame was loyal to them and to their causes.

Before Teame had arrived on the scene another of Teame's relatives, Auntie Aberash Debessay, had provided hospitality and support for the village elders for the previous twenty-five years.

The life of the newly married couple was to take a new twist – once more fired by Teame's academic ambitions. His role as co-ordinator at the Institute meant he had to attend regular meetings of the other co-ordinators at teacher training institutes in other provinces – Debre Berhan, Harrar, Jimma and Addis Ababa. The meeting would be held in Addis Ababa. They were all influential people in their institutes – in many ways more so than the directors because of their hands-on experience with the students and local schools. They, and the Institute Directors, were directly responsible to the Director of Teacher Education at the Ministry of Education in Addis Ababa, rather than to the Provincial Education Officers.

It was whilst attending one of these conferences that Teame heard that the British Council in Addis Ababa were holding interviews for places at British universities. It was a tremendous opportunity to achieve his aim to study for a Master's degree. He quickly applied.

He was called in for an interview followed by a written examination. Another interview followed with a group of British Council specialists. Shortly afterwards Teame heard to his delight that he had been selected.

He had now to convince Ato Matewos, the Director at the Asmara Training Institute, to release him. The Director, who by now had grown to like and respect Teame, was reluctant to let him go. He told him he was doing a good job and the student teachers appreciated his approach and his commitment to the profession.

Teame pleaded that he needed to further his education. He needed new experiences as he had given his best at the Institute. Now he needed to be invigorated so he could give the institute more.

The Director could have vetoed Teame's hopes, but he relented and told him: 'You have a bright future ahead of you. I don't want to destroy it. But he asked, will you come back to Asmara after graduation?'

Teame promised that he would. So they had a friendly understanding. He felt the Director had shown a wise understanding of his situation and was acting in his best interests. Ato Matewos, whose respect for Teame's teaching methods had grown during his time at the TTI, was now clearly anxious not to lose him permanently.

A few months later Teame was on a flight to London. He had one regret, Teblez was expecting their second child and he would not be there for the birth. He felt he had no option but to accept the scholarship he had been offered. But this did not alleviate the distress he felt at leaving the family. For Teblez's part there was sorrow at his leaving but, despite the hardship it might cause, she supported the move knowing it was important to both their futures. His marriage to Teblez might have started as an 'arranged' union but it had grown into one of love that became a rock solid partnership.

(At the time of writing Teame and Teblez were approaching their 50th wedding anniversary.)

CHAPTER FIFTEEN

Bristol Masters

Teame arrived in London full of hope but also a sense of loss at having to leave his family behind. It was a huge culture change from Asmara. He had his first sights of Buckingham Palace, the Houses of Parliament and London buses. Teame, and other teacher educators from Asia, Latin America and Africa, spent three weeks in London on an introductory course explaining university life in Britain. It was only then that they were told which university they would be going to.

The British Council's aim was to broaden the experience of the teacher educators. They were keen for Teame to specialise in teaching mathematics. Ethiopia, including Eritrea, needed more teachers in the subject. Teame, however, was keen to continue his studies in Teaching English as a Second Language (TESL) as well as Teaching English as a Foreign Language (TEFL). He had studied both subjects at the American University in Beirut along with his specialisation of teacher education.

His assessors from the British Council recognised that English and Teacher education were his main strengths although he agreed to take the mathematics course as well. Initially he was assigned to a university in the north of England. But at the end of the assessment Teame was told he would be going to Bristol at the other end of the country.

Bristol was then, and still is, one of the country's most prestigious red brick universities. Teame was immediately impressed with the quality of the academics who would be responsible for their courses. The man overseeing the programme for the British Council Scholars was Professor Roger Wilson who at the time was also Dean of the Faculty of Education. He had spent many years in Malawi teaching at the University of Blantyre. His reputation there accounted for the twenty or so Malawian teacher educators on the course.

Teame discovered his fellow British Council scholars, who came mainly from other African countries, were to take a Teaching Certificate which was a disappointment for him and some of the other students. He already had a Diploma in Education from the American University in Beirut where he had also obtained his degree. What he really wanted to do was take a Master's degree which would give him a higher status, and increased salary, back in Ethiopia/Eritrea.

But, despite his reservations, he realised he had no option but to accept the course on offer. In fact, as he soon discovered, this tailor-made Certificate course did take his knowledge up to new levels. The main focus was teacher education with the emphasis on child development and psychology of education. It might not be providing the extra qualification that Teame wanted, but his knowledge of the subjects was being enhanced. He also had a five week attachment to Redland Teacher Training College (now closed with the building redeveloped as flats) as part of the course. After his attachment to the Training College he had written a lengthy report on how primary school teachers were trained in the UK.

The international group of British Council students taking the Teaching Certificate course found themselves isolated from the local students. There were two groups – the larger contingent of post graduate students doing their initial teacher training and the small groups of experienced teachers attending an In-Service programme.

The large numbers of students meant there was not space for all of them to share coffee breaks in the cafeteria of the Woodhouse Building where they and their studies were centred. Teame felt unhappy that there was no chance to meet up with his British counterparts. It would be a chance not only to improve his English but also to discuss education and the views and experiences of the British students.

There was another bone of contention. The thirty or so experienced British teachers were taking a slightly higher qualification – a Diploma of Education. Once in possession of that students were able to apply to take a Master's degree. Although he already had his Diploma of Education from Beirut, it was not recognised under the British system.

During the Christmas break that year he and the other British Council students were invited to Professor Wilson's holiday home on the coast. Because some of the lecturers, and even fellow Africans, had trouble pronouncing Teame's name he agreed to have it shortened to Tom. At the time he had been quite relaxed about it although when he later realised the connotations of a black man being called Tom, he had put a stop to it.

As the students enjoyed the hospitality, Professor Wilson called Teame aside. By this time he had been selected by his counterparts as their spokesperson. The Professor said: 'Tom, how is the course going?' Teame told him he was very happy with the course. But all he ever heard was African voices. He would like the chance to hear voices of English students and to find out what their thoughts were on education. They were not getting any cross fertilisation of ideas never mind integration.

Professor Wilson listened sympathetically and said he would convene a meeting to discuss Teame's worries and decide if anything could be done. The outcome was that Teame was told that he, and any other interested students, would be given the opportunity to take the Teaching Diploma course if they performed well in their current course and also met the entry requirements. But there was another condition. Those accepted for the Diploma Course had to continue with the Certificate of Education course as well. It would mean the workload would be almost unbearable.

Teame was the only one who accepted the challenge. But, as he was later to acknowledge, it was a nightmare. Some of his African colleagues had turned down the opportunity and Teame thought they might have made the wiser choice. But having chosen to do the extra work he knuckled down to it. He had never worked harder in his life. Every evening was taken up with his studies. There were no visits to pubs, no sightseeing. There was not just one dissertation to write but two. He had only four hours sleep a night and understood the truth of Einstein's much quoted words about his own enormous achievements, attributing them to '1% inspiration and 99% perspiration'. The great man's sentiments gave him the inspiration to keep going.

He finally completed his two dissertations and submitted them. He passed both. More importantly he had scored sufficiently high marks in the Diploma course dissertation to go on to take a Master's programme in the next academic year. It was what he most wanted to do. But it would mean extending his stay in Bristol for another year and he had promised Ato Matewos, the Director of the Asmara Teacher Training Institute, that he would return after a year.

Professor Wilson was delighted at Teame's success. He, and other members of the university staff, took him out for a meal with their families, to celebrate. But Teame still had to overcome the problem of needing to stay another year having made a solemn promise to return to Asmara.

The situation in Eritrea had deteriorated. Fighting between the Ethiopian Army and the Liberation Front was continuing with killings on both sides. Teame was worried for the safety of Teblez who had by then given birth to their second daughter, Esther Mebrahtu. Aida their first-born was now just one year old. Teblez was still working at the Locust Control Office in Asmara with her sister and other relatives helping with the care of the children. The fighting and bloodshed was happening close to the area where the family were living. As Teame got news of events at home he became increasingly worried.

So not only did he face the problem of delaying his return to Asmara, despite his promise, he was now concerned about the safety of his family. And if he was to stay and take his Master's as he hoped to do, he would have to find an additional scholarship.

First though he had to explain the situation to Ato Matewos. To his relief the Director of the Institute in Asmara was understanding. He wrote a letter in support of his staying in Bristol. He could see that Teame needed his Master's degree. It would be good for the Institute as well as for him. So he wished him well and gave his permission for Teame to stay another year. Teame promised that he would return in a year. Although with events in the Ethiopia-Eritrea conflict he could not be sure that would be possible.

The British Council also agreed to extend his scholarship for another year. Professors Wilson and Ben Morris, along with Bill Tyler had been helpful in putting forward his case.

Everything was in place for him to stay in Bristol. Teame decided that he also needed to get Teblez and his two daughters out of the country to join him. At first they had problems getting an exit visa. But Teblez's brother, an influential businessman with links in Addis Ababa, was able to smooth the way. The situation was also helped by the Minister of Education's delight at Teame's success. He was happy to extend the duration of Teame's stay for one more year – albeit without pay.

So Teblez, Aida and Esther, who was just a few months old, arrived at Heathrow for an emotional reunion. Teame saw the new baby for the first time. They were given accommodation in Zebra House, one of the university residences for married students with families. The British Council staff, assisted by some university secretaries, would take the wives and children of the students out for tea from time to time. There was a playground nearby for the children. The family settled happily into life in Bristol and made friends with their neighbours from Colombia, Uganda and Egypt.

Teame found the Master's course very demanding and tough. He was given new insights into Anthropology, a subject he had studied in Beirut, by Bill Tyler who had worked in Africa studying tribes in Ghana and Uganda. In Beirut, the focus had been more on cultures of different societies from life to death which was part and parcel of the discipline known as 'Cultural Anthropology'. What Teame was now learning from Bill Tyler was 'Social Anthropology' with focus on the structure of society and how it functioned. He found the approach much more interesting.

Teame was fascinated to learn more about African tribes like the Nuer and Acholi in Uganda. Bill Tyler would describe the beauty of the African countryside and talk about the many different cultures. Having never visited any other African country this was an eye opener to Teame.

Bill Tyler, who undertook extensive research in the eastern part of Africa, described how arbitrary boundaries set up by colonial powers affected the structures of traditional societies and how conflict could be caused when tribes with different cultures or religions were lumped together. He used South Sudan as an example.

It reminded Teame of the situation in Ethiopia where Eritrea had been swallowed up after annexation resulting in the liberation struggle and bloodshed. He began to develop a deeper understanding of the consequences of 'the scramble' for the Dark Continent of Africa by the European powers starting from the 1870s.

His studies for the Master's degree had gone well. He had been stretched and stimulated. The theme of his dissertation revolved around the lessons that can be learnt from the Teaching Practice Programme in the United Kingdom and on how to improve the professional development of primary teachers in Ethiopia. At that time, Eritrea was still part of Ethiopia.

Despite the pressures he was working under Teame had still managed to cultivate lasting friendships with some of his colleagues on the Master's course like John Hayter, Stuart McFarlane and Steve and Sue Ferguson. Towards the end of the course his friends decided to organise a farewell party for Teame and his family at Steve and Sue's home.

Unknown to Teame, one of the hidden agendas was to test his alcoholic capacity. The party was certainly fun for Teame but proved an embarrassment for Teblez when she saw her husband – not used to a large intake of alcohol – being helped into the car of one of his friends and ferried back to Zebra House. All was forgiven later.

Teblez, in fact, had made many friends too. Whilst working hard looking after the young Aida and Esther, she had also regularly seen several of the secretaries at the university including Marie Taylor and Anne Mallitte.

With the term ended Teame started making arrangements for him and his family to return to Asmara. He had not yet got his results. But after attending a Viva by the External Examiners of the Bristol programme, which he thought had gone well, he was confident that he had done enough to get his Master's degree. This proved to be the case.

On the way home to Asmara, Teame organised a four day stop-over in Rome. He felt Teblez deserved a short holiday after all her hard work looking after the family while he concentrated on his studies.

They took in the sights including the Colosseum, the Vatican and the Trevi Fountain. One of their favourite memories is the delight at seeing fruits – oranges, paw paws and mandarins – from their part of Eritrea, (Mai Aini) on sale in the local shops.

They had a shock when it was time to get a taxi back to the airport to continue their journey home. Teame had overspent his budget for the trip and could not find the money for the fare. In desperation he searched all his pockets. It was his custom to keep a few coins tucked away for emergencies. He did indeed find just enough to cover the fare. The two of them jumped into the air with delight and relief much to the confusion of their young daughters.

They boarded their Ethiopian Airlines flight with a sense of gratitude and achievement. But their emotions were tinged with a sense of anxiety as to what would await them on their return. On arrival at Asmara Airport they were met by members of the family and close friends and were taken to stay at the home of Teame's brother-in-law, Ato Tewolde.

Teame now had to wait to be told by the Ministry of Education what his next job would be.

CHAPTER SIXTEEN

Director

Shortly after arriving in Asmara, Teame was instructed to go straight to the Ministry of Education in Addis Ababa. Leaving his family with his brother-in-law, Ato Tewolde Medhane a business executive, he set off and at the Ministry was met by the Director General of Teacher Education, Ato Getachew Mekuria.

The Director General welcomed him warmly when he arrived at about 11 o'clock in the morning offering him coffee. To Teame's surprise he took him out to lunch – an unusual honour from a man so high up in the government. Teame had only briefly met Ato Getachew in his previous capacity as the Co-ordinator of Asmara Teacher Training Institute. But the Director General, who was responsible for all the Teacher Training Institutes, appeared to know a lot about him.

Over lunch he told Teame that he thought the Ministry could benefit from his experience in Bristol. Teame told him of the report he had written about the training of teachers in the UK which the Director General was anxious to see. Then he said he wanted him to take up a role at the Ministry in Addis Ababa. He didn't specify what it would be but hinted that it could be a big step up for Teame and could result in him climbing up the ladder within the Ministry in a few years.

It was a big temptation which would mean being close to the sources of power in the government along with opportunities not available to people in the provinces. But Teame was not at ease with it. He was reluctant to work in Addis Ababa, a city he did not know well and where a good grasp of Amharic was needed. Above all, though, he did not want to disrupt his family life with Teblez and the girls whose home was in Asmara.

He explained his doubts to the Director General. He replied that Teame would be foolish to turn down the offer and hinted that he could be in danger in Eritrea because the liberation fighters might think he was in league with the government. But he agreed to discuss the situation with his superiors before making a final decision on Teame's future. He made it clear he would be fighting for him to join the In-Service Section of teacher training in a senior capacity.

However, despite the Director General's reluctance, a few days later Teame was told he could go back to Asmara to the Teacher Training Institute. He was told he would be informed of his new appointment. The Director General refused to give any hints of his new post saying it had to be decided by the Minister of Education. Two weeks after Teame arrived back at the Institute a telegram arrived. He knew straight away what his new appointment was because it was addressed to Teame Mebrahtu, Director, Asmara Teachers Training Institute. He was to be the new Director. It was a shock but a happy one. This was a job that he had trained for.

His predecessor, Ato Matewos Gessesse, had already been sent to a new post as National Director at the new Academy of Pedagogy in Bahir Dar.

Teame worried how the rest of the staff would receive his new appointment. He need not have worried. They happily congratulated him. He had known most of them well during the previous time at the Institute.

The assistant director of the TTI formally welcomed him and there was a small party with cakes and tea. Teame told them not to think of him as their boss. He said he wanted to work with them for the good of the Institution. They should not stop discussing problems with him in the way they had done when he was the Co-ordinator at the Institution. He promised to always inform and involve them in any decisions he took.

Full of ideas, and anxious to begin making a difference, he soon set to work. First, he changed how the Institute was run by improving liaison with staff and introducing forward planning. The administrative structure was streamlined. There were also meetings with student leaders – not something that happened during his predecessor's regime.

A new channel of communication was put in place. It took the form of a set of weekly meetings with the teacher-trainees and their leaders in order to discuss real or perceived problems. Care for the students – a large majority of them Ethiopian – was still important to him, as it had been in his days two years earlier when he was the college co-ordinator.

Relationships with both local primary and secondary schools were improved to the mutual benefit of their teachers and the staff at the Institute. Student-teacher activities – sports clubs, music and dance – were expanded. The relationship between the TTI and the local community was enhanced. Each trainee was required to assist at least three illiterates in reading and writing by the end of the academic year.

In-Service courses were introduced during the summer for experienced but under qualified teachers. Teame also gave lectures to members of the Eritrean Teachers Association in Asmara dealing with issues like coping strategies in the classroom and posing the question: 'What makes a good teacher?'

His view of the role of Director was that he needed to be a team builder. He likened the job to that of the captain of a football team, leading by example on the field and involved in the game, rather than a manager standing on the sidelines, observing and giving orders.

One example of his care for the personnel of the institution involved an Ethiopian trainee, who had a heart problem and needed an operation. Teame took the seriously ill student to Kagnew Station, the American base in Asmara, because the Eritrean hospital in Asmara did not have doctors who could do the heart operation at that time. There was a private hospital that could do it but that would have been prohibitively expensive.

He saw the education officer, an American, explained the problem and asked for his help. The officer listened carefully then asked: 'Is he a relation?' He seemed to be inferring Teame was asking a favour for a relative. This angered Teame who emphatically told him: 'No.' He said he was embarrassed being asked the question. The American officer clearly suspected he was part of the corruption and bribery that went on. Other Eritrean or Ethiopians had probably approached him before asking for favours.

Teame pointed out that he was Eritrean and the trainee was from Wollega in Ethiopia. He said that he was asking the American to help for reasons of humanity. Teame added that he felt both professionally and personally responsible for the trainee whose parents lived hundreds of miles away.

At last the American officer realised the request was genuine and said, yes, he would help. Much to Teame's delight he agreed to send the trainee off for an operation at a hospital in America. After the complex operation the trainee returned to the TTI to resume his studies. Teame was proud of what he had achieved which had, almost certainly, saved the young man's life.

On another occasion Teame found himself in the unexpected role of a matchmaker. An Indian lecturer, a High Caste Hindu, fell in love with his Eritrean maid who, like many Eritreans, was a Coptic-Orthodox Christian. Unlike the well-educated lecturer she was semi-literate. The intended match had not gone down well with the other Indian and

Pakistani members of staff who were ostracising him. But the lecturer was determined to marry the girl and asked Teame to assist.

So he found himself attempting to reconcile the differences in religion, education and status and the inherent prejudices that came with them. He went several times to the potential bride's village near Mendefera about 65 kilometres away to talk to her relatives. They, too, were unhappy about the match claiming that they had never heard of a Coptic marrying a Hindu. But finally they consented after Teame made the point that their daughter was benefitting from the arrangement.

Teame then pleaded with the Chief Priest at St Mary's Orthodox Church in Asmara to perform the marriage. In fact the Hindu groom did convert to Christianity. Whether he was acting from conviction, or taking the pragmatic route to ease the passage of his marriage, Teame was not sure.

But on the day Teame found himself with dual roles. As well as acting as Best Man for the Groom he also gave the bride away as her father had died some years earlier. On top of that he organised the wedding reception. The happy couple stayed in Asmara for a couple of years and had two daughters (the eldest of them was Aunty Azieb's God-daughter). The family later emigrated to Canada.

During his first few years as Director at the TTI Teame found himself, much to his surprise, apparently elevated up the social ladder. Out of the blue he received an official invitation to a lunch in honour of Emperor Haile Selassie at the Imperial Palace in Asmara to celebrate the Emperor's birthday.

He came down to earth when he discovered that not only he but all civil servants holding the rank of Director and above were invited. But the memory of attending what turned out to be a very lavish lunch under the watchful eye of an Emperor sitting on his throne, was an experience he never forgot.

Teame had become a popular and well respected figure at the Institute. He was to find out just how much his staff and students thought of him when he faced the devastating news of his mother Wagaye's death. She had been taken ill and came to Asmara for treatment in the local hospital and stayed with his family for several months. The long term affects of malaria and the hard working life she had experienced, bringing up her eight children, had taken its toll. She was only in her mid fifties.

Teame's grief at her passing was compounded by the fact that she had died so young. She would never get to know her grandchildren who would have benefited from her experience of life and wise counsel. He felt empty and at a loss. He had been very close to his mother and missed her deeply.

But he was glad that during the last two weeks of her illness Teblez had arranged for Wagaye, who she respected and loved, to take Holy Communion at her hospital bed. This gave her a great sense of relief before she died and she blessed her daughter-in-law for her kind and thoughtful action.

It was decided to take Wagaye back to Adi Ghehad for burial. The tradition for Eritrean funerals is for the cortege to be escorted by mourners. As it set off Teame was astonished, and very moved, to discover that about four hundred staff and students were lining both sides of the road for a length of 2 kilometres. There were also four bus loads and fifteen cars full of mourners who accompanied the cortège all the way to Adi Ghehad. Teame was deeply touched by the showing of sympathy.

Teame was both grief-stricken and exhausted. The traditional mourning in the Coptic tradition is a long process. Mourners, about eighty of them, would assemble in a huge marquee where they would sleep for two weeks. They would rise at 5.30 am to greet fresh mourners arriving from surrounding towns and villages.

Teame had fond memories of the love and kindness of his mother who, because she married so young, always looked upon him, her first born, as more of a brother than a son. She was not widely travelled or schooled but he fondly remembered her as someone with a big heart filled with her Christian faith.

She was renowned for distributing bread and milk, under cover of darkness, to widowed mothers and orphans during Eritrea's bitterly cold rainy season. She would give her last possession to someone in need even at the expense of her own children. Teame concluded that his mother's death reminded him of his own mortality, but it also had taught him about the need for compassion for others which had been one of his mother's hallmarks. Teame considered her qualities were personified in the contents of a beautiful Arabic poem which goes, '*Umi umi, hiat Ainee wa hiat Gelbi*,' meaning, 'My mother is my eye and my heart...'

But, amidst his grief at his mother's passing there were more problems to deal with at the TTI. During the two years he was in Bristol the buildings, which were in poor condition then, had deteriorated still further. There were cracks in the walls and the compound was badly in need of cleaning and smartening up. He wanted to do something about it but requests for the funds he needed were held up by government bureaucracy.

Looking after budgets and being responsible for administration was not something Teame enjoyed. He was much more interested in the academic and professional side of his new job. Dealing with the Education Ministry officials 1,000 kilometres away in Addis Ababa was never easy. Sometimes the phones did not work. It was very time consuming and telephone costs were high.

In view of the difficulties in obtaining funds for the Institution Teame became convinced that the answer was for all five of the Teacher Training Institutions in the country to be given financial autonomy. They should each have a trained accountant responsible for the budget. It would allow them to make their own decisions on where money was spent without delay and without the usual bureaucratic tactic of saying in Amharic, '*Bagetu temelash honewal*,' which means in English, 'The budget is withdrawn.'

It was a radical idea. He raised it at one of the regular meetings of institute directors arguing that it would make their establishments more efficient. Because of their proximity to Addis, some of them were not convinced. Teame, though, did not give up. He documented the problems he had persuading ministry officials to part with money.

When part of a roof at one of his buildings collapsed and fell on the head of a trainee – fortunately not injuring him seriously – he took photographs and used them as evidence of the need for financial autonomy. He kept up his campaign. It took about three years but he and his fellow directors did eventually win the argument.

Meanwhile he campaigned to get mini buses for all the five Institutions to be used for transporting trainees to local schools during their teaching practice. This, he argued, was vital because the trainees needed experience in the nearby rural schools, where most of them would be allocated after graduation. He was delighted when his idea was accepted and the buses were provided.

But, to Teame's dismay, the first three buses that arrived were allocated to Addis Ababa and neither he nor the other provincial TTI directors got one. The Director of the TTI in Addis Ababa, who was very powerful and influential, had clearly used his influence for his own institution's benefit.

Teame was furious. It was yet another frustration. The situation was not made any easier by the political situation in Asmara and the ongoing struggle between the Ethiopian army and the liberation fighters. It meant recruiting new staff was proving difficult. Potential lecturers from Ethiopia were reluctant to come to Asmara because of the dangers. And some of the international staff were not renewing their contracts, unwilling to extend their stay because of the uncertainty of the situation and the potential dangers.

The situation was fraught with difficulty and Teame was beginning to wonder if the time was fast approaching when he should seek another job. But a series of events, both personal and national, were to take precedence.

CHAPTER SEVENTEEN

Mengistu Coup

On September 12, 1974 Teame was in Addis Ababa to attend one of the regular meetings of Institute Directors at the Ministry of Education. He was to witness an event that day which changed the history of Ethiopia.

Walking from his hotel to the Ministry at about 9.00 am, he noticed a lot of agitation among the shoe shine boys, unemployed youngsters who made a humble living around the city centre. They were shouting, 'Down with the Emperor' – something unheard of during Haile Selasie's reign and which would normally have brought serious consequences.

Puzzled and wondering what was going on, Teame continued on his way to the Ministry for his meeting with the other directors and Ministry officials. Towards midday they heard a commotion outside. The windows of their meeting room in the Ministry overlooked the Trinity Cathedral adjacent to the Imperial Palace.

Teame and his colleagues saw a mob of people who had surrounded the area and were also shouting against the Emperor. Then they were shocked to see Haile Selassie being driven slowly past them in a humble Volkswagen, not his usual official limousine. He had been marched out of the Palace and down the steps after being arrested by the Dergue, a committee of low-ranking military officers and enlisted men who had launched a coup. The most prominent officer was

Colonel Mengistu Hailemariam who was to become the leader of the new Marxist regime.

It took a little time for Teame to understand the implications of what he was seeing. But the soldiers on the streets and the demise of the Emperor soon brought home the realisation that a military coup was underway. Life in the country was to change dramatically and Teame`s immediate emotion – although he could not have anticipated the horrors to come – was one of uncertainty about the future and what it would mean not just for Eritreans like him but for the whole of Ethiopia.

So what started as a routine day of meetings for Teame and the other Directors had become a momentous moment in the long history of the country – the end of Haile Selassie`s reign. He was the last emperor in the 3,000-year-old Ethiopian monarchy and had ruled for half a century. Now the old Royal autocracy was to be replaced by Marxism.

Teame recalled later that he had heard the crowd of demonstrators outside the building, shouting: ' Death to the Emperor!' He believed that they had been paid to swell out the crowds since ordinary Ethiopians would not, at that time, have joined a demonstration against the Emperor.

The Emperor was taken into captivity and died in mysterious circumstances in August 1975 at the age of eighty-three. State media reported that it was from 'respiratory failure'. But there were rumours that he had been assassinated. In 1992, after the fall of the Dergue, his bones were reportedly found buried under a toilet at the Imperial Palace. The cause of his death remains a mystery. In November 2000 his body was laid to rest in Addis Ababa's Trinity Cathedral.

There had been unrest against the Royal regime for some years. The army were protesting against low pay and were not pacified by a 33% wage increase. The famine in Wollo in north-eastern Ethiopia –

highlighted by Jonathan Dimbleby's documentary in 1973 *The Unknown Famine,* had added to the Emperor's unpopularity. The documentary, retitled *The Hidden Hunger* was constantly shown on Ethiopian television right up to the day of his overthrow.

Teame was uneasy at the turn of events. He was no fan of the Emperor who had annexed Eritrea. But he did not consider he had been treated fairly. He considered he should have been given respect and a fair trial. But under the new Marxist regime that was not going to happen.

He realised that change was needed in the country. But, although there were many academics at that time who thought that Mengistu would be the saviour of the country, Teame believed that human life was important, whether an Emperor or a beggar. The Emperor, he felt, should be treated in accordance with the law not the rule of a dictator.

The new regime took away land from the Balabats, the landlords, throughout the country. They were like aristocracy with huge power and influence. The regime slogan was Land to the Tiller. Ordinary farmers were told: 'The land is yours.' Teame had some sympathy with this. There was a lot of poverty and injustice. But he was horrified by other bloodier aspects of the Mengistu regime.

Mengistu's Dergue started a programme of sending youths to the villages. Any who refused to go were arbitrarily shot in front of their parents who then had to pay for the bullet that had killed their sons.

Back home with his family in Asmara, Teame found the streets were patrolled by soldiers loyal to the Dergue. An evening curfew had been introduced. Food prices had rocketed. There was a great deal of fear and anxiety. Teame was very worried about Teblez and the girls – especially when he had to leave the city on business. He would ring home whenever he was away to check that they were safe. He was careful what he said for fear that a government agent might be listening.

He did not feel free to talk about the situation except to a few trusted friends. Only fellow Eritreans inside and outside the Institute were taken into his confidence. But he would be careful what he said to the Ethiopians. Many of his international colleagues did not renew their contracts so worried were they at the situation in the country.

The Mengistu regime was as opposed to the Eritrean Liberation movement as the Emperor had been. Liberation fighters, both the Eritrean Liberation Front (ELF) and the Eritrean People's Liberation Front (EPLF), continued to operate in the area around Asmara and there were killings and kidnappings.

But life at the Institute carried on, albeit with some limitations caused by the curfew. Evening classes in the Secondary Schools, including the one attached to the TTI, had to be cancelled. But Teame was determined to be professional despite all that was going on around him. He continued teaching in the daytime as well as in the evening before the curfew, whilst also carrying out his duties as Director. A great believer in hands-on education he took the view that he should not stay in his office and pontificate. He should do it himself, he thought, determining that a good teacher was a doer as well as a reflective thinker.

Shortly after the Emperor's overthrow by the Dergue the conflict between the Ethiopian Army and the Eritrean liberation fighters had escalated. The fighters were approaching the outskirts of Asmara. An army outpost had been attacked and destroyed. There had been a massacre by the army of the population of a little village called Sheeb because they were suspected of harbouring the liberation fighters. Colonel Mengistu was threatening further bloody retributions, by breaking a bottle full of blood in one of his mass rallies in Addis Ababa.

He had appointed as chairman of the Dergue a former Royalist, General Aman Andom, who had become the public face of the regime.

He was a popular figure having fought in the war against the Somalis in the Ogaden desert. He was at odds with the Dergue who wanted to crush opposition in Eritrea by force. He persuaded Mengistu to let him make an attempt to solve the crisis in Eritrea peacefully.

Although a member of the Mengistu regime, and a supporter of the Ethiopian cause, his parents were Eritrean and the family lived in Sudan where he had been brought up and educated.

He said he would address a mass rally at the football stadium in Asmara and hoped to head off further trouble and bloodshed. The rally was announced on local radio and on the day the stadium was packed with Eritreans hopeful that he would bring a solution to the misery they were suffering.

Teame, as Director of the Teacher Training Institute, was invited to be there. He was given a seat with the VIPs but decided instead to sit in the crowd where he would not be noticed. Sitting in a prominent position might be seen as a political statement and he was aware of the need to remain neutral in the eyes of his many Ethiopian students.

On the ground in front of the stands thousands of soldiers were lined up. The army were ready to act if there was trouble. Teame saw the General's helicopter fly over the stadium announcing his arrival. He remembers a great sense of anticipation among the crowd and he thought the General was a brave man to come to Asmara at such a dangerous time.

When the General arrived in the stadium he ordered the soldiers to keep their rifles at their sides. A tall man, over six feet, he stood on a rostrum in the middle of the stadium. He spoke to the crowd in Arabic initially. This generated a feeling of both surprise and optimism among the crowd, many of whom were Muslims. Then, in his broken native Tigrigna and finally in the official language of Amharic. It should be noted that Arabic and Tigrigna had been banned by the Mengistu regime.

The General said that the end of the Imperial Regime was also the end of old practices towards Eritrea. He said a government dedicated to national unity and progress would restore peace and prosperity in Eritrea.

Then he said something that was both very courageous, and would have registered with the Eritreans in the huge crowd. He condemned those soldiers responsible for the massacre at Sheeb as well as other crimes against Eritreans. The guilty would be punished he said.

As he spoke those words Teame could see that many of the soldiers were looking uneasy. He knew that in condemning the massacre the General was likely to anger Mengistu. Newspapers and television reported his speech. In an effort to regain the media advantage Mengistu launched an attack on local landlords, the balabats.

The General, who had disagreements with the Dergue, launched a campaign to seek support from elements of the Army and around the country. He sent a message to military units highly critical of the Dergue. A few days later he refused Mengistu's order to send 5,000 troops to Eritrea and to execute sixty imprisoned Imperial officials.

He resigned and went to his house in the countryside, sending appeals for help to his supporters. But Mengistu forces intercepted them. The house was surrounded by troops loyal to the Dergue. The general died in the ensuring gun battle. It's not known whether he was shot or committed suicide.

Teame, like many of his countrymen, recognised that the death of the general was the end of any chance of a peaceful solution to the conflict in Eritrea. There would be no hope of reconciliation. The problems were going to be solved militarily and there would be yet more suffering for the ordinary Eritreans.

CHAPTER EIGHTEEN

Student Death

A study day out at a local reservoir for a group of students at the Asmara Teacher Training Institute should have been a pleasant interlude in their studies. But it turned into a tragedy with potentially dangerous consequences for Teame.

The students, accompanied by an Indian lecturer, had gone to the area to study butterflies. It had been Teame's idea to go there after the lecturer had complained he couldn't get models of butterflies for his science classes. Teame told the lecturer the students could study the local butterflies in the wild and they didn't need expensive models brought in from Europe.

It was a sound idea and the students had set off in Teame's official van accompanied by the lecturer. All went well, there were many butterflies in the area as Teame had said. But it was a hot day and one of the students decided to go for a swim in the river which ran from the reservoir. He got into difficulties, was swept away by the current, and drowned.

It was a tragic accident. Teame was devastated. He felt responsible. Although he had not been at the scene the trip had been his idea. No student under his care had died before. It was like losing one of his family. But the situation was to get worse.

The dead student was Ethiopian. He had died in Eritrea. Rumours started flying around the city that the student had been killed by the Eritrean liberation front fighters operating in the area. Many of the Ethiopian student-teachers had contacts with the Ethiopian army soldiers based in the barracks right next door to the Institute. The situation threatened to get ugly.

Teame pondered what to do. It was a big test for him. He followed all the protocols. The body was sent to the mortuary for a post mortem which confirmed that the student had drowned. But still the rumours persisted despite the students who had been on the trip confirming what had actually happened.

The Ethiopian soldiers next door as well as the few Ethiopian trainees who for one reason or another did not join the field trip started making threats, saying they would seek revenge for their countryman's death. They blamed the Eritreans and said they would have to pay. It may have been just bravado but it was a dangerous situation.

As he considered what to do next, Teame decided the Institute must have traditional ceremonies of mourning for the dead student. He encouraged the Eritrean students to join the Ethiopians to show their respect. The ceremonies went on for four nights. Teblez, Teame's wife, cooked food and some of the staff provided provisions. Teame attended all the ceremonies himself, staying until the lights were switched off at 11.00 pm. Gradually, the rumours died down and relations with the Ethiopians improved. They had appreciated the period of mourning and the participation by the Eritreans, led by Teame.

He wanted to mark the death in the proper way. For him that meant returning the body to the student's home village, deep in the heart of Ethiopia and thousands of kilometres away. But that could be very dangerous. News of the death had reached the area and feelings were running high. There had been a riot in the local secondary school and, since the Mengistu coup, some of the pupils had got hold of arms.

Despite the dangers, and warnings from close friends and colleagues, Teame was determined to fulfil what he saw as his responsibility to the student and his family by taking the body back to his home village himself.

Armed with the death certificate and all other necessary papers he took the body to Addis Ababa by plane. He was met at the airport by the Director General of Teacher Education Ato Getachew Mekuria. The coffin was taken to the Ministry of Education awaiting transport back to the village.

On hearing of Teame's plan to take the body back to the village himself the Director General said: 'Are you a fool? What are you doing?' He knew just how dangerous it would be for Teame to go into what would be hostile territory and, fearing for his safety, tried to persuade him not to go.

But, although he had great respect for him, Teame was adamant. He told the Director General: 'All I am doing is following my responsibility. I would do it for anybody.' He had promised his students, many of them Ethiopians, that he would return the body to the village for burial. He would not want to lose face by not doing so.

The Director General, realising that Teame was determined to go said: 'You do this at your own risk. Don't say I didn't warn you.' Teame thanked him for his concern. The next day he set off.

The village was 600 kilometres away from Addis Ababa and was not accessible by air. So the journey had to be made by car. The Ministry provided him with a driver and an interpreter – the local villagers spoke Oromigna, a local language which Teame would not understand. They carried the coffin in the back of the car.

Arriving in the village was an experience that Teame describes as the most frightening he has ever known. They had notified the parents of their imminent arrival via the Ministry of Education office in the locality. When they got there they were met by a huge crowd of angry villagers and students. Women were wailing in their distress.

Unknown to Teame many members of the Ethiopian army from the village had been killed in the conflict with the liberation fighters in Eritrea. Tempers were running high. Some of the crowd were shouting in Amharic: 'Here is an Eritrean in our village.' Others were brandishing their newly acquired pistols.

Finally, a group of about ten young men representing the students, demanded to see the body. They said they would not allow a burial until they had examined it themselves. Some of the students had pistols. Teame explained that they had doctor's certificates certifying the death. But the students shouted: 'Doctors, what doctors? Are they Eritrean doctors? We don't care about them.' Teame feared for his life. There was little rule of law in the area at the time.

The students wanted to open the coffin. Teame advised against it. He said the coffin was sealed for hygienic reasons. They would have to take responsibility for whatever they did. His job was to see that the student was given a proper burial. Then he asked to talk to the boy's parents.

They were brought forward and, through the interpreter and speaking mostly to the mother, Teame explained what had happened to their son. He produced photographs of the ceremonies of mourning that had been held in the Institute which showed they had done their duty and shown their respect according to tradition. He apologised for what had happened but said it was an accident.

There had been a collection among staff and students at the institute which had been generously supported. The total came to over a thousand Ethiopian dollars. More money than the family would have ever seen. Teame handed it over to the mother saying it was to go towards the burial ceremony. He made sure he handed the money over in front of witnesses.

The mother was grateful for the money and seemed to believe Teame's account. Teame also thought it was likely that some of the Ethiopian students in the Institute, with links to the area, had sent word back that the story was genuine and that Teame was to be trusted.

Meanwhile the student representatives came up with a compromise to partially open the coffin to ensure the identity of the dead trainee. But, as it was getting late, it was mutually agreed that the body should be buried. Soon after that Teame borrowed a megaphone from one of the student representatives and addressed the huge crowd of mourners – about 2,000 of them – speaking in Amharic. He said that the loss of the young man was a loss to all Ethiopians including Eritreans.

Things began to quieten down. It was nightfall by now, too late to start the long journey back to Addis Ababa. So as tradition dictated, Teame, his driver and the interpreter, were all invited to spend the night in the family's small hut in the village. There were no hotels nearby.

Teame and the others did not spend a comfortable night. The food was not what they were used to. Smoke from the fire in the hut made it difficult to sleep. In the morning after a breakfast of milk they set off back to Addis Ababa.

Teame was grateful to be still alive. As the car crossed the boundary back into the next province he said a quiet 'Thank God' to himself.

He was met by the Director General when he returned to the Ministry. He was angry with him saying: 'I thought you were a wise man.' He told Teame he had been foolish. But Teame was still convinced he had done the right thing and later the Director General admitted he respected his decision.

At the next meeting of the five Teacher Training Institute directors Teame gave a full report of what had happened. The other Directors commended him on his actions and said he was brave and that they would not have done it.

Teame replied: 'I am Eritrean and foolish!' They all laughed. But he knew that things could have turned out differently and he thanked God that they hadn't.

CHAPTER NINETEEN

The Academy

'Report to the Minister of Education immediately' said the telegram delivered to Teame's office in Asmara. It was both intriguing and worrying. Why did the Minister want to see him at such short notice? His mind was full of questions.

He was right to be worried. Others who had received similar summonses had ended up in prison or just disappeared as the Mengistu Marxist regime conducted a brutal campaign against landlords – the balabats – and others they saw as political opponents, including academics. Rumours were rife about their fate.

The Minister, Dr Hailegabriel Dagne, was a Mengistu appointee, a leftist who had studied in East Germany. Teame knew and respected him, but it did not assuage his fears. The man was, after all, part of the regime. He agonised over whether he should go. Would it put his life in danger? Would he ever come back?

Teame consulted trusted close friends and relatives including his brother in law – Teblez's oldest brother – who was very close to him. Opinions were divided. Some said: 'Never go! There is no guarantee that you will come back.' Teblez, too, was very concerned. Others felt he had no option but to accept the summons.

In the end time ran out. A decision could be delayed no more. The

Mengistu regime was coming down hard on those who refused their 'invitations' to meet the committee. Teame realised that if he refused to go it would infer he was guilty of something. So, with great trepidation, he packed a small suitcase and boarded the first available flight to Addis Ababa.

Arriving at the airport he went straight to the Ministry of Education. A commissionaire took him to the Minister's office. He knocked on the door which was opened by the Minister's personal secretary, a man who Teame had met before when he was secretary to the previous Minister. He had always found him arrogant and unhelpful. A member of the old guard who expected visitors to bow several times – something Teame, although always respectful, would never do. There was no love lost between them.

But this time things were different. 'Oh, Ato Teame,' he said, 'come in.' He was very polite. The opposite of what Teame had expected. He shook his hand – something he had never done before – and ushered him into a large hall where many others were sitting awaiting their turn to meet the Minister.

The Secretary picked up the phone and reported to the Minister that Teame had arrived. Shortly afterwards, to Teame's surprise, he was beckoned to go up to the Minister's office, walking past the others who had been waiting for hours to see him and who whispered angrily to each other as to why this man was getting priority over them.

Arriving at the Minister's office he was greeted with great respect by Dr Hailegabriel Dagne who stood up to greet him – an unusual honour. The Minister was very polite. Teame showed him the telegram he had received and said he had got there as soon as flights allowed but the Minister brushed aside his apologies and said: 'You are here now. That is all that matters."

The Minister seemed to sense his anxieties and the tensions within him. He had, after all, arrived at the Ministry fearing the worst. But

Hailegabriel Dagne attempted to put his mind at rest, asking him about himself, his experience in Asmara and his visits to the other Teacher Training Institutes.

All Teame wanted was to discover why the Minister wanted to see him. He was not interested in talking about himself. But he could not ask him straight out. That would have been impolite.

The Minister asked him if he knew of the Academy of Pedagogy in Bahir Dar. It was a prestigious new institution set up with support from the United Nations and the World Bank with the aim of providing a prototype of advanced teacher training for the Third World. The academy students were experienced teachers being given more training to further their careers.

Teame told him he knew little about the Academy as it was quite new. But he did know his predecessor as Director of the Asmara Teacher Training Institute, Ato Matewos Gessesse, was there. The Academy had both Ethiopian and international staff with two directors. Matewos was the Local Director. Coincidentally Teame also knew the International Director, Dr Barrington-Kaye, a Briton who had been in charge of the Redland Teacher Training College in Bristol where he had been attached whilst studying at the city's university three years earlier.

Finally, the Minister got to the point. He explained that there had been a student revolt at the Academy. They had gone on strike and taken Ato Matewos hostage claiming he was cheating them of food and resources. The Minister said that a Select Committee had met and, after long deliberations, had chosen Teame to go to the Academy and attempt to resolve the crisis. He said the decision was not his, but that of the Select Committee.

Teame was taken aback. This was not what he had expected. He had a mixture of emotions. Firstly, absolute relief and joy that he was not on his way to prison. Secondly, a sense of the enormity of the task he was being asked to perform. It could be difficult and dangerous. But to be asked was a sign of the high regard in which he was held by his Ministry peers and was an unexpected honour from Ethiopians for an Eritrean.

However, he expressed a reservation about his skill at speaking Amharic which would have been the mother tongue of most of the Ethiopian students at the Academy.

In fact, his Amharic was better than he was prepared to admit. But what was in his mind was the need to have someone at his side as he attempted to tackle such a tricky and potentially dangerous venture. He needed someone he could trust and who knew the local situation better than he did. It might have been a ruse but it was one that Teame considered, in view of the scenario, was entirely justified.

Whatever the reasons for his reservations the Minister was in no mood to accept his doubts. 'You will do as you are told and you will be going this afternoon,' he said. Teame made one last attempt to get a companion – ostensibly someone who spoke fluent Amharic. The Minister replied: 'Who would you like to take?'

Teame knew hardly anyone at the Ministry who might help. Then he remembered one person he did know – a former head of the Haile Selassie Secondary School in Asmara, Messele Metiku, who was now a Director General in one of the Ministry Departments. He was Ethiopian and fluent in Amharic as well as Teame's mother tongue Tigrigna. He was much older than Teame and a man he respected for his straight forward honesty and integrity. Someone he felt he could trust.

The Minister picked up the phone and requested Ato Messele Metiku, who had an office in the Ministry building, to report to him immediately.

When Messele arrived, somewhat mystified by the summons, he was surprised to find Teame there and then to be told by the Minister that he was to accompany him on the mission to the Academy. He would not have known about the problem there since news of the student revolt was being suppressed. But, like Teame, he had no option but to obey the Minister's orders.

He asked for permission to collect some clothes from his home and was given a government car and driver to do so. Then by the afternoon the two of them set off, in two jeeps with armed soldiers, for the Academy which was several hundred kilometres away.

These were uncertain and dangerous times in the provinces of Ethiopia. Their route took them across the province of Showa, home of the capital Addis Ababa, and into Gojjam where the Academy at Bahir Dar was situated on the banks of the Blue Nile. Along the way were villages still loyal to the Emperor. There had been incidents of sabotage and conflict between Royalist and Mengistu supporters.

Soldiers were also inciting villagers to violence – sometimes providing them with arms. The Army was not popular at that time and they were trying to win support. Factions in student movements around the country were also supporting the regime's campaign against the landlords and involving themselves in the political movement of the day. Soldiers in one of the two jeeps only accompanied them until they had crossed the most dangerous part of the region where skirmishes were continuing.

The group had orders to check in at police stations in villages and towns along their route to ensure it was safe to travel further. All went smoothly until they reached a bridge which separated the two provinces and discovered it had been sabotaged. There was no alternative but to take a long detour through farm tracks and rough ground. Finally after two days they arrived at Bahir Dar.

Barhir Dar is one of Ethiopia's most beautiful cities on the banks of the Blue Nile and close to Lake Tana. The city is renowned for its wide avenues lined with palm trees and colourful flowers. The

Academy was a huge complex, with modern blocks of dormitories and lecture rooms standing by the river. But Teame had other things on his mind than the beauty of the area.

Teame's jeep with the two armed soldiers aboard drew up in the Academy compound. The institution had been closed down by the student strike and the international staff withdrawn to Addis Ababa. The local, mainly Ethiopian, lecturers had fled to their quarters in the town. The students were in control of the academy building.

Sending the soldiers away to avoid provoking the students Teame approached the buildings, but was warned by local residents to keep away. He was told it would be dangerous to go further.

So he and Messele withdrew into the town to consider what to do next. He wondered who he could contact among the staff who might help him. Messele remembered there was a lecturer there who Teame had selected to run a summer In-service programme at the Institute in Asmara, some years previously. Teame had been impressed by his attitude. His name was Lema Arity, a common name in the country and Teame wondered whether it could be the same man at the Academy. Assured by Messelle that it was indeed the right man, he sent word to arrange a meeting with him.

A curious Lema Arity turned up to meet Teame and his colleague from the Ministry of Education. They gave each other a traditional hug of greeting but he was full of questions, asking Teame what he was doing there. Teame explained their mission. He asked for assistance and suggested Lema nominate two or three trusted colleagues who might collaborate with him in persuading the students to let him talk to them.

Agreeing to help, Lema went off and returned with several other lecturers. Teame and Messele outlined their plans. It was suggested that it would be useful if they could meet some of the student leaders before attempting to get into the Academy. Lema expressed doubts that they would be willing to talk to him. Certainly not outside the building. But then he mentioned three Eritreans among the student teachers at the Academy all of whom Teame knew well. Two of them were Ato Abraham Ghebremariam and Ato Bissirat Teclehaimanot. The third was Ato Zeray Abraham who had trained with Teame at Asmara Teacher Training College. They were all people Teame felt he could trust. He decided to enlist their help.

Word was sent and they met Teame that evening. At first the students were suspicious. Why had the Ministry sent this fellow Eritrean to do their business? Was he a spy? Teame explained to them that they were there as professionals and had no political intent. They wanted to listen to the students and hear what their grievances were.

At both his meetings, with the lecturers and the students, the message they gave him was clear: 'Your mission is too big. It is a major issue and we don't think you can solve it.' They warned that some of the students had guns. Factions in the Mengistu regime were arming them.

It was never going to be an easy assignment. Apart from the immediate challenge of persuading the students to call off the strike and release the director, there was also the issue of conflicting interests within the Mengistu regime. For as Mengistu's Education Minister was asking Teame to solve the student crisis, other elements in the regime were inciting students to riot and arming them. It was incongruous. But Teame recognised that the Minister and his team, although members of the regime, were also professionals who felt a wider responsibility both to the country and the education system. The Academy was, after all, a huge national asset and its demise could affect Ethiopia's reputation around the world, not to mention backing from the UN.

Teame knew he had to tread carefully. But despite the difficulties and the doubts expressed by the lecturers and students of his chances of success, he was determined to carry on with his mission. He would not return to Addis Ababa without doing everything he could to end the crisis. He pointed out to the staff and students he met that he was not a political animal. He was a professional who was seeking a professional solution to a problem in an academic institution.

Eventually, with the help of Lema and the other lecturers, a meeting was set up with some of the student leaders who had initially been reluctant to talk to him. He asked them if they would agree for him to address all the students. They asked: 'How long will the meeting take?' Teame replied: 'As long as you want it to last. It can be five minutes or an hour. It is up to you.' But he emphasised: 'I am here to tell you the truth the way I see it. I want to solve a professional problem.'

To Teame's relief the students' representatives agreed to give him an hour to talk to the students. A meeting was arranged in the auditorium at 4.00 o'clock that afternoon.

At the appointed time about eighty students turned up. They were angry and boisterous. Teame could see that some had pistols in their pockets. He decided to make the meeting as informal as possible. So, instead of standing on the rostrum to address them he had the chairs arranged in a circle with him and Messele sitting among them instead of looking down on them.

He started off by explaining that he would love to talk to them in Amharic but that was not his first language. They could speak in English if they wished. And he raised some laughs by saying that they could also speak in Oromigna although he would not be able to understand them. Oromigna is the majority tongue in Ethiopia but not one used by the Amharas, some of whom feel theirs is a superior language.

The ice was broken. But the students were still suspicious and noisy. Teame said he was prepared to listen to their grievances, but when he spoke to them he was not prepared to be ignored or interrupted. A solution to the problem would only be found as a result of the process of their discussions. He added that the future of the Academy was at stake and that problems could not be resolved by kidnapping a man and taking him hostage.

'What exactly is it you want?' he asked. They complained they had already sent their grievances to the Minister but had not received a reply. Teame responded by saying it was the Minister who had sent him and he wanted to hear from them himself about the nature of the problem.

They started to list their grievances and demands and most of them revolved around the Director, the man they had kidnapped and held hostage. They accused him of misusing money meant for their food and teaching aids and claimed the quality of the food they were given was not good. They said they were being treated like secondary school pupils not experienced teachers and that there were not enough meetings with the National Director. The students also claimed they were not involved in the decision making process which affected their daily lives.

Then they said if nothing was done they were going to kill the director. It was a threat that Teame had to take seriously in view of the number of students in the auditorium with guns. He also knew that hidden elsewhere in the building, keeping an eye on what happened in the meeting, were some of the more militant Marxist students, also armed, who could well have intervened.

Teame asked where they had imprisoned the director. They refused to tell him. It was by now 5.30 pm and the meeting had been going for an hour and a half – well over the time allotted by the student leaders. Teame decided to call for a break for refreshments and offered to pay for them to be obtained from a local café as the Academy kitchens had been closed down.

As he sat talking to the students, many of them not much younger than him, he told them he realised they were serious about their grievances to have taken such radical action. But he said he did not think they were taking the right course. They needed to release the director. He appealed to their conscience asking if they would want blood on their hands if the director was killed. He felt they were acting against the normally courteous nature of the Ethiopians. However justified their grievances might, or might not, have been he worried that it might escalate into violence whipped up by regime militants.

Then he offered his solution. He would get the director out of the academy and send him to Addis Ababa where the Ministry officials could deal with the grievances against him. If he was guilty of what he was accused of, he would be dealt with. He promised to send him on the first flight out of the town.

The students discussed his suggested solution. There was a lot of argument and different opinions. But after the tea break finished, the students asked to be given time to consider. Teame and the eight or so teaching staff who had attended the meeting withdrew to allow the students privacy.

Eventually they came back and said: 'Yes we agree to the proposal, but we want it in writing.' The crisis had been averted. Teame felt a huge sense of relief, not least because the life of the director had been saved. Had the situation not been quickly resolved there was every chance that the more militant students who boycotted the meeting would have stepped in, putting Teame and Messelle's lives in danger.

Teame handed his written promise of what he had proposed to Lema Arity and the following day the director was released and put on a flight to Addis Ababa. Teame did not meet him. He felt it would be a blow to Ato Matewos's pride if he, someone who had been his junior at the Teacher Training Institute in Asmara, had confronted him. And since he did not meet him he was not able to discover Ato Matewos's side of the story. But he considered he had completed the task he had been set – resolving the crisis and in the process almost certainly saving the Director's life.

Teame meanwhile went back to Addis to complete his report and submit it to the Minister Dr Hailegabriel Dagne. The Minister offered his thanks for the way Teame had resolved the crisis. He told him if he was happier writing his report in English, to go ahead. It was an unusual step for an Ethiopian, the rulers of the country with Amharic their official language, to make. For Teame, it affirmed the existence of realpolitik among the Amharas.

The Minister later wrote a letter of thanks to Teame for his 'service to the country'. And, although he had not expected thanks for what he had done – to him he was just acting as a professional – he couldn't help thinking of occasions in Asmara when a letter of thanks would have been appropriate but had not been forthcoming.

He met Ato Matewos briefly sometime afterwards in Addis Ababa and received his thanks for saving his life – although Teame diplomatically did not discuss what had happened at the Academy. Matewos was in a hurry and could not stop to talk further. So Teame never did discover whether he had been censured by the Minister or whether it was decided there was no case to answer. He was saddened to hear some years later that he had died.

They might not have always seen eye to eye on teaching – Matewos the strict traditionalist, Teame always seeking new ideas – but Teame remembered with gratitude how Matewos had been supportive of him leaving the Teacher Training Institute to get his Master's degree at Bristol. By then he he'd begun to appreciate Teame's worth and Teame had discovered qualities in Ato Matewos he had not at first recognised. So Teame held no grudges against him – even after the tricky time he had experienced at the Academy. He believed Ato Matewos deserved respect.

Before he left for Asmara after his time at the Academy Teame had met with the Director General of Teacher Education who had also received a copy of his report. He wanted to discuss Teame's future. Although nothing was said directly, Teame could sense that he was being sounded out to discover if he would be interested in taking over the role of Local Director at the Academy. It was a job with a salary four times greater than he would receive back in Asmara, came with a villa, a car and driver, and the chance to attend international conferences. The temptation to accept was high.

But Teame did not feel it was the right move for him. For one thing the situation in the country was volatile which put the future of the Academy under threat. But, more importantly, he felt he had to put his family first. He did not want to take Teblez away from her family in Asmara where she had support. She had made sacrifices for him as he advanced his career. He felt he owed it to her to put her interests first this time. So he turned down the opportunity. It turned out later to be a prudent decision as the Academy never returned to its former status.

A new chapter in Teame's life beckoned as he returned to Asmara in an entirely different mood from when he had left. There was a joyful reunion with his family. His journey home had been one that, a few days earlier, he had feared he might never make.

Now safely back home, and having turned down the offer at the Academy of Pedagogy, he could consider his future. There was already, in fact, another opportunity. Shortly before his summons to solve the crisis at the Academy, Teame had been surprised to receive a call from the Dean of the Social Science Faculty at the University of Asmara, an American nun, Sister Luella Wall, asking to meet him. Asmara University was situated in a large modern building right next door to the Teacher Training Institute which was much smaller and less impressive. Teame invited her to his office for coffee. A tall, impressive lady, she held a Doctorate from an American university.

As they talked, Sister Luella said she had heard positive things about Teame from students, both Ethiopians and Eritreans, she had met from the University and the TTI. Teame assumed she was referring to his efforts to improve the curriculum and his introduction of new ideas such as students being taught how to use their own vegetable plots. She had seen Teame planting flowers in the compound to make it look nicer. Sister Luella might also have heard about the pastoral work Teame carried out with the students.

She asked if she could come to the Institute and to learn more about Teame's methods and to sit at the back of the classroom and see him teaching. Teame said he would be honoured and added he would welcome her feedback as it might help him improve his teaching.

A few weeks later Sister Luella arrived at the Institute to see Teame teaching. As she arrived in the classroom Teame instructed the class to all stand up – an act of courtesy and respect which he insisted on whenever a guest came into the classroom. It was something not all his lecturers agreed with, saying it was treating the students like elementary school children. But Teame's view was that the students were going to be elementary school teachers and they should learn the principles of respect so as to instil them into their own pupils.

Sister Luella, who fitted her tall frame into one of the classroom chairs, attended four or five sessions in Teame's classes over several weeks. At the end she asked Teame to have lunch with her at the University. (It would not have been considered appropriate for a Nun to lunch in a public restaurant with him). They had a wonderful Italian meal followed by ice cream – not a normal accompaniment in an Eritrean meal – and fine Italian coffee.

Sitting in a quiet corner of the restaurant, away from other diners, she gave Teame some feedback from her observations in the classroom. She said she had appreciated the interaction with the students which Teame practised in his teaching, involving them in the sessions rather than giving them a lecture. Her one suggestion for improvement was Teame's writing on the blackboard. She felt he was writing too much making the blackboard overcrowded. Teame was grateful for her input.

It was then that Sister Luella revealed what was really in her mind. She told Teame the University wanted to set up a new Education Faculty. Having now seen Teame in action she would like him to run it.

It came as a total surprise to Teame. But he had, for some time, had an interest in joining the staff at the University. Although his time at the TTI had been fruitful and stimulating, he thought he might enjoy the academic life and the fresh challenges it would bring. The frustrations he was facing in his role at the TTI had reinforced his desire for a change.

It was, though, still a huge decision. Despite the difficulties he was facing at the Institute, leaving would be a wrench. He had thanked Sister Luella for honouring him with the offer of such a prestigious appointment. But he asked for time to think about it.

His adventurous and testing time at the Academy had subsequently taken precedence, diverting his mind from Sister Luella's tempting offer. He could now give it his full attention.

CHAPTER TWENTY

University and
the Death of a Friend

It did not take Teame long to make up his mind. Shortly after his meeting with Sister Luella he got back in touch to tell her he would accept her offer to join the University as an assistant professor running their new Faculty of Education.

Having already turned down the chance to become Director of the Academy of Pedagogy the formalities of resigning his post at the Teacher Training Institute and accepting the University offer were quickly attended to. Sister Luella also recommended Teame's wife Teblez for a secretarial job at the American Embassy which she was offered and accepted. New opportunities for both of them were opening up.

But before leaving the Teacher Training Institute as director he had won one last battle. He had long fought for the erection of a new building for the Institute. It was much needed to replace the existing one which was old and too small for its purpose. In his final months as director he had heard that his efforts had been successful and a site had been found for the new building. He had been assisted by Dejasmatch Haregot Abbay, the Lord Mayor of Asmara and the then deputy Governor General, Dejasmatch Tesfayohanes Berhe. He had the honour of cutting the first turf as the builders started work accompanied by Ato Getachew the Director General of Teacher Education. He felt honoured to have done so and was glad to have left the Institution with a bright future.

As for his arrival at the University he was joining at a difficult time not just in the academic world but throughout the country. The curfew, introduced by the Mengistu regime, was continuing in Asmara. Killings by both the Ethiopian army and the liberation fighters were a constant reminder of the conflict between them. Mengistu's death squads were a threat to any who opposed the regime.

The particular problem that Teame encountered soon after he joined the University was the decision by the Dergue to implement a policy of sending students out into the villages to work on the land with farmers harvesting and maintaining crops. It was not popular with the Asmara University students – 99% of them Eritrean – who were already opposed to the Mengistu regime.

Teame found himself pulled into the controversial new policy when the President of the University, Dr Assefa Tekle, a former head of the Pasteur Institute in Addis Ababa, received a letter from the regime ordering him to implement the new policy. Dr Tekle asked Teame and another Professor, Dr Petros Habtemichael, to take on the respons-ibility of telling the students what was asked of them and to report back to him. Petros was an old friend of Teame's whom he had first met at the student conference in Bologna during his time at Beirut.

Teame was not comfortable with the idea. But he and Dr Petros had no option but to comply with the request from the University President who, although Eritrean by birth, had spent most of his life in Ethiopia and was perceived by many, rightly or wrongly, to be a unionist.

The two of them called a meeting of the students in the university auditorium. There were angry protests when the plan was outlined.

Teame told them they were perfectly within their rights to be angry, but not to turn their anger on him and Dr Petros. They were just the messengers. But the order from Mengistu was that the following week the university would be closed and the students sent to the villages.

There was a lot of shouting. The students asked why Mengistu didn't come and tell them himself. Teame and Dr Petros suggested breaking up into smaller groups to discuss the idea. They offered to give them time to reflect. But the students didn't want to be split up and said: 'Tell the authorities that we are not going to do this.' They said they would let their student leaders deal with it.

They were warned that refusal to co-operate could mean the army stepping in and forcing them to go to the villages or throwing them out of the university. The students replied: 'They can do whatever they like.' The next day the students boycotted their lessons and stayed away from the University fearing they would be arrested.

Teame later described the meeting as the most difficult moment of his academic career. He wrote a report to the university President explaining what they had done and the reaction of the students.

Teame had, from the start, been sceptical of the success of the plan to send students to the villages. He knew that a similar scheme by President Julius Nyerere of Tanzania in 1960 had failed. So, although he did not feel free to tell this to either the President or the students, he considered the idea was a non-starter.

He did feel able to discuss his concerns about the situation with Dr Petros who he had known since his days at the American University in 1964 in Beirut. Petros had joined Teame in distributing propaganda protesting at the annexation of Eritrea by Ethiopia whilst attending the conference of student leaders in Bologna in Italy. At that time Dr Petros represented Switzerland, while Teame was representing the Middle East. Teame knew he could trust Petros.

The students' fears of arrest, meanwhile, proved well founded. Soldiers turned up at the University with a list of student leaders they wanted to arrest. They read out the names and asked where they were. But where did they get the names from? Rumours spread that some members of the Ethiopian air force who attended evening classes at the University, might be responsible although there was no evidence that this was the case.

Teame had taught an Ethiopian military officer in one of his classes and had no problems with him. But Dr Petros, who taught him in his economics class, got into constant arguments with him – particularly when he expounded his view that Eritrea could be self-sufficient economically. The country had, he said, copper and gold as well as petroleum in the Red Sea. He was giving an honest opinion (which history has since proved to have some substance). But it was dangerous politically. It went against the Ethiopian view that Eritrea could not survive on its own and needed Ethiopian support.

The Ethiopian officer would angrily confront Dr Petros. They would have fierce arguments with Dr Petros challenging the Ethiopian propaganda of the time which also claimed that Eritrea got its cereals from Ethiopia. Dr Petros put forward the view that, with the right resources and support, Eritrea could be the bread basket of East Africa.

But whatever the rights and wrongs of the argument, Teame was worried that his friend was being a little too honest in putting forward his views so forcefully at a time when the Dergue did not react well towards critics of the regime. He understood that he was thinking of his Eritrean students when he spoke out. But he feared Petros was being politically naïve. He seemed unwilling to keep his views to himself and was determined to keep to principles of human rights and freedom of speech. His principles would have been easier to uphold in Western universities where Petros once taught, but were dangerous notions in Mengistu's Ethiopia.

The hunt by the army for the student leaders continued. The university staff were asked to produce those on the list. But they said they had no idea where they were. An army captain came into Teame's office one day and asked for information about the students. He had a pistol which he put on the desk. Teame didn't like his arrogance and could feel his anger rising at the officer's manner. But he kept his feelings under control.

The captain said: 'I am asking you to bring these students to me.' Teame replied that it was not his job to do so. He told him that he was employed to teach the students not to know where they lived and said he was not talking to the right person.

The captain seemed shocked to be confronted like this by an Eritrean. Teame told him: 'Of course you are in power, you can do whatever you like as long as you hold a gun. But you can do it in a different way. It is not giving you a good image.' His words seemed to have an effect and the captain's attitude softened.

The soldiers did eventually find some of the students they were looking for although many of them had just disappeared. They also rounded up students who had remained on the campus. There was a disturbance with the students shouting that they should have sanctuary in the university – terra sancta – a tradition that goes back to 13th-century universities in Europe. But their claims that they should have freedom of expression were to no avail. They were arrested and, for a while, imprisoned.

The village scheme eventually fizzled out, with the government, although not actually cancelling it, not forcing it through in Eritrea. It did operate for a few more months in Ethiopia where the students there did not oppose it.

With the situation now calmer the university returned to something like normal. Teame and Petros along with other staff, including a brilliant Accountancy lecturer, Ato Woldetsion Kelati, went back to teaching their classes. Part of the regular routine, both at the university and in the civil service, was to break from work at about 1.00 pm and go home for lunch returning at 3.00 pm.

Petros did not have a car. Teame had a small Volkswagen and would drop him off at his home for lunch en-route back to his own house. He would pick him up again on the way back. Petros lived in a small flat in an apartment block above shops. He had a wife and small child with another one on the way. Teame and Teblez had been instrumental in persuading him to get married and organised the wedding with the support of the relatives of both the groom and the bride. One of those on the bride's side was Memher Hailemichael Ghebreyesus, the man who taught Teame at Dekemhare Elementary School and who played a great part in shaping his future role as an educator.

One day Teame arrived back from lunch to pick Petros up at his house. He rang the bell and Petros's wife appeared at the window upstairs to tell him that Petros had already gone. He had left the flat to wait outside for Teame whilst enjoying a smoke – a habit Teame had been trying to make him give up.

Apparently another car, also a Volkswagen had drawn up and driven off with Petros. His wife thought it was Teame picking him up as usual. Now worried about his friend, Teame returned to the university to discover that Petros was not there. He sometimes walked back from lunch. Teame reported his disappearance to the university authorities. With no signs of him after several hours the alarm was raised and the police were called in.

The police found two witnesses who said they had seen Petros being picked up by the occupants of a Volkswagen. He had been heard to say: 'Who are you?' He was then pulled into the car which drove off. It had all the signs of a kidnapping by the Mengistu death squads who operated in the city and often left bodies of their victims in the gutters in the early hours of the morning. Teame felt that the kidnappers must have been watching Petros and noticed his habit of waiting outside the apartment block near Cinema Roma to be picked up.

Search parties were organised to look for him. Relatives and friends took part. Teame joined one which went to a large park on the road to Massawa. To their horror, although not completely to their surprise, they found Petros's body. It had the tell-tale marks around the neck which showed he had been killed by strangulation with piano wire, a trade mark of the death squads.

When the police investigators arrived they discovered that he still had his expensive watch and a large sum of money which would have been the bulk of his wages that were, at that time, paid in cash and would have been collected a few days earlier. Clearly it had not been a robbery. His outspokenness had caught up with him.

News of the murder quickly spread around the city. Dr Petros was very well known in Asmara. The student population knew him as a prominent nationalist. His death was greeted with shock and anger. Rumours started that the Ethiopian air force officer he had argued with in his class might have had something to do with his death.

Petros was a Catholic and his funeral was at the Tsetserat Catholic cemetery in the city. Thousands of people turned up. Many of them were wearing the traditional white Eritrean dress.

Teame felt somebody ought to address the mourners. But he was warned by friends not to say anything himself. Mengistu agents might well have been in the crowd. The situation could very well turn ugly. But he felt he had to say some words about him. If there was no-one else he had to speak on behalf of the family and the university.

'I can't let him down,' he told his friends. 'I ate with him, I laughed with him. He was my friend. Now that he is dead I have to say something.' He kept his remarks to a brief account of Petros's life. He thanked the mourners for their sympathy and kindness and spoke of the traditional belief of Christians in Eritrea that the dead man's soul would be on the right hand of God. It was not political. It was the normal things that were said at funerals.

But his friends remonstrated with him afterwards saying: 'What have you done, we told you not to get involved.' They feared reprisals. Teame replied that he could not have abandoned Petros. He was dead now. Tomorrow it could be his turn. In fact, when he got back to his car after the funeral, he discovered that a window had been broken. Nothing had been stolen but he suspected it could have been Mengistu agents looking for something to incriminate him. There was nothing there for them to find but it was a warning to Teame that he might be under suspicion. His relatives advised him to go into hiding. But Teame ignored them and went back to the university as normal the next day.

The killings did not stop. The liberation front fighters had got word of the murder of Petros. They wanted revenge and blamed the Ethiopian air force major for Petros's death. Within weeks he had been assassinated too. There was a note saying: 'This is your reward for what you have done,' left at the scene.

It was a dangerous time. The Mengistu death squad got word that sympathisers of the liberation front were holed up in a house in Asmara. They stormed the building and killed the four men in it. Shortly afterwards an Ethiopian general was killed in retaliation.

Teame knew, as a close friend of Petros, it was possible that he could be targeted too. He kept out of politics and concentrated on being professional. His aim was to serve the country as an educationist. But in those uncertain times, when one never knew if a government agent might be following them, danger could be just around the corner.

One day Teame was approached by one of the students, a member of the Ethiopian forces. He wanted to meet him for a coffee. When they met up he asked to go somewhere quiet away from the crowds.

He was complimentary about Teame's teaching. But then he looked straight at him and said: 'I don't want anything bad to happen to you.' Teame realised right away that, without actually saying so, the man was warning him that he was next on the death list. The man repeated: 'I do not want anything bad to happen to you.' He did not elaborate, but he had said enough.

Teame recognised that the Ethiopian officer had taken a big risk. It confirmed to him that there were many Ethiopians who were sickened by the bloodshed of the Mengistu regime whatever their political views. The officer had made a brave gesture Teame would never forget and for which he would be for ever grateful.

The two men shook hands and went their separate ways. But he knew what he now had to do. He had only been at the university for about a year but his time there had to end prematurely. His life was in danger and it was time to get out of the country.

CHAPTER TWENTY-ONE

Leaving the Country

The meeting with the officer had left Teame in a state of shock and anxiety. He had sleepless nights as he fretted over what to do next and he was not eating well. He kept his worries to himself not wishing to trouble his wife, Teblez, or other close relatives.

Returning to the university, now closed down following the student revolt over the villages scheme, he kept a low profile as he pondered his options. The coded warning following Petros's death, that he could be next on the list, had left him feeling insecure. He was constantly looking over his shoulder fearing the death squad could be round the corner.

There was no-one at the university whom he trusted enough to talk to. The officer who had bravely warned him of the dangers he could be facing, was no longer there. He was never to see him again.

Eventually, he took Teblez and close relatives including his brother-in-law Tewolde Medhane and his father, into his confidence and told them what the officer had said and of his fears. With Teblez now fully aware of the dangerous situation Teame faced – although she must have guessed from his silence and worried demeanour – they now spent many long nights discussing what the future held for them and what they should do. At times Teame felt desperate and feared not just for his own future but for that of his wife and children.

As they talked it became clear what he had to do. He must leave the country. But that was easier said than done. Crossing the border into neighbouring Sudan was dangerous. It was patrolled by the army, bandits operated in the area as well as spies for the government. There were gangs who smuggled people across but they too could be dangerous to deal with, sometimes robbing those they were supposed to be helping.

Amidst all the political turmoil the university had by now been closed down although it would later reopen. The closure meant Teame now found himself facing a different challenge. The Ministry of Education, faced with scores of lecturers with nothing to do decided to spread them around the country doing other work for the education system.

Teame was sent to Addis Ababa to work on a new curriculum for secondary schools. His fears for his life continued. He had no idea whether he was being watched but, away from his office in the Ministry, he was careful of where he went and what he did in the city. His evenings were spent in his hotel room and, with time on his hands, he began to plan his next moves.

Deciding against trying to cross the border into Sudan he realised his only other option to get out of the country was to get a scholarship to gain a PhD at a foreign university. Not only would it be a way to leave Ethiopia where his life was in danger, but it would be a legitimate advancement of his academic career which would also benefit his employers, Asmara University. But first he had to get a grant.

Having already received government support for his first degree at the American University in Beirut, and a British Council Scholarship to later study in Bristol, this time he would be reliant for financial backing from his current employers, Asmara University.

He began to prepare his case pointing out that a PhD would make him better able to fulfil his role as assistant professor setting up the new Faculty of Education on solid foundations and running it. At this point, despite the current fears for his life, he was convinced that the situation in Ethiopia would improve and he would be able to return after getting his Doctorate. He was also confident that the university would by then have re-opened. He made it clear to the university that he saw his career there as a job for life. He planned to remain at the university until his retirement, given the chance.

His experience at Beirut and Bristol had shown him how institutions in the developed world operated. They had resources for research, modern libraries, staff to run them and adequate finances. Teame knew that things would be different in Asmara as they would be in most other universities in the Third World. But he was convinced the focus could be extended to include his ideas for research oriented education even though it would be difficult with limited resources.

He was amused by those Ethiopian graduates he met in Addis Ababa who had come back from foreign universities sporting pipes (the UK based students) and graduation rings (the American colleges). Their personal taste was not something he would ever criticise. But he wanted to generate a spirit at Asmara University more in keeping with the Eritrean culture and able to work within the limited resources available. He felt that trying to be someone you are not erodes your integrity as a professional.

He laid out, in his grant application, the kind of university faculty that he would like to see and that he wanted to work for. The teaching function was obviously a key factor. University staff were there to teach. But beyond that he wanted to introduce into the courses, an element of research. This should include the behaviour of children, in and out of the classroom and the way teachers – primary and secondary – are trained.

He also wanted to conduct research into how you organise a teacher training college and why you should involve the University Students

Association in the decision making process. And finally how a teaching practice programme is run. These issues were all an encapsulation of many of the things he had picked up on his own educational journey.

Asmara University had started life as a Catholic institution run mainly by nuns and priests. Emperor Haile Selassie had become the Chancellor at a time when Ethiopia had wanted to show their support for the university and its importance in the country's academic system. This had not always been the case. There had been many critics in Addis Ababa of there being another university in the country. But the ongoing liberation struggle and unrest in Eritrea had meant a change of policy both in Haile Selassie's government and the Mengistu regime who overthrew him. The Emperor even remained as Chancellor, in name at least, after his overthrow and arrest and up until his subsequent demise.

Teame's attempts to gain a grant from the University were conducted through the university offices in Addis Ababa. They had set up offices there after Haile Sellassie became Chancellor. There were a series of meetings. Teame wrote letters to Sister Luella, the American nun who was Dean of the Faculty of Social Sciences and had been instrumental in him joining the University. She distanced herself from the negotiations but passed the letters on to the Committee in Addis Ababa– and probably was privately supportive of Teame's case.

Teame was subjected to vigorous examination by the Asmara University Committee in Addis Ababa composed of an international group of nuns and priests. They were very knowledgeable, and asked many questions. Teame outlined his vision of the new Faculty of Education he had been asked to run and described how he thought the PhD would help him achieve it. He made the point that, with the university currently closed down, it would be a good time to take his

PhD, and the University would benefit. The discussion went on for several weeks.

Finally, after much deliberation, Teame received the news he had been hoping for. His grant application had been successful. It was a big moment for him and a huge relief. He could now safely and legitimately leave the country and the dangers he faced there.

All that was left was to decide which University to apply to. There was plenty of choice. In America the Ivy League Harvard University and Columbia Teachers College which had a good record for teacher education. He applied to both. He also applied to Bristol University where he had gained his Master's degree.

He had reservations about the American PhD courses. He considered they were narrow and included initial modules which were compulsory and prepared students for the research which was to follow. The result would be a longer course and he did not feel he needed to take the earlier modules. At Bristol University, however, the PhD courses were totally research based with the student guided by a supervisor but left to their own devices as they conducted their research.

He had offers to study at all three universities. It was an easy decision in the end. Teame already knew Bristol University and many of the staff in the Faculty of Education. This, allied with the totally research based PhD course, which he preferred, persuaded him to choose Bristol. He wrote to the Dean of the Faculty of Education, Professor Ben Morris, accepting their offer and asking if he could find him some accommodation.

All seemed to be going smoothly. But there was another snag which threatened to jeopardise everything. He had expected his visa application to go smoothly. But, to his dismay, it was refused. Armed with his documents, approving both his grant and his acceptance by Bristol University, he had gone to the Foreign Office to collect the visa, and get his Ethiopian Passport stamped assuming it would be a formality. But it wasn't.

He was told by the Foreign Office officials that university staff, like him, were being sent out to the villages with the students as part of the regime's policy which, although abandoned in Eritrea, was still operating in Ethiopia at that time.

He argued that because the policy had been abandoned in Eritrea it did not apply to him. But his protests were to no avail. He spent the time in his hotel room feeling disappointed and frustrated, worrying about what to do next.

He repeatedly returned to the Passport Office to try and get the decision reversed. Every time he was told, *'Eshi Nege,'* 'Yes, tomorrow.' It went on for a month with Teame getting increasingly frustrated. Fortunately for him the monotony, not to mention the frustration, of life in a hotel in Addis Ababa was broken from time to time by invitations to many Eritrean homes including that of his brother-in-law, Abraham Medhane.

Eventually salvation came from an unlikely source – a committee of educators acting for the *Dergue*, the secretive regime committee who ran the country. By now the running of Asmara University had been taken over by the government.

Some of the committee members would have known Teame. Although part of the feared Mengistu regime, he felt they were open minded and would act as academic professionals rather than politicians. No doubt there would have been some hard line supporters of the regime on the committee who could have opposed Teame's application. But there must have been others who were sympathetic to his case because, much to his delight and relief, he finally got a letter of approval saying his exit visa had been granted.

After all the worry and the waiting it was a moment to savour. Teame was delighted that he could now continue his studies and get his PhD. He travelled back to Asmara to give the news to Teblez and the rest of his family. It was a wonderful moment for both Teame and Teblez. In the privacy of their home they celebrated wildly and with great relief – it would not have been wise to show their joy too publicly. Asmara was full of Mengistu's troops and Teame was only too well aware of the warning he had received from the Ethiopian serviceman.

But with his exit visa finally in his hands he began making plans. Within a few weeks he was ready to leave. He was anxious to depart the country as soon as possible. Having seen the body of his great friend Petros in a gutter after being strangled with piano wire, he was not keen to be in the country for any longer than necessary.

As he reflected at the time, he could only go to Bristol if he was still alive.

PART TWO

CHAPTER TWENTY-TWO

Return to Bristol

It was with mixed emotions that Teame boarded an Ethiopian Airlines flight to Heathrow. It was the summer of 1976 – a year which would herald further twists and turns in his already incident packed life. He was relieved to be leaving the country after fearing his life was in danger and to be achieving his ambition of gaining a PhD. But he also felt guilty that he was leaving Teblez who had only recently given birth to their third daughter, Zeb Mebrahtu.

He feared he was betraying his wife and daughters and asked himself how he could leave them in the chaos which prevailed in the country for the sake of his education. But he was determined they would join him in Bristol as soon as it could be arranged.

Arriving in Bristol, which he had got to know well during the two years gaining his Masters degree, he was met by someone from the University who took him to accommodation at Meridian Hall in the Clifton district of the city, where students from all over the world had rooms. It was self catering accommodation and Teame had never learnt to cook. That was not part of the Eritrean tradition where men were not welcome in the kitchen and relied on their womenfolk to provide meals. By his own admission Teame did not even know how to peel an onion and looked upon food as something to be quickly eaten before moving on to something more important.

He was quickly befriended by two West Indian post graduate students – both educators like him. They were excellent cooks and helped Teame prepare some basic meals. They laughed at his lack of interest in food but often included him in their well prepared meals which he soon began to appreciate. Their West Indian style of cooking included plenty of meat.

But whilst settling into his new surroundings the situation back in Asmara where Teblez and the girls were living was never far from his mind. He was not enjoying being away from his family. The situation there was still bad with conflict and bloodshed continuing. Mengistu, who many Eritreans like Teame likened to Pol Pot, the Cambodian dictator who had been responsible for the mass killings of his people, had stepped up his campaign against the liberation forces. There were constant battles and instances of atrocities against the civilian population of Eritrea.

Areas of the country were heavily mined, including the countryside close to Adi Ghehad where liberation fighters were active. He heard with alarm that sometimes villagers had lost limbs, or worse, after stepping on a mine.

As Teame heard the latest news, it would only worsen the turmoil he felt. There were so many things going on in his mind. He would lie awake at night worrying about Teblez and his three daughters, Aida, Esther and baby Zeb. It had been difficult to leave them all in Asmara. He would ask himself, why did I come? Had he put his ambition to get his PhD before the needs of his family? He certainly had regrets and agonised over whether he would ever see them again. He wondered about the future of his beloved country and was both angry and disturbed by the support the Mengistu regime were getting from Russia. How could tiny Eritrea stand up against a superpower, he asked himself.

He also viewed with dismay the internal battles for power between the two Eritrean liberation groups – the Eritrean Liberation Front (ELF) and the Eritrean Peoples Liberation Front (EPLF) – which he feared would hinder the liberation struggle.

There were occasional phone calls to Asmara when he would limit his conversations with Teblez to how they all were. He was mindful of the fact that as an Eritrean the Ethiopian authorities could be monitoring his conversations and was careful not to say anything that could get him, or Teblez, into trouble.

At the heart of his worries was the deeply held belief in the Eritrean tradition of family and the responsibilities that came with it. An Eritrean family is an institution that links the youth with society at large by instilling in them traditional values and ethos.

In the villages at that time a man was not considered an adult until he had a wife and children. The concept of the family extended beyond close relatives, which included aunts, cousins and their own off-spring. It also embraced old retainers and some who had been taken into the home and looked after. In the case of the Mebrahtu household that included a shepherd who worked on the farm and an elderly blind nun who they had taken under their wing.

Teame, as the eldest son who was earning a comparatively high salary in Eritrea, had taken much responsibility for feeding and clothing them which was an expected part of the family culture. When he left for Bristol he had given his father money to continue the tradition of care and continued to send money for some years.

This deep and instinctive commitment to family had only served to increase Teame's anguish as he struggled with coming to terms with his future.

One thing he was absolutely sure about was that it was essential to get Teblez and the three girls out of the country to join him in Bristol. Not only would it be safer for them but he was desperate to see them all again.

There had been delays in getting them exit visas and Teame worried that a politically motivated official might be holding things up. The visas had to be issued at the government offices in Addis Ababa. Teblez, with her three young daughters to look after, was unable to get there. But, eventually, with the help of relatives and friends in the city, the visas were obtained. At the Bristol end Teame had to confirm he could look after his family financially, which thanks to his generous grant from Asmara University, he could. He sent off their plane tickets and awaited their arrival with huge relief and great anticipation. At least one of his major worries would shortly be removed.

Travelling with three small children is no easy task for any parent on their own. Teblez, when she boarded the flight for Heathrow was clearly having difficulty. Two other Eritrean women on the plane came to her rescue and offered to help look after the children. As they introduced themselves it turned out the two women were sisters of Teame's old friend from the American University at Beirut, Yemanu Tesfayohannes, who had first met him and taught him to swim.

The plane stopped over at Rome where Yemanu was now living. He met his sisters at the airport and, discovering that Teblez was with them, took them all on a tour of the city and put them up at his home overnight. It was a happy coincidence which made the journey a lot easier than it might have been.

Teame met them at Heathrow for a heartfelt reunion. He had been desperately worried about the safety of Teblez and his daughters and was delighted and relieved to see them again. His friend Jim Baynard-Smith, who he had first met in Asmara, came over from his home in Oxford to meet them and drive them back to Bristol.

Teame had managed to rent a flat in Dublin Crescent – a row of Victorian terraced houses in the Henleaze district of Bristol. His West Indian friends had helped him clean it up in readiness for the family.

They arrived – the girls exhausted and asleep in the car – to be met by other Bristol friends who gave them a welcome party.

To Teame's delight he had discovered that there was already a fellow African family living in the upstairs flat above their ground floor apartment. Omer Osman was a Sudanese architecture student at the university. His wife Asia and their two daughters, slightly older than the two eldest Mebrahtu girls, were with him. They became good friends and the girls all went to the same local school.

Teame's mood was vacillating from one extreme to the other. On one hand he was immensely encouraged by having his family around him. But on the other hand, it was around this time that he had heard of the cruel death of one of his former staff, Ato Zeray Bocurezion and five other teachers who were tortured to death and their bodies hung in the Edaga Hamus Area of Asmara near the university.

But at least having his family around him was an answer to his prayers. He and Teblez were thankful for the friendship and support of many in the local community as well as fellow students and staff at the University.

He did not stop worrying about the situation in Eritrea – although he was still convinced it would improve and he would be able to make good on his promise to return to Asmara University. But in the meantime, he and Teblez were able to enjoy the friendship of those who were only too willing to help them settle into their new surroundings. They still look back with gratitude at the welcome they received.

Among those who offered friendship and aid was a secretary at the University where Teame had now enrolled for his PhD, Anne Mallitte, who would regularly go to the local market and get them fresh vegetables. A former M.Ed colleague but now a member of staff, John Hayter, gave them the use of his caravan for family holidays. Another British fellow student, Carl Harris, would invite the Mebrahtus for Sunday lunch. Carl also provided Teame with huge amounts of scrap paper on which he drafted his PhD dissertation. It saved him the considerable cost of having to buy paper.

One evening another friend Peter Newman, who lived with his wife Mary, close to the Primary school attended by the Mebrahtu girls, arrived on their doorstep carrying a huge television. He had heard the Mebrahtu's hired set had broken down and the girls were missing their regular dose of the popular American soap *Dallas*, so had brought round his spare set.

They also became firm friends with a local church minister, Rev Fred Pope, minister of Trinity-Henleaze United Reformed church just round the corner from their home, and his wife Rose. The Mebrahtus attended the church and Teblez would often meet Rose, who also had a young daughter at Henleaze Junior School, outside the school gates. When Teame was suddenly struck down with appendicitis and had to be rushed to hospital, it was Fred Pope – himself suffering ill health at the time – who ferried Teblez to see him. Rose was also invaluable in collecting the girls from school, feeding and looking after them whilst Teblez was at the hospital visiting Teame. Teame and Teblez were distressed when, sadly, Fred later died from his illness.

All these acts of consideration and kindness had deeply moved the Mebrahtus. And with the family together again Teame was able to fully concentrate on the reason for his being in Bristol. He had already held a series of meetings with the Select Committee at the University who scrutinise PhD candidates and discuss the quality and parameters of their research.

He was now entirely focused on what he wanted to achieve with his PhD. His aim was to prepare for what he was still convinced was going to be a lifetime commitment to Asmara University.

He had some theories he wanted to research and explore during his time in Bristol based on his view that education is a tool for national development. He wanted to grapple with the question of what were the requirements of a university in a developing country like Ethiopia or another African country compared with those of the more developed nations in the Western World.

He was given a supervisor to guide him through his research – Dr Bob Thompson, a specialist in African higher education who had taught in a number of universities in East and West Africa. Teame respected and got on well with his mentor. They were on the same wavelength. By a happy coincidence he turned out to be living close to the Mebrahtu's flat in Dublin Crescent and would often entertain the family in his home. He also had young children who became friends with Aida, Esther and Zeb.

His conviction that education is a tool for national development was at the heart of his research. From the African point of view he felt Western universities could be seen as a luxury. Universities in the developing world could never afford to have the kind of facilities enjoyed in the West. He asked: 'Where would you get the resources, the accommodation, the funding for the students? And what sort of education would you provide?'

He wanted to develop a model which would be relevant to the developing world. One that would embrace the key functions of Western Universities – teaching, research and management of services – but to modify it to suit the particular needs and resources of the home country. He remembered the time at the Asmara Teacher Training Institute when he had suggested a teacher should use the local butterflies as an example for his students rather than buying expensive models of butterflies from Europe.

But halfway through the course there was a bombshell. He received a letter from the Ministry of Education in Addis Ababa ordering him to return to the country. It was totally unexpected.

The letter from a government official said there was a job waiting for him and he was expected back immediately. Teame did not know what to think. Why did they want him back? What was the job they had for him? Would it be dangerous to return?

He was at a crucial stage in his PhD course having had his research proposal accepted. He had already started drafting his dissertation but there was a lot more work to do. He had no intention of giving it up. He wrote back to the Minister saying he had been given the opportunity to get his PhD in order to carry out his new role at Asmara University. To leave now would be a waste of the resources and time he had already put in. He said he had every intention of returning to the country, as promised, once he had gained his PhD.

But the reply from the Ministry was unequivocal. They insisted he come back saying they were not interested in the PhD. Writing in flattering terms they said they knew his reputation, he was a known entity and there was an important job awaiting him.

Teame asked for further explanation of the job and said he couldn't see the logic of what they were asking. His supervisor, Dr Bob Thompson, wrote a letter in support of him staying explaining the importance of his research which, he said, would contribute to the whole of Africa not just Ethiopia.

Angry at the situation in which he now found himself, Teame questioned the motives of those in the Ethiopian regime who were demanding his return. He was furious that they were seeking to impose their will on his life.

But neither his anger or Dr Thompson's efforts on his behalf were able to change anything. Another letter arrived saying: 'Report back immediately.' It was followed by an ultimatum. If he did not return, his grant would be stopped. With the Ethiopian government then running Asmara University and in charge of the purse strings it was a threat they could carry out. Teame was faced with a heart-rending decision.

CHAPTER TWENTY-THREE

Refugee

Teame agonised for days over what to do. He was being asked to make a decision that could change not just his life but the lives of his wife and children. Refusing to go back would mean cutting himself off from the Eritrea he loved and still wanted to serve. But if he refused how would he survive without his grant?

He was wary of the motives for his recall. Still fresh in his mind was his hurried departure from the country following the death of his friend and colleague Petros at the hands of the Mengistu regime and the warning that he could also be on the death list. His chief worry was that the recall, with the offer of a big and important job, was merely a ploy to get him to return to the country. He feared he could then be at the mercy of the Mengistu regime with their reputation of dealing violently with those they opposed – although Teame had always been careful to act professionally in his dealings with the government and never dabbled in politics.

The letter he had received was not signed by the Minister of Education, Hailegabriel Dagne, a man he knew well and who had personally thanked him for his work in solving the crisis at the Academy of Pedagogy at Bahir Dar. Instead the letter had come from an unknown bureaucrat who he thought was probably a member of the Dergue.

Teame had, up until this point, still been planning to return to take up his post at Asmara University after his PhD. Now, for the first time, he was having serious doubts that it would ever be possible.

He worried that, if he refused to go back, he would be saying good-bye to his past in a country he loved and with people he loved and respected. But then he also agonised about his, and his family's, future.

If he went back what sort of future, if any, would he have? He was at a crossroads and was beginning, for the first time, to consider the implications of refusing to go back. It would mean applying for asylum.

He looked up Article 14 of the Universal Declaration of Human Rights which goes: 'Everyone has the right to seek and to enjoy in other countries asylum from persecution.'

He considered, in view of what happened to his friend Petros and the implied death threat to him, that he had good grounds for applying for asylum.

But still the doubts continued. What would happen to him, he worried, if his application was turned down? Would he be deported? And if so what would be his fate back in Ethiopia? Then, conversely, he would agonise over how he and the family would survive if he did become a refugee but lost his grant.

His state of mind had not been helped when he heard that the family possessions he had stored at Asmara University – which included Ibrahim's handmade furniture, their wedding presents, photo albums and his many books – were likely to be thrown out if they did not return soon. It might have been a small thing compared with the decision he was faced with but it just added to his sense of despair. (The possessions later disappeared and the family, to their great sadness, never discovered what happened to them.)

He felt he was in a complete state of limbo. His mind was buzzing with all the different possibilities of going or staying. It was his wife

Teblez, with whom he had spent many hours discussing what to do, who finally helped him make up his mind. She saw things clearly in terms of the family and asked Teame: 'Are you not a responsible father? Think of the future of your children?' She reminded him of the time he had protected them with his own body under the bed when there was shooting at night between liberation fighters and Ethiopian troops back in Asmara. Teblez did not want him to end up like Petros and wondered why he was even hesitating.

Teame realised she was right. The children should be his first priority before even his academic ambitions. He knew he could not go back to Ethiopia and would have to hold to his decision not to take up the job offer. The fears for his life were a strong motivation not to return but it had been his daughters' future which had crystallised his thoughts. He and the family must stay.

He realised that without Teblez's wisdom, support and determination he would not have been able to cope with the situation and his life would not have been complete.

Even then he still felt a huge sense of loss. He was, and still is, a proud Eritrean steeped in the country's culture and traditions. It had been his home for better or worse. Cutting himself off from the country did not come easily. He wondered what his friends and relatives back home would think. But, despite his heartache, he now started making plans to stay. It was not going to be easy.

He was now in the country without the backing of the government in Addis Ababa. Without the grant he had no means of support. His only option was to apply for refugee status. Matters were further complicated when the landlord of the flat they were living in announced he was selling the property. Teame would have to find other accommodation for the family as well as seeking to convince the British authorities to allow him to remain in the country as a refugee.

Teame, like other foreign students at the time, had to regularly report to the local police station – in his case New Bridewell in the Broadmead area of the city. It was there that he went to make his application for refugee status.

The police officers he met were polite and arranged a meeting with senior officers and a civil servant who Teame presumed was from the Home Office. A few days later he was interviewed for several hours and had to return again some weeks later for more questioning. The officers wanted to know all about his life and asked to see his qualification documents. They insisted on inspecting the original copies of his degree from the American University at Beirut and his Master's degree from Bristol.

Teame's application wrested on his contention that his life could be in danger if he returned to Ethiopia. He told them of the assassination of Petros and his fears for his own life under Mengistu's murderous regime.

Finally he had to travel to the Home Office department in Newport to answer further questions. He was relieved that Teblez and the girls were not involved and did not have to be interviewed.

He was grateful for the respect he was given during the process. The officers who interviewed him had shown patience and under-standing especially when he had trouble expressing himself in English. It was in sharp contrast to the conduct of the police in Ethiopia and Eritrea at that time. He remembered the Ethiopian officer in Asmara who had threatened him with a pistol when he was searching for university students protesting about the plans to send them to the villages.

He was of the opinion that if you have no respect for another person you have no respect for yourself. The Italians, he thought, had a nice way of putting it: 'The person who is the biggest burden to our planet is an ignorant man.'

Eventually, to his great relief, a letter arrived with the news he had been hoping for. His application to stay had been accepted. He had been granted asylum. Eventually he and his family would receive full British citizenship.

It was a wonderful moment but was tinged with a mixture of emotions. When he had managed to get backing to come to Britain and study for his PhD – and escape the threat to his life – he had still been convinced that he would be able to return safely to Eritrea as an academic. Now, having been granted asylum, he was a refugee from his homeland. He was enormously grateful to Britain for granting him and his family a new life and was keen to give something back to the country. But he still thought, at that time, that his 'refugee status' would be only temporary. He saw himself not as a refugee but a global citizen and, above all, an educator whose life was committed to sharing knowledge with those less fortunate than himself.

His immediate priority, though, was finding the means to support himself and his family. Relatives and friends from Eritrea came to the rescue giving him financial support and loans to tide him over for a few months. They all clearly understood and supported Teame's decision to stay despite his worries at their reaction. With the help of his PhD supervisor Bob Thompson, he also got some minimal help from a number of charities.

As a refugee he would have been eligible for state benefits. But Teame, despite his perilous situation, decided not to take them. For him it was a moral issue. He felt that as he had not contributed to the State he should not benefit. As he put it: 'Why should I get something from a pot I have not put in to?' It was partly a question of pride. But he had always made decisions on the basis of it being right or wrong. In this instance he thought it was wrong to accept benefits he hadn't earned. He was determined to find other ways of surviving without his grant.

He was still working on his PhD research and the course fees had been postponed for a year to enable him to continue. Stacking shelves in a supermarket, which he would have gladly done, would have made it impossible to continue his research. So he was considering trying to get a job cleaning toilets in hospitals. A fellow African student at the University was doing just that. His view was as a fit and able young man he was prepared to do anything to feed his family and not be dependent on receiving what, to his mind, he did not deserve.

The exception was the child benefit which Teblez, his wife, received. They had not applied for the benefit nor expected to get it. But they were told that their children were eligible – the two older ones Aida and Esther were by now attending the local St John's Primary School. Since it was for his children Teame did not feel this was a benefit he should turn down. He never saw the money and had no wish to, leaving Teblez to administer it. To this day he doesn't know how much it was.

Apart from earning enough to live on making money had never been a big issue in Teame's life. A big car and a large house did not appeal to him. Some of his contemporaries at the University could not understand his disinterest in financial success. But he would argue that his only interest was in using his skills as an educator. There were moments when he would regret not making money – perhaps this was one of them – but he had decided he could not stick by his convictions and be a rich man as well.

They had persuaded their landlord to give them a month's grace to allow time to find other accommodation. Their plight had not gone unnoticed. In the nick of time they were offered the chance of a new home in the city. A couple who had become good friends, Geoff Sanders, a Bristol businessman and his wife Freda, said they would like to help. They had a basement in their house, a large Victorian building in Hurle Crescent, which could be converted to a family home.

Teame accepted with gratitude and the basement was quickly renovated, with other friends – John Hazell, Arthur Merriot, Dennis Price and Les Tweney – pitching in to help get it ready for the family to move in just before the deadline expired on their flat. For Teame and Teblez their home was not a basement flat. It was a palace. They felt it was a God-send as they embarked on their new life in Britain.

Teame, meanwhile, was still searching for ways of earning. At the suggestion of Bob Thompson he took up an opportunity to give adult education lectures in evening classes conducted by the University. One was entitled *Does Aid Work?* In it he explored inequalities in the North/South divide and what happened to foreign aid in under-developed countries. He did not fail to mention the despots in charge of some countries who siphoned off much of the aid money. Another theme was on what was for Teame a subject close to his heart, *Promoting International Understanding through Education.* He would sometimes show slides and films and there was always a lively twenty minutes discussion with questions and answers at the end of every session.

The lectures – there were ten of them during the Spring term – were advertised around the university and were popular and well attended both by a large number of British students as well as interested local residents including both serving and retired teachers. Teame continued the lectures for two years as they were much in demand. With his help some of the adult students went on to do BA and MA courses.

He also helped Bob Thompson with lectures on his Master's programme, sometimes leading discussions. It was good experience and Teame was grateful for the opportunity. He had great respect for his PhD supervisor who was a constant source of encouragement and support.

However, his work with Dr Thompson, although valuable, was unpaid. He still needed to earn something with the money from the loans running out. Despite his thoughts of an eventual return to his

Homeland, he was determined to throw everything into proving his worth to the country that had taken him in.

He realised his good fortune and was determined to repay it by using his skills as an educator. But he was also beginning to understand the complex issues faced by those seeking safety in a new country. Along with his commitment to education, he now had a strong motivation to help other refugees. It would be a defining part of his new found citizenship.

CHAPTER TWENTY-FOUR

Rowntree Trust

Teame was still determined to find ways of surviving without claiming benefits from the country which had welcomed him as a refugee. He had been prepared to clean toilets in a hospital. But, at the suggestion of two university colleagues, he found an opportunity to get back into the classroom instead.

Professor Roger Wilson, Dean of the Faculty of Education at Bristol University and a lecturer, Nicholas Gillett, who Teame had got to know during his earlier Masters course, suggested he should apply for funding from the Rowntree Trust, a Quaker charity which supported social justice.

Funding would be dependent on Teame putting forward a project that fitted the aims of the Trust. Nicholas Gillett, himself a Quaker, took Teame under his wing and helped him prepare an application.

Teame decided he would like to go into Primary and Junior schools to introduce the children to the Africa he knew and give them an idea of the African people and what it was like to live there. He aimed to change the stereotypical views of Africa which many in Britain had at that time. He also wanted to give children a global awareness which would help them to better understand the rest of the world – especially his own continent of Africa. The project was in line with Teame's conviction that education was a tool for creating international understanding.

203

He applied for funding from the Rowntree Trust and, to his delight, his project was accepted. The first hurdle was negotiated. Now he had to convince the schools to let him in. His friend and mentor Nicholas Gillett cautioned him about trying to get into Primary schools. He warned Teame that he might find it easier to get into Secondary schools as Primary School heads, at that time, had a great deal of autonomy and might not accept the project.

Teame appreciated he was trying to be helpful, but he was adamant he wanted to target the Primary schools. He was convinced the best place to start was with the very young.

It was to be no easy task. He circulated schools in Bristol and the surrounding area asking to be given an opportunity to explain his project to head teachers. Taking a bus out to the schools who wanted to know more about the project – he had no car – he was received with courtesy but caution. He would explain what he wanted to do saying he needed forty-five minutes with a class and would like the head or a teacher to be present to assess what he did. The heads asked him what he hoped to achieve. Teame told them he wanted to give the children the chance to talk to a black man, an African, and introduce them to a different culture.

The response was usually a polite thank you and a promise to let him know. But, after a few weeks, he began convincing schools to give him a chance. One of the first was Colston Juniors in the Cotham area of the city. There was a buzz of excitement as he walked into the classroom. Teame sat in one of the tiny school chairs with the children sitting on the floor around him and a teacher observing.

He started off by telling the children his name and its meaning – sweet, succulent and kind – explaining that all names in Eritrea are meaningful. He asked them if they knew where Ethiopia was – he didn't expect them to know of Eritrea. Then he showed them the country on a map he carried around with him. His aim was to keep things simple, concentrating on what the children would understand and relate to. The session went well and, as word got round, other schools began to invite him to visit them too.

As interest in the project grew Teame needed an office. With support from the Rowntree Trust he was given one at the University which he shared with Simon Fisher, a Quaker, who was involved with a project on Conflict Resolution, also sponsored by the Rowntree Trust. He was, like Teame, working in local schools.

Additional help came from Marie Taylor, Professor Roger Wilson's secretary at the University. She offered to take the phone calls from schools as interest in Teame's project grew and invitations from schools began to increase. The schools were spread out over a wide area which included Bristol, Gloucestershire, Somerset and Dorset.

Marie Taylor would help Teame to travel around the area by bus, working out which ones to catch and the timetables. He found himself going to places named Air Balloon Road and Two Mile Hill. The travel times meant he could only fit in two school visits a day.

Teame was invited back to many of the schools. The children had trouble pronouncing his name so he would often find himself being called 'Dr Tom'. He did not object to the name, despite the unfortunate connotations for a black man, realising it was entirely innocent.

For many of the children Teame's arrival in their classroom was their first sight of a black man close up. At one school a little girl came up to him and gently touched his hand as he talked. Teame realised with some amusement that she wanted to see if the black would rub off! Needless to say it didn't. The classroom teacher observing Teame's lesson was embarrassed and worried that Teame might be angry. But he encouraged other children to come up and rub his hand too. 'Come and see for yourselves,' he told them. Soon there was a queue.

Teame would often take something with him to interest the children. Sometimes it would be one of his daughter's traditional

Eritrean dresses. He would ask one of the girl's to try it on resulting in much laughter from the others. Teame would point out the special decorations on the dress and ask the little girl to twirl around.

He would teach them the ABC of the Tigrigna alphabet asking them to recite it. His aim was to keep the children interested and never bored. He knew that once they became restless he would have lost them. If they started shuffling their feet and looking around the classroom he knew he was in trouble.

He would make a point of gently encouraging the shy children. It would often be one of the shy girls who would be asked to wear the dress. Others would be asked their name or to tell something about themselves.

Teame would ask the children what they would like to talk about. And, more often than not, they asked about the animals of Africa. 'Which ones?' Teame would ask. Back would come the answers: 'A giraffe.' 'A lion.' 'An elephant.' 'A hippopotamus.' They would examine pictures and Teame would ask them to draw the animals. He would organise the children into small groups where they would be asked to talk to each other about the lesson with Teame moving from group to group encouraging them and answering questions. He held sessions with children whose ages ranged from five-year-olds to ten and eleven-year-olds – tailoring what he discussed to suit the different ages.

He would set them tasks for his next visit, asking them to give their views on what they had been learning and talking about. Teachers co-operated – a sign of the success of his project and the confidence the staff had in him. The children would write to him saying what they wanted to talk about next time.

Some of the older ones would go home and look up some of the issues they had talked about and write to Teame about what they had discovered. It helped them to exercise their writing skills and expanded their knowledge and understanding.

Teame was invited by teacher Ray Harris to talk to pupils at Hanham Abbots School in Bristol which at that time was in a largely white, middle class area with few immigrant families. Teame, as he always did on these occasions, spent time helping the youngsters better understand the multicultural and multiracial world in which they were growing up. Ray Harris remembers that at the end of the talk one of the pupils, a girl of Chinese background, came up to him to offer her thanks to Teame. She said it was the first time she had heard someone talk about the challenges of fitting into a new country. She felt Teame had understood her own concerns and had helped her to see how she could fit into her adopted country.

Whilst working to sow these seeds of understanding among young people in the country he had also adopted, Teame was keeping a close eye on events in Ethiopia and the war of liberation raging in Eritrea. He would talk to the children about the refugee camps in Sudan where thousands of Eritrean children were living after fleeing with their families from the liberation war across the border. Teame would discuss with the children how lucky they were compared with the children in the refugee camps. He would tell them that whilst they enjoyed breakfast, and often a midday break with a bar of chocolate, the refugee children would have a glass of powdered milk as their only meal for the day.

He would ask the children: 'Should we care for these people or should we forget about them?' 'Oh no!' would be the answer. Teame was encouraged to see decency and humanity in the young children. He would ask them to find out more about the situation, to discuss it with their parents and tell him what they thought at the next session. As a humanitarian activist, Teame wanted to motivate teachers and children to gain awareness of the needs of children in another country and to share their own resources to help them.

With the help of the children, many of whom were by then feeling concerned about the refugees, he started collecting teaching materials for the schools in the camps. The materials were stored at Bishop Road Primary School with the enthusiastic help and support of Ray Harris, now an advisory teacher there, and lead adviser Rex Beddis who were working with School Links International – a charity which pioneers links between UK schools and schoolchildren around the world creating awareness of each other and an understanding of the issues faced especially in developing countries. It was an innovative project which Teame embraced as part of his own philosophy of giving children a wider view of the world. In the School Links International handbook Teame is pictured carrying boxes of pencils, paper and books to the van heading for London and then on to the refugee schools in Sudan.

They would collect pencils, pencil sharpeners, rubbers, paper used on only one side – the refugees could use the other one – and textbooks. Teame would take a pencil and cut it into four and hold up one of the short pieces saying: 'This is the pencil the refugees use.' The children were astonished. But they began to understand the plight of the Eritrean refugees.

Some of the children wanted to raise money for the refugees. But Teame, reluctant to be responsible for receiving and distributing cash, asked them to buy more pencils and paper with any money they raised.

The supplies for the refugees were sent out to Sudan via the Eritrean Relief Association (ERA), which had a base in London. They would pay for the shipment to the Sudan. The refugee children would write their thanks helped by their teachers who would transcribe their words into English – the Eritreans would speak only Arabic or Tigrigna. The English children would write back asking the refugees about themselves. What sort of games they played for instance. What they had for tea (although they would find out that tea was not on the menu for most refugee children). Bishop Road School was among a number who formed links with the refugee schools in Sudan.

When talking, in particular, to secondary school children, he would sometimes come up against stereotypical views. He would ask the students to write what they knew about the Third World. The results were illuminating.

One wrote that 'the Third World is a place of half naked can-can girls in grass skirts', another that 'the people who lived there are illiterate, hungry, thirsty, diseased, skinny, deformed, pot-bellied and black'.

Instead of trying to put them right at once Teame would congratulate them on their honesty whilst inviting them to attend additional seminars when they could further discuss the issues and understand each other better. He would then paint a picture of the other side of Africa. The modern cars, airports, petrol stations in African cities. He would tell them about the modern streets and beautiful Italian architecture of the Eritrean capital of Asmara. In time, the misconceptions changed and the students discovered a side of Africa they did not know existed.

He would never say this himself but, in truth, Teame's own obvious learning and academic expertise must have also been a sign to his young listeners that their stereotypical views of Africa and Africans was not the whole story.

The Rowntree Trust project went on for two years. Teame visited over a hundred schools in that time. After the initial reservations the project blossomed. Towards the end he could not accommodate all the requests and had to turn some down. He felt a sense of achievement that he was helping children, in a country he had now embraced and cared for, to increase their understanding of humanity and of the wider world they were living in.

The children would often sing songs for him which he would tape and play back to other schools. One of the songs he recorded was: 'The Family of Man', written by English musician and peace campaigner Karl Dallas. Teame felt the song – with its inspirational lyrics – accurately reflected the ethos behind his project in the schools.

> The family of Man keeps growing
> The family of Man keeps sowing
> The seeds of a new life every day
>
> I belong to a family, the biggest on the earth
> Ten thousand every day are coming to birth
> Our name isn't Davis, Hall, Groves, or Jones
> It's a name every man should be proud he owns
>
> I've got a sister in Melbourne, a brother in Paris
> The whole wide world is dad and mum to me
> Wherever you go you'll find my kin
> Whatever the creed or the colour of the skin
>
> The miner in the Rhondda, the coolie in Peking
> The men across the ocean who plough, reap and spin
> They've got a life and others to share it
> So let's bridge the oceans and declare
>
> From the North Pole ice to the snow at the other
> There is not a man I wouldn't call brother
> But there isn't much time, I've had my fill
> Of the men of war who intend to kill
>
> Some people say the world's a horrible place
> But it's just as good or bad as the human race
> Dirt and misery or health and joy
> Man can build or can destroy.
>
> Karl Dallas

CHAPTER TWENTY-FIVE

PhD and University

As Teame worked with the Rowntree Trust visiting schools he had also been continuing to research and write his PhD dissertation. He entitled it *The Role of the University in National Development* and placed an emphasis on Ethiopia – which at that time still included Eritrea – as a developing country.

The original intention had been for him to go back to the University of Asmara to use the results of his research to serve the country. Events had conspired against that with his asylum status after refusing to comply with the government summons to return to the country in mid-course because of fears for his safety if he did so. But his commitment to investigate how universities in developing countries, including Ethiopia, could be used for national development had not dimmed.

He wanted to discover how the universities in the developing world of Africa, the continent he knew best, but also Latin America and Asia, could better serve their peoples. Using the model of the Western universities he was keen to investigate how it could be adapted to the particular needs of a developing country which did not enjoy the resources of their Western counterparts.

Teame had felt that his PhD dissertation needed to be two volumes long which was twice the normal length expected. He considered he needed the extra volume in order to be able to adequately explore his subject. His aim was to examine the role of universities going back to the original academic institutions in 12th or 13th-century Europe. It meant a great deal more work which took longer to complete.

A dissertation for a PhD, as opposed to a thesis, was the more usual route at Bristol University because it gave wider scope for elaborating the candidate's own new and unique research and depth of knowledge. A thesis concentrated on a narrower form of research with less depth of knowledge required. A dissertation was particularly useful in Teame's case for both his PhD, and his earlier Master's degree, in view of the length and depth of his research.

He found his supervisor, Professor Bob Thompson, helpful and supportive, encouraging him and holding his arguments up to close scrutiny. Teame found him a good listener. They were very different. Teame was talkative, Prof Thompson said little. But, as Teame observed, when he did say something it was a 'pearl of wisdom'. The Professor became a very influential person in Teame's life and he had great confidence in him.

The Professor had been supportive of him writing his dissertation at such length and broadening his research. Teame realised that another supervisor may have taken a narrower view. But, whilst being supportive, Professor Thompson made it clear that Teame would have to justify the reasons for the length and depth of his research.

Typing up his thesis as it developed became something of a family affair. With money tight employing a professional typist was out of the question. So Teblez, who had strong secretarial experience when working in Eritrea, took on the task. She would type up the drafts with her two older daughters Aida and Esther reading out the text for her as she typed. Aida, incidentally, would have been about ten years old and Esther a few years younger so quite an achievement. They were getting a taste of the academic life early on. No wonder they and their younger sister Zeb all went to University later.

The mammoth task of typing up Teame's two volume thesis went on for several years. Teblez would fit it in during spare moments from running the home and looking after the girls while Teame would either be out on his Rowntree visits to schools or with his head down in the library conducting his research.

There was heavy use of Tipp-Ex correction fluid, now the saviour of all secretaries in the days of typewriters, as mistakes were rectified. Long words were attempted, spelled out then rechecked. The girls, despite their lack of years, found themselves becoming familiar with a variety of academic terms even if they didn't know what they meant.

It was a family joke that Teame's drafts had so many arrows pointing in different directions all over the text as he made constant revisions. Poor Teblez would sometimes have trouble understanding them.

Meanwhile Teame's research took him into every aspect of university life and its place in society. He did not see universities as an 'Ivory Tower' isolated from the rest of the community. For him the model university was one that was development orientated – i.e. was at the service of its host society, a servant of humanity with a responsibility to work towards alleviating poverty by improving the condition of the country.

In his dissertation he examined what he saw as the four key principles of a university: discovering new knowledge; contributing to the socio-economic welfare of the society; curricular reform – for primary and secondary schools; and promoting freedom.

This last principle was to him, with his experience of an oppressive regime, especially true for some African countries. Freedom, he believed, was an essential tenet of academic life. The freedom for academics to speak their mind and not to be afraid of telling the truth particularly in the developing countries of Africa, Latin America and Asia but also, to some extent in Europe, including the United Kingdom.

Teame was using his experience in the classroom and college lecture rooms in Asmara as he developed his thesis. But he wanted to expand his theories. It was hard work with long hours spent in research. He relished the academic challenge and opportunity to learn. But he would sometimes feel guilty that he did not have the time to help Teblez in the home and would acknowledge that without her help and encouragement he would have found it difficult to complete his thesis. It was one more example of the rock-like support from Teblez which has been a cornerstone of their union.

Bob Thompson understood the significance of Teame's research and what he was attempting to achieve. As he neared completion of his dissertation, all two volumes of it, he told Teame: 'When you have finished, this will be a very important book not only for Africa but for the entire developing world.'

Teame recommended that universities needed to tackle issues which threaten the 'global village' or the survival of humanity. He reminded Universities in both the North and the South that they had a moral obligation to respond justly to the issues affecting humanity including the plight of refugees and the multitudes of displaced people, and the injustice of selling arms to dictatorships.

Ethnic minorities, who profess a different religion from their host societies, should be made to feel valued and accepted. It might lead Universities to an analysis of a civilisation different to the Western model – which for all its merits still tended to be divisive and exploitive – and form a basis for an alternative vision of human society.

He urged educators to be less concerned with the development of education, and more with the role of education in development. His study also criticised educators who believed that their primary duty revolves around the intellectual growth of the individual, rather than with national economic and political goals. Finally, in line with the Brandt Report of 1981, he recommended educators in higher education institutions to be at the centre of shaping the common future of humanity, rather than leaving this vital duty to governments.

In June 1980, his work completed after four years of concentrated effort, the time came for Teame's viva – the oral exam when he would appear before an external examiner who would decide the fate of his PhD aspirations. Everything would now rest on the next three hours when he would have to defend his dissertation which would be closely scrutinised by a distinguished academic in his field of research. Teame was well prepared and confident of the veracity of his two volumes of research. But he still awaited the external examiner's arrival in a state of nervous anticipation. Bob Thompson had told him: 'If you get through today, the world will be your oyster.'

The examiner was Professor A. Taylor, from Cardiff University. Teame had never met him before. He had a reputation for strictness which did nothing to improve Teame's nervousness. He waited in an anteroom at the University while his supervisor Bob Thompson collected his fellow professor from the station.

When the two men arrived Teame was called in to the room set aside for the examination. Bob Thompson was there but, as he warned Teame, he was present as an observer taking notes. He could not help Teame even by a nod of the head if he got something right or, worse, something wrong. Teame was on his own.

As Teame was to say later, it was the most difficult few hours of his life. The Professor started off by questioning the length of his two volume dissertation. He challenged him to justify why it was necessary. Teame defended his work, saying it was necessary to write at that length in order to fully explore the nature of universities down the ages, how they had developed, and how they could play a role in national development.

His nervousness disappeared as the conversation flowed. Professor Taylor was a highly experienced external examiner and his questions probed Teame's theories and thought processes. He would find contradictions in his arguments and ask him to explain them. Teame, he said, was talking about a university which was Western in origin yet he was focussing on how a university could serve the peoples of a developing country. Was he not contradicting himself by transferring the 'Ivory Tower' from the West into a developing country context?

It was a challenging question, but Teame had anticipated it. He replied that, yes, his model was Western in its orientation – although he also pointed out that many universities actually had their origins in the Middle East. But as these were the only models available, he had adapted them to the needs of the developing world. He was talking about a university that was suitable to the particular needs of a developing country which took account of the lack of resources. He pointed out that the universities in Africa – in Nigeria, Ghana, Uganda and Kenya for example – had all been established during the colonial period and followed the 'Ivory Tower' model. He wanted to make them more relevant to the African context.

His dissertation suggested that one role of these universities he was advocating would be to tackle the diseases that were endemic in many African countries. One was malaria which killed many thousands of people world wide. Tuberculosis was another common disease that could be tackled.

Universities, he said, should adjust their teachings to serving the people. So when he talked about national development he was advocating that they should take a lead in improving the health and living conditions of the population, especially the many who lived in poverty. (Teame had been inspired to hear about the work of Mohamed Yunis who, during the Bangladesh famine of 1974, had made loans to poor families to enable them to start up their own businesses. It was the forerunner of the Grameen Bank set up in 1983 to help poor farmers.)

He said he wanted universities in the developing countries to 'come down from their Ivory Tower into the basement where the farmer was ploughing the land.' If nothing else, the quality of the plough could be improved. It could be made lighter to make it easier for children and women to use it. These were questions universities could conduct research into. Chemistry departments could look into producing medicines to combat malaria and other diseases. If they could not find the answer themselves they could develop contacts with universities in the West, learn from them and then adapt to the specific needs of their people.

As well as health and education he also talked of what he felt was the need for the universities to have democratic principles in their teachings. Universities, he said, should be politically conscious in the sense of educating their own citizens to seek the truth. For lecturers to test and challenge the way things were done. Were curricula prepared with national development in mind or with passing the School Leaving Certificates exams?

The morning had gone swiftly. After three hours of close questioning and Teame's responses as he defended the results of his research and his conclusions, Professor Taylor called proceeding to a halt and he and Professor Thompson left the room to discuss Teame's performance. He waited anxiously for them to return with the verdict.

When the Professor returned he knew straight away that the outcome was positive. With a smile on his face the professor shook Teame's hand and said: 'Congratulations Dr Mebrahtu.' He had been awarded his PhD.

It was a huge relief. He had been confident that the work he had put in would be enough. But knowing that it had finally been successful brought him great joy. He took particular pleasure in the knowledge that he had been able to articulate his views and defend them in a language, English, which was not his mother tongue –

although the professor had clearly had no trouble in conversing with him. His English, in fact, was excellent and he need not have worried.

With the formalities of the viva complete the three of them, Teame and the two professors, walked into an adjoining room to find that Teame's colleagues had organised a party in the confident belief that there would be something to celebrate. It was a chance to finally relax after what had been a stressful morning. The first thing he did was to ask the department secretary, Margaret Lole, to get his wife Teblez on the phone so he could give her the good news. She had been waiting at home in an even worse state of nerves than him. After all, she was very much part of the exercise having spent many hours, assisted by Aida and Esther, typing up Teame's huge thesis.

It had been a remarkable day. As Teame later reflected: 'A great achievement for a humble villager from Adi Ghehad.'

CHAPTER TWENTY-SIX

Sudan and Refugee Schools

Teame's links with the refugee schools during his time working with the Rowntree Trust – facilitated in large part by Ray Harris of School Links International based at Bishop Road School – brought an opportunity to visit Sudan to experience at first-hand how the resources they sent out were being used and experience the conditions the children lived under. He was to make five visits, the first of them in the summer of 1981, followed by others in subsequent years up to 1985.

He was assisted by the Eritrean Relief Association who were responsible for shipping supplies out to Sudan for the refugees. He was given a small grant from Christian Aid, just enough to cover his expenses for a two week trip. He would assess the situation in the schools and advise on how best they could be further helped. It would also be a chance to visit some of the schools receiving the classroom supplies from Bristol.

His journeys would take him not just into the camps where thousands of his fellow countrymen were now living. Former trainees and colleagues of his from Asmara who had joined the liberation fighters and been injured in the conflict, were now teaching in the refugee schools. There would be a chance to meet them and, when he made his first visit in 1981, he wondered how they would react on seeing him again.

Arriving in Khartoum he met aid officials and was briefed on the situation. He travelled out to the town of Kassala where most of the refugee camps and the schools were sited. Situated on the banks of the Gash River, Kassala was close to the border with Eritrea from where thousands of refugees had crossed to escape the fighting. The age of the children in the schools ranged from toddlers of three or four up to teenagers. Many of them had been orphaned. It was not unusual for some of the older children to leave the camps and go back to Eritrea to join the liberation fighters.

Teame soon discovered that there was a wide divergence of schools divided on both political and religious lines. Some were supported by one of the two wings of liberation fighters – the Eritrean Liberation Front (ELF) and the Eritrean People's Liberation Front (EPLF) – others were Koranic schools, *madrassas*. Most of the refugees were Muslim, the dominant religion in the border area of Eritrea that they came from and where some of the heaviest fighting in the liberation war was taking place. There were two main Muslim groups, Shia and Sunni, with their own allegiances, and beliefs and the divisions which are continuing to cause conflict in the Muslim world today.

There was a hotchpotch of ideas and Teame realised he would have to be careful not to take sides. His arrival was already being looked on with suspicion by the various factions who wondered what his agenda might be. He was determined not to show preference to any of the schools but to act purely on his professional views.

He visited a number of the schools, including those already receiving pencils, paper and other supplies from Bristol. At those he was delighted to see the pencils and paper, sent out from Bishop Road and the other schools being put to good use. He encouraged the teachers to help their children to continue writing to the Bristol children to thank them and tell them about themselves. The teachers would translate the words from Tigrigna into English. The letters and pictures they sent, taken by the camera donated by Bishop Road, were then sent back to Bristol where they were posted up on the walls of classrooms.

The refugees would answer questions about themselves from their Bristol pen friends who were surprised to discover the kind of lifestyle that existed in the camps. Some of the younger ones couldn't understand why their Eritrean counterparts had to walk miles to get water or firewood. Or why they didn't watch TV programmes or have a meal when they came home from school. Many of the Bristol pupils also commented about how 'weird' the languages spoken by Eritrean refugees, and how 'odd' their alphabet looked. Their eyes were being opened to a world very different from theirs.

As he visited the other schools in the refugee camps Teame's aim was to establish which ones could best be helped by the limited resources available from aid programmes. He was also ready to offer advice on curriculum and school administration, although he trod cautiously not wanting to incur the displeasure of religious or political groups who had their own very fixed ideas.

He was taken first to a *madrassa* school on a Friday, the Muslim day of prayer, which was supported by UNHCR, the United Nations Refugee Agency. The school was well run. But whilst Teame understood why they were taught in Arabic, the language of the Koran, he would have liked to see them also taught Tigrigna to enable them to converse with non Muslim Eritrean children in the camps. Teame was convinced there would be better integration between the two groups if they were taught Arabic and Tigrigna which were the official languages of Eritrea prior to Federation with Ethiopia.

He quickly realised that some of the schools were better organised than others. A few – especially the Koranic schools – appeared to be well funded, although Teame was not sure where the money came from. Buildings varied greatly. The poorer ones had classrooms open to the elements exposing the children to the baking Sudanese sun with teachers and children perspiring in the heat. There were fewer Christian schools where the children were taught in Tigrigna. The ELF and EPLF ran many of the schools and had their own political slant in the curriculum with the EPLF being more orientated towards Marxism.

Politics apart, Teame discovered that some of the best run were those run by the EPLF which by the mid 1980s had become the dominant group among the liberation fighters. The EPLF was to go on to eventually win victory and independence in 1991.

He suggested that Arabic and Tigrigna be taught at all schools and recommended that this should be a requirement for a school being eligible for assistance. In view of the problems of working in the intense mid-day sun Teame also suggested that lessons should start earlier and finish at 11.30 am before recommencing later in the afternoon.

He realised it was unrealistic to attempt to work with all the schools in view of the differences in resources, beliefs and curriculum and the limited funds available. In the end he decided he would have to concentrate on the better organised ones. This meant those run by the EPLF whose schools were better run than many of the others. In the light of the need he would have liked to support all the children and their teachers. But, in the end, recognising his time and resources were limited, he took the pragmatic approach. It came down to the art of the possible.

He also focused his attention on a school in Khartoum run by the United Nations which was for all Eritrean refugees, both Muslim and Christian, unlike most of the other schools in the camps at Kassala. The school sent students, on grants, to Atlantic College in St Donat's, South Wales – founded by the German educationalist Kurt Hahn, who also established Gordonston School in Scotland. Some of the students went on to study at British universities.

Teame knew the then Headmaster of the School in Khartoum, Michael Jaber, and many of the Eritrean teachers, who were totally dedicated to their jobs. Impressed and full of hope for the future, Teame ran some sessions for all the staff on themes they identified. He also spoke to the students in their classrooms in order to make up his mind how important this school was for their future survival. When the UN funding was threatened Teame campaigned vigorously to save the school from closing. It kept going for another two years before it finally did close.

Teame was also instrumental in gaining a small grant from aid charities to buy simple, inexpensive cameras for some of the schools to be used by the refugee children for educational projects. The films they took came back to Britain for developing and printing. Copies were posted up in the classrooms in Bristol for the children to study.

Teame's pragmatic decision to support the EPLF school was partly influenced by the fact that he already had links with teachers in the EPLF schools. He knew many of them from his days both as a trainee and as a teacher-trainer at the Asmara Teacher Training Institute and also from his time at Asmara University. They had joined the liberation war and been injured in the fighting. Some had lost limbs, others an eye, a few were in wheelchairs. Unable to fight they were sent to the refugee schools to put their teacher training to good use.

Teame was at first concerned about their reaction to him. He had always supported the liberation cause and still did. But he had been able to escape the country when his life was in danger. He had now been accepted as a refugee in the United Kingdom and was safely living there with his family. His former colleagues had risked their lives to join the liberation struggle and now were injured and facing an uncertain future. Many of Teame's relatives, including his brothers Hagos, Bereket and Tekie and a number of cousins were liberation fighters and Teame did not know whether they were alive or dead.

But whilst admiring their bravery and commitment to liberation, Teame remained convinced that his philosophy of staying out of politics and working towards change through education, was the right one for him. Despite that he worried that they would look upon him as someone who didn't have the courage to fight and instead had pursued his own personal aims.

His concerns proved groundless. The ex-fighters greeted him warmly. They told him he was among the first educated Eritreans now living in the developed world who had taken the trouble to come out to Sudan to see the situation for themselves and to try and help. Some of them may have been jealous of Teame's situation compared with their own – he wore better clothes and was better fed – but they showed no sign of it. They expressed gratitude that he had not forgotten them. And the fact that they knew him and were aware of his reputation for honesty and integrity – some remembering his courageous action in returning the body of the dead student to his home village – would have counted in his favour.

Teame felt the teachers needed hope. They were despondent at the continuing bloodshed in the war. Many were even so despairing they said they wanted to go back to the war and end their lives in the fight for liberation. Teame, whilst respecting their dedication to the cause, thought in this instance it was misplaced. He considered they underestimated the important contribution they were making to educating Eritrean refugees who were the future of Eritrea.

The refugees, including the teachers, lived in tented camps with groups of up to half a dozen sharing a tent. Whilst staying in the Kassala area Teame also lived in the camps sharing a tent with other teachers and living on the same food. A staple diet in the camps was milk – powdered not fresh. For many of the refugee children it might be the only meal they would get.

He and the teachers would talk about the situation in Eritrea, with the liberation still underway. Teame suspected that some of the ex-fighters – particularly those from the EPLF – would have considered him not 'Marxist' enough. Having read Marxism in the early 1960s, as part of his Philosophy course at Beirut, and having seen the havoc it brought in different parts of Africa subsequently, he would stress that he was not a supporter of the ideology.

On the other hand, he would make it clear he supported the liberation struggle. But he would say he was not political and took little interest in it. By his own admission he was politically naive. He hated the fragmentation that politics produced and would tell the former fighters he was not a member of either the EPLF or the ELF. Admitting that education in its widest sense is a political decision, he would stress that he wanted to serve his country through education and considered that was the best way to achieve change.

He was a great believer in the words of English author Edward Bulwer-Lytton who in his play *Richelieu* written in 1839 wrote: 'The Pen is mightier than the sword.'

> True, This! —
> Beneath the rule of men entirely great
> The pen is mightier than the sword. Behold
> The arch-enchanters wand! — itself is nothing! —
> But taking sorcery from the master-hand
> To paralyse the Cæsars, and to strike
> The loud earth breathless! — Take away the sword —
> States can be saved without it!

His view was that if a different route had been taken by solving conflict through education and negotiation, Eritrea would not have succumbed to the state it was then in. Equally important, he felt, if the two wings of the liberation movement had listened to the prayers and pleas of the ordinary Eritreans in the early 1970s, the bloody conflict that took so many lives could have been averted.

But the visit ended well with Teame and the Eritrean teachers running the refugee schools, taking a good deal of hope, in the knowledge that the Eritrean youth in the Sudan refugee camps would at least have access to some basic education. Teame left them some reference books and a few of his lecture notes on a variety of disciplines including classroom management, lesson planning and pupil-centred teaching.

During one of his visits Teame met Englishman, Hugh Pilkington, who was staying in the same hotel in Khartoum. He was a member of the Pilkington family and had set up the Windle Charitable Trust to support needy students in Kenya and other parts of Africa including Eritrea.

Like Teame, he believed that good education could equip the people of Africa to meet the challenges they faced. Teame was impressed by Hugh Pilkington's frugal lifestyle. He insisted on sharing the same leaves for their cups of tea, wore simple clothes, walked rather than taking a taxi around the city and booked the cheapest room in the hotel. The two, with their shared vision, got on well. Teame would later help Hugh by consenting to join the Selection Committee of the Windle Trust based in Oxford. Its primary function was to assess and select candidates from Africa to study in Britain funded by the Windle Trust. (The Trust later became the Hugh Pilkingon Charitable Trust after his tragic death in a car crash in Canada in 1988.)

Teame would prepare reports on all his visits to the Sudan camps during 1981 and 1985 making recommendations about the way the schools were run. He had great admiration for his fellow Eritrean teachers who were working in the schools and wanted to do all he could to help prepare the young students for life back in Eritrea once it was liberated.

His visits to the Sudan camps and refugee schools had brought him in touch with key members of the Eritrean Relief Association (ERA), who had organised his time in the Sudan. Among them Tekie Beyene, and Paulos Tesfagiorgis, head of the ERA schools in the Sudan and Osman Saleh, Head of the Education Sector in the liberated part of Eritrea.

They talked at length about the situation in the liberated part of Eritrea. It was then that Teame heard for the first time about the 'Zero School' which had been set up there to educate orphans and children of the liberation fighters, many of whom had their families in camps in the liberated territory. Was there something that he could do to help them he wondered. His visit was coming to an end but he left with the feeling that he could soon be returning – this time to liberated Eritrea.

CHAPTER TWENTY-SEVEN

University Teaching

Ever since his first teaching job in Eritrea, at Adi Keyh Elementary school in 1960 – and even before that when he set himself up as a personal tutor aged sixteen – Teame had a passion to be an educator. He saw teaching not just as a job but a commitment. He relished the chance to change young lives and empower them through education.

Over the years as he honed his skills in the classroom, both as a teacher and teacher trainer, and sharpened them further at university level culminating in his PhD, he had developed his ideas and convictions on the nature of education. These included identifying the aims of education on both the national and international stage, considering what the essential elements of the curriculum were, and how the well-being of the students could contribute to fulfilling their potential.

After gaining his PhD Teame had begun standing in for Professor Thompson, taking Master's classes during his absences whilst travelling to other countries promoting the university courses. With the work load increasing, and following a rigorous schedule of interviews, Teame's appointment became full time.

It had been a difficult time financially after the Rowntree Trust project finished and he had been making do with part time lecturing work. With three young girls to look after it would have been impossible for Teblez to get a job either. Teame was continuing to keep to his resolution not to claim state benefits, even if he was entitled to them. So getting a full time job was a welcome boost to the family budget and was the subject of rejoicing, and much relief, in the Mebrahtu household.

Teame worked at the Graduate School of Education at Bristol for the next twenty-four years taking on increasingly responsible academic and administrative roles. He was able to put into practice his philosophy of education and to play an important part, along with other experienced and talented colleagues, in the success of the School.

He taught a variety of different courses and modules at Advanced Diploma in Education, Bachelor of Education and Master's level for both United Kingdom based and international students. Many of the courses he taught were tailored to the particular needs and backgrounds of the international students with modules which were relevant to the education systems in their countries.

Among the International students taking these tailored courses were a group of teacher trainers from Gambia – co-taught by Teame with colleague Tricia Broadfoot – with a primary aim of improving the quality of teaching in the country. There was a course for Educational Administrators from Nigeria where more schools were being built and extra teachers needed, thanks to extra revenue from the country's oil industry as prices rose in the 1970s. The Nigerians, dressed in flamboyant African costumes, brought a touch of colour and gaiety to the department's Berkeley Square buildings.

Teame found much common ground with the Africans. As an African himself who had come to study in Britain with no knowledge of the country or its university system, he understood the issues they faced in settling in. For their part the Africans – and later students from other continents – were grateful to find an empathetic lecturer from whom they could not only learn their subject but who also was willing to listen to their problems and go out of his way to help.

Experienced educators came from Egypt to improve their proficiency in English. Teame this time co-taught with Simon Pratt who had been one of his tutors during his own student days. The course had special emphasis on key planning terminologies and concepts. To highlight the point that any planning process is characterised by different theories, motives and alternative routes, they discussed at length with the Egyptians the pros and cons of the late Tanzanian leader, Julius Nyerere's remark, 'to plan is to choose'.

With Professor Bob Thompson he ran a course on Education and Development which focused on education services in developing countries. The Professor's profound expertise and experience from his time working in Kenya, Tanzania and Nigeria meant most students, initially, came from African nations. But as the course developed it grew to include students from other developing countries. After Professor Thompson retired in the mid-1980s Teame took over responsibility for the course and considerably extended it.

There had been a threat to the future of the Graduate School of Education at about this time. But the threat was averted due in large part to the efforts of the then Head, Professor Peter Robinson – a man Teame had a high regard for who had been supportive as he developed his career there.

The reputation of the courses dealing with Third World issues, which the Graduate School of Education in Bristol had developed, resulted in Teame being invited by Professor Arve Brunvoll to lecture for several weeks at Bergen Teacher Training College in Norway. Another link, developed by a colleague, was with Oslo College in Norway where Teame taught for two weeks as a guest lecturer. It led to a dozen Norwegians doing part of the M.Ed course in Bristol.

His remit for other professional duties also increased by leaps and bounds. He sometimes wondered whether it was due to his inability to say 'No' to any request. It is probably the case that his willingness to take on everything he was asked to do sometimes resulted in a few less scrupulous colleagues taking advantage of his willingness to help. So the requests would just keep flooding in.

His style is remembered by one fellow academic, who admired and respected him, as 'polite, gentle' but also 'lengthy'. That latter point a friendly acknowledgement of Teame's penchant for using not one word but two (or perhaps three) in order to get his point across. It may not have always gone down well with some of his more impatient colleagues.

The other side of the coin was that Teame's natural wish to find out about people and chat to them were the qualities that made him such a respected Student Adviser to the international students. If that meant more words than some would like it was a small matter compared to the value of his care, thoughtfulness and commitment to spend enough time with people.

His polite and gentle ways meant that he would never give vent to the inevitable feelings of frustration, even anger, the pressures of the job could bring. But that did not mean he did not experience them – and it would be Teblez who would hear about them when he got home. In her wise way she would help him to put things into perspective.

Those who worked closely with him valued him highly and respected the work he did with the international students. Another colleague remembers him as being 'highly committed to supporting his students and he devoted considerable personal time and energy to this.'

One of his former students from Barbados, describing him as a 'compassionate soul', adds: 'This dignified gentleman was the bright spark which made homesick foreign students feel a sense of belonging in the grandeur of the University of Bristol.'

He took on a university-wide role as Recruitment and Admissions Officer – considerably adding to his administrative responsibilities which already included his duties as Adviser to Post-Graduate international students and chair of the Education and Development Line of Study at M.Ed level. He was in demand as a speaker at secondary and primary schools in Bristol and the surrounding counties of Gloucestershire and Somerset where he would talk to the pupils about the developing world.

The international students were a diverse group. It was a challenge that Teame and his colleagues had to face. The students came from a huge variety of nations in Africa, Asia, the Middle East and Latin America. Students had different cultural and social backgrounds. For many of them English was not their first language and their limited communication skills sometimes made it difficult for them to understand lecturers or for the lecturers to understand them. Teame made special efforts to accommodate their needs.

He was a firm believer in the view that teaching is not merely an occupation but a profession which requires total commitment. His view was that anyone who goes into teaching without being prepared to put their heart and soul into it, and to really want to pass on knowledge to their students, will end up being frustrated – and not good teachers. He saw teaching as a calling. Not just a job but something you have to really want to do.

His philosophy of education, based on his experience in the classroom and what he had learnt from his own training at college and university, would form the basis of many of his lectures.

Teachers, he believed, are imparters of knowledge but also craftsmen in the way they guide their students through the education process. His years in teaching – especially his time in the education system in Eritrea with its scarce resources and limited opportunities for schooling – had convinced him of the value of good and committed teachers.

He knew that the best teachers could hold the attention of a class throughout the lesson or tutorial. He developed his own techniques for keeping his students at the university awake and interested during a 90-minute tutorial starting at 9.30 am. Instead of giving streams of information for the entire session he would break things up and involve the students by changing his teaching style. Recognising that some minds might be detouring to the next essay they had to write – or one they still had to complete – and others could be still befuddled by the previous evening's excesses in one of the city's bars or night-clubs, he would break his lectures up into segments.

So he might talk for twenty minutes on the subject in question, then break for a discussion, or throw questions at the students. He might show a video, or play some music and ask the students to diagnose the content. Anything to break the monotony and keep the students interested. He was always keen to involve the students, to challenge them to think, and above all to learn. They would be broken down into small discussion groups, asked to give seminar presentations – not always easy for the more diffident – and was keen to encourage team spirit amidst the inevitable, and understandable, competitiveness of ambitious students.

Sometimes he would liven things up with a joke to make a point. Once, mindful of the Muslims among his audience, he told the apocryphal story of a boy who was told by his father to buy a sheep. The boy bought the sheep but then sold the head – a delicacy in the Arab world – and returned with only the headless body to the consternation of his father. The father asked where the head of the sheep was. The boy replied that the sheep was like a teacher, without a head! It was a euphemistic way of emphasising that a teacher who does not use his head is no good to his class. The students got the point. And the Muslims were amused rather than offended.

He saw teaching as both an art and a science. At times using painting, music, even dance to aid the learning process and develop skills, values and attitudes. But also scientifically creating and passing on knowledge. Teaching also, he believed, included problem-solving. He was always looking out for anything troubling his students. It might be a problem with their studies, a health issue, and in some cases a personal issue. He felt it was his job to look out for the signs and to take whatever action was necessary to deal with them. And he would explain to the teachers and teacher trainers whom he taught that they needed to be problem solvers too. So he would attempt to equip them with the problem solving skills for the classroom as well as life outside it, which would make them better people and more effective teachers. He would take issue with academics who considered that teaching was purely the act of passing on knowledge which he saw as 'just filling up an empty vessel'.

His view was that teachers are made not born – although some may have a more natural aptitude than others. Teaching, he believed, was a role which needs the teacher to be motivated by their inspiration to pass on knowledge which in turn inspires the student. But they needed training.

Teame felt his role was also to empower his students to do their own thinking. He was among the educators who strongly believed that their students should be able to find out things for themselves. So they were not being filled like an empty vessel but helped to both learn and become self-reliant.

He was mindful of the need not to make assumptions about students if they didn't initially make a good impression. This was particularly the case with students who, perhaps through shyness or lack of confidence – often because of their lack of language skills – held back from group discussions or from asking questions. So he would not pre-judge them and would do his best to help them to fulfil their potential. Many of them did, returning to their countries to become key figures in the academic system.

He was keen for his international students to go back to their countries and seek ways of improving the education systems and policies. To interact with their own students in the way he had with them.

Teame also believed in the reflective side of his teaching and welfare role in the classroom. He would make a point of asking himself after every tutoring session: 'Have I done my job properly?' And he would encourage his students to reflect on their performances too. For him the reflective attitude meant he would assess himself and his performance in front of the class before he went off to his next class which could be on the same subject with a different group of students. He would ask himself: 'Do I need to change anything?' Did he have to adjust his teaching and the way he did it because these were students with different needs, perhaps different levels of under-standing. He believed that the more he reflected the better teacher he would be.

The mark of a successful teacher, in his opinion, was the amount of time they spent in preparation before a class. He saw that as the crux of good teaching. They needed not only to have their lessons – what they were going to teach – but also a strategy of how they were going to do it. And afterwards there was reflection on their performance.

His teaching would differ from class to class depending on who was sitting in front of him. If he was teaching UK-based students with good English understanding he knew he could move through the lesson faster because there would be no problems with communi-cation. But if, as was sometimes the case, there were international students who had difficulty understanding English, he would slow down his presentation giving time to ensure everyone was following. He would understand that those with better English might get frustrated and want to move faster, but would explain his reasons. It was sometimes a compromise but he did his best to make it work for everyone in the class.

He took a humanist approach which meant he was primarily concerned with the humanity of the students he dealt with, their self-worth, and with the problems and qualities that made them human. He was not a humanist in the conventional sense.

His methods were laced with his Christian beliefs, instilled in him since childhood by his parents and grandmother and the culture of the Coptic Church in which he had been brought up. It had given him his strong sense of not only the power of a Supreme Being but of the need to care for the individual above all else – often to the detriment of personal ambition – which permeated through all his dealings. But he was respectful of people of other religious convictions and would happily acknowledge that everyone should have freedom of thought and belief and be able to worship, or not worship, in their own way.

His approach to teaching was to be what he described as a 'life-long hungry learner'. Becoming more aware of the cultural and linguistic background of his international students which could affect their learning he would adjust his teaching accordingly. He saw the need to appreciate the students' multicultural diversity. His lessons had a multi-disciplinary approach allowing him to weave together different lines of thought and keep the students interested. He saw himself as a learning catalyst – rather than an authoritarian controller of knowledge – which meant tolerating new ideas and encouraging the students to be life-long learners themselves. And finally he always felt the need to identify his own imperfections. His aim was for his students to thrive, not just survive.

He looked upon teaching as producing the future generation. Teachers, he said, can be a lubricant like the oil in the machine which makes the engine function more smoothly. It was a job that has to be taken seriously and was exciting and intellectually stimulating. But if you don't inspire your students they can't, in turn, inspire those they go on to teach.

He would offer his students some food for thought, which seemed to encapsulate his educational philosophy, reminding them of the need to:

- Earn your credibility;
- Be a part of not apart from;
- Reflect before you point your finger at others;
- Be a bridge builder;
- Foster independence of thought.

With the conflicts around the world much in mind he also urges students to:

- Assist in the development of sound conflict prevention strategies;
- Be aware of the wide ranging impact of global interdependence.

But he also campaigned for the careful selection and recruitment of teachers. The teaching profession was a calling, something that someone really wanted to do. It should never be an option taken because others were not available. Neither should teaching courses be a dumping ground for students who had been rejected by other faculties – something he had noted with dismay was particularly prevalent in some developing countries. Although, in those cases, he also believed that low salaries were not attracting the highest candidates and that more resources for education would result in better quality teachers.

In March 2013 – eight years after Teame's retirement in 2005 – the centenary of the Bristol Graduate School of Education was celebrated with a one day event where memories were shared of how the centre had become a hub of excellence in the field of teacher education. Teame was among those asked to speak along with Professors William Taylor, Eric Hoyle, Tricia Broadfoot, Philip Gammage, Dr David Satterley and Elspeth Gray.

Teame focused on how the Bristol model of teacher training had influenced the programme of training teachers in the developing countries. Being the modest man he is he would never have mentioned the contribution he made to the model by creating and teaching a new module on Teacher Education for Development. But the invitation to talk about it was a fitting recognition of his work at the Graduate School which spread out to the wider world. He felt honoured to be included.

As new research on the nature of learning continues Teame has, if not changed his views, acknowledged that there are new ideas emerging – some of them contentious.

For instance, when he started teaching in the 1960s he understood the nature of learning was essentially based around the ideas of philosophers and psychologists who mostly associated learning with teacher-centredness and motivating the students.

But with the advent of brain-imaging technologies and genetic research starting in the 1990s he recognises that neuroscientists had come up with new concepts of how learning takes place. They have identified the brain as a 'living organism that grows and reshapes itself as it develops and is used'. The research has radically changed the concept of learning.

This debate continues. But for his part Teame concludes that learning is a continuous process and is not about memorising but understanding the knowledge accumulated. Moreover learning is not, as many believe, the exclusive domain of the intellect. It is influenced greatly by, among other things, social, psychological, genetic and linguistic factors.

His main motivation as a teacher revolved around the success and well-being of his students and the degree of understanding that he could help them achieve. He would happily acknowledge being first and foremost an educationist focussing on strengthening the ability of his students to learn. Even in his time as Director of the Teacher Training Institute at Asmara, where he had big administrative responsibilities, he could not resist taking a teaching role as well.

In fact it was during those early days in Eritrea that he developed his firm belief that he could best teach people by sitting amongst them rather than being a distant figure preaching down at them. It fitted his values and he knew it worked.

One fellow academic describes him as an 'educational evangelist' whose actions are rooted in his strong values and sense of the importance of education, particularly in the developing world.

His motivations were not for personal advancement and he had no wish to be rich – although the higher salary from promotion would have helped the family budget.

He never became a professor at Bristol – although he had been an assistant professor at Asmara University at the young age of thirty-six and, truth to tell, took on a professorial role in many of his duties at the Graduate School of Education. He would say, with a wry smile, that there were already too many professors in the university hierarchy and you had to wait for at least one of them to die before there was a vacancy. He reflects today that in the 1980s and 1990s the post of Professor was not as down-graded as he believes it appears to be nowadays. He would be quick to point out though that this was a comment on the system rather than the quality of individuals.

For him, the business of teaching and the welfare of students was a greater priority than spending time researching which would have added to his credentials and his chances of getting a professorship. Instead he saw his role as being a facilitator, helping his students to discover knowledge for themselves. For him, this was more important. He understood the need for such research, and respected why others would take that route, but felt it was not for him.

His level of commitment to the teaching and other roles he undertook was never in question and his work was much appreciated by Heads of Department as well as the many students he taught and mentored.

His prioritising of teaching and mentoring also reduced opportunities to further enhance his academic credentials by writing and publishing. But despite his busy, sometimes self-enforced, schedule he did find time to accept invitations to contribute to a number of academic publications where his work was greatly respected. These included the prestigious International Encyclopaedias of both Education and Higher Education respectively and various professional journals. In addition he wrote three books, *Learning from the South* (1984), *Swann and the Global Dimension* (1987) and *Globalisation, Educational Transformation and Societies in Transition* (2000) with Michael Crossley and David Johnson.

He wanted to be true to himself. Always speaking his mind, albeit diplomatically. He knew that the world of academia – both in Asmara and in the UK – can be a rat race. Like other professions it is highly competitive. So, although he would often entertain friends and sometimes colleagues, in his home it was not his custom to regularly socialise in the hope of cultivating professional relationships which could be to his benefit.

So, did his career advancement suffer? It clearly did. And at times he could have been forgiven for feeling undervalued and under rewarded in view of the work load he took on – some of it albeit voluntarily and because of his inability to say 'No.' As one close friend astutely said of him: 'His one weakness is his generosity.' But he had no regrets. He acted knowingly and willingly. He would say his reward was to be seen by his students to have been a professional who served their educational needs and aspirations to the best of his ability.

CHAPTER TWENTY-EIGHT

Student Adviser

Soon after Teame joined the academic staff of the Graduate School of Education at Bristol University in 1981 he found himself increasingly becoming not just a tutor to the international students but also their mentor and, in some cases, confidante when they got into personal difficulties.

His work with the students, outside the classroom, started informally and unofficially. As someone from the developing world and also a former student at the University the international students, many of them fellow Africans, saw him as someone who would understand the academic and personal issues they faced in an unfamiliar country far from home. It was a natural extension of his philosophy of putting the well-being of the students first as a platform for helping them to achieve academic success.

Teame had a large office at the Graduate School of Education in Berkeley Square a stone's throw from the university's famous Wills Memorial Building with its clock tower, a Bristol landmark. The international students had an induction programme in the first week to introduce them to life at the university. But there were still questions to be answered. A steady stream of students would arrive seeking advice. His willingness to help no doubt encouraged the flow still further. He would find time, amidst his teaching duties and a growing administrative role in the department when he became Admissions Tutor, to sit down and talk to students with a problem on their minds.

His time at the university, as he took on more senior roles with increased responsibilities, was defined by his principal motivation which was the welfare of the students. To him that took priority over the demands of their course work. He firmly believed that if the students were happy in their personal lives it would naturally follow that their studies would benefit. It was a philosophy that had been honed during his days at the Asmara Teacher Training Institute. There he had introduced social events, music and, when necessary, a personal heart to heart chat with a student, to sit alongside his desire to see them achieve high academic standards.

In time the university authorities, recognising the value of the work Teame was doing with the students, and his obvious suitability for it in view of his background, experience and above all his empathy with them, formalised the situation and appointed him International Student Adviser. It was a further responsibility in addition to his teaching role which by then included his work with the international students teaching modules such as Education and Development in the Third World, a course he inherited from Professor Bob Thompson. He was also running M.Ed and Advanced Diploma in Education courses for the wider group of students in the Graduate School of Education.

So it was a busy time but one that Teame threw himself into with his customary vigour and enthusiasm. In his role as International Student Adviser he became something of a father figure to the international students who came not just from Africa, but from Asia, the Far East and Latin America. Drawing on his own experience of settling into university life in a new country with a different culture and traditions, he was keen to point them in the right direction and head off potential problems.

New students, most of them teachers or teacher trainers on British Council scholarships, as Teame had been as a post graduate student ten years earlier, would come to him for advice on their courses. Teame would help them decide which modules would best suit them. The courses were very intensive and included the Advanced Diploma of Education with the chance to upgrade to an M.Ed if they reached the required standard in the first four months.

Teame was the link between the British Council and the students they were sponsoring. Every three months he would assess each one and submit a report on their progress which would go to the British Council offices in Bristol. From there it would be sent on to the Ministries in the student's home country.

But it was on the personal level that Teame found his adviser's role most challenging. As the Student Adviser he was the first point of contact when there was news from home for the students. And it was more often than not bad news such as the death of a family member. Teame would have to break the news and help them deal with the inevitable emotional implications – made more difficult by being so far away from home and unable to return to grieve with other family members.

Homesickness was a common problem he would help the students to cope with. They would miss a loved one at home, a wife or children, and want to go back to see them in the vacations, which of course they couldn't. It would be expensive and their breaks from classes had to be used for study and writing their essays so intensive were the courses.

Some of the fear and anxiety that he had to deal with related to the pressures students faced by a return to studying. Senior teachers, administrators and teacher trainers, who had not studied or written an essay since their college days many years previously, would approach Teame and tell him how worried they were about the four essays they had to write as part of the requirements of their first term. They feared they might fail. Many of them also felt under pressure to do well because of the support from relatives and villagers who had high expectations of them.

A case in point was that of a young Kenyan student whose fees were being paid by his village under the 'Harambe Scheme'. The fact that he had won the trust and support of his village community was an uplifting experience for him. On a number of occasions, he told Teame how proud he felt to have won their respect. But at the same time the huge pressure such support placed on him – especially when he could only manage two Grade C's for two of his four modules at the end of the Christmas term – was hanging heavily. The pressure showed. He could not sleep at night due to his anxiety. He also started doubting not only his ability to meet the high demands of the one-year diploma course, but also his capacity to transfer the knowledge and skills gained to his home community.

This complex case of health and learning issues which had concerned Teame so much, was passed on to a psychiatrist, who was able to help the student. The psychiatrist convinced the distressed student that he would not lose face in the eyes of his community if he returned home. And the student did indeed return home without facing the repercussions he feared.

Teame considered it was his responsibility to help the students to fulfil their dreams. It was his firm belief that the students under his care would not start their learning process until they had established positive relationships with their tutors.

The different cultural backgrounds of the students could also cause difficulties. This was true of some of the Chinese students Teame taught who had problems with communicating in English. They held back in group discussions and were losing out in their studies. Teame would take time to draw them out to discuss their problems and give them confidence. He would recommend some of them to take a three-month English course to improve their language skills.

He made a host of friends among the students and was regularly in touch with some of them thirty years or more later. Many of them returned to their countries and went on to hold important posts as Director Generals, Ministers of Education and as Professors.

One of them was a Tanzanian. He suffered a tragedy while studying in Bristol. His wife – the mother of his four children – died. Teame helped him cope with this crisis. He had wanted to give up his studies and return home to look after his children. Teame understood his need to do that. But he was able to arrange a leave of absence from the university for him to return home to look after his affairs and then to return to complete his studies. The student had, at first, been reluctant to return but finally accepted Teame's advice and came back to complete his degree.

Many years later Teame visited Tanzania, as Principal Consultant for Merganser – a British consultancy group – to help set up links between British and Tanzanian schools. One day he walked into a meeting to find himself shaking hands with the man he'd persuaded to continue his education after his wife had died. He told Teame: 'Thank you for persuading me. Your advice was good.' He was by then a Director General in the Department of Education. He expressed his gratitude in front of a crowded meeting of educationists and said that without Teame's advice he would have missed the opportunity to achieve his position.

As well as dealing with the personal issues, Teame ran study skills sessions when he would reintroduce mature students to the art of academic essay writing, preparing their arguments, justifying them and acknowledging sources. He would also teach them how to under-take qualitative or quantitative research and to construct a bibliography of their source material.

It ought to be noted that the Graduate School of Education had an extremely supportive and sympathetic staff, not least in the university library. There the library staff understood the anxieties of some of the international students. They would recommend the right books for a particular module, often going out of their way to assist.

Another sector where badly needed help was provided to the students – some of whom had never seen a laptop or a personal computer – was the IT department. The experienced and well trained staff on the fourth floor of the department building would, with a great sense of humour, allay the students' fear of technology. They were able to assist 99% of them to use the university computers to complete their essays by the end of their first term. Not all international students had problems with IT. Those from Japan, China, Malaysia, Hong Kong and Taiwan were very computer savvy unlike their counterparts from Africa.

Occasionally students suffered mental health problems. Teame would ensure that they had the right support and medical help. Several students, including one African woman who suffered badly from loneliness and homesickness, had to be treated in a local hospital. Teame would visit them in the evening after his lectures had finished and would keep a check on them.

The change of culture and social mores was often a mystery to students arriving fresh from Africa and other parts of the world with different customs and attitudes. This proved particularly tricky for some of Teame's African students whose idea of saying 'Hello' to someone was to stop for an extended chat. So they were surprised and a little perplexed to get no more than a brief 'Hi' from their British counterparts – both students and lecturers – before they quickly moved on. Teame had to explain to them that this was the custom among the more reserved British and, in any case, they probably didn't have the time for an extended chat. By the time the Africans had finished their year-long course they were happily making do with a brief 'Hi' as well.

Teame, with his natural aptitude to socialise and talk, was no stranger to the British liking for brevity having had to cope with it himself as he settled into the country years before. At least he understood the issue sufficiently to be able to point his fellow Africans in the right direction.

Cooking, too, was something that many of the overseas students had not experienced – although they were not alone in that as many a mother of British students would confirm. But Teame, remembering his own early days as a Bristol student who could not cook, would give them a few tips – mainly on the cheapest places to buy food.

Fitting in his advisory role between lectures, Teame looked upon it as troubleshooting. He could never be sure what issues he would have to deal with from day to day. Sometimes it would be a student in financial trouble. Many of those not on grants relied on family support to pay the £6,000 a year course fees (as they were in the 1980s) in instalments. If a payment was late Teame would liaise with the university finance office to give them more time to pay.

His efforts to help the international students also extended to ensuring they could get access to the books they needed to read from the university library. With as many as fifteen students all wanting to read the same book for one module there were not enough copies for all of them. In collaboration with the education department library staff he instigated a system whereby students could only borrow a book for a maximum of three days. Or some books were restricted to be read in the library whilst others were borrowed for only one day.

He was a great believer in the personal tutoring system which enabled a small group of students to meet with a tutor – usually drawn from their study discipline – to help with any problems they might have either academically, such as queries following a lecture, or personal issues which might require some gentle teasing out by the tutor. The Graduate School of Education already had a personal tutor system in place and Teame soon joined their ranks which enabled him to put some of his ideas about personal development into practice.

He viewed the tutorials he was leading as an opportunity to listen to the students, attempting to identify concerns that they might have. It was not always easy. The African students in particular, including the more mature teachers and teacher trainers that Teame taught, were brought up in a culture where the teacher was a kind of 'demi-god' who could not be questioned. They would have difficulty expressing what was really on their minds. Teame would encourage them to speak their minds and be frank about anything they did not understand or disagreed with. His own African origins helped to break down the barriers.

Teame recognised that the tutorials were a valuable resource for the students because of the chance they provided for them to have one on one discussions with tutors which did not always happen in the hectic schedule of lectures and staff meetings. He also knew that not all tutors were able, or prepared, to make the time to answer student's questions, or to get to know them better on a personal level. So the tutorials were an opportunity to address those issues. He felt they were a valued link between students and academic staff which meant the students, particularly some of the less confident ones, felt valued and listened to.

Judging from the feedback that Teame received from his seasoned colleagues like John Hayter, Roger Garrett, Bob Smith, Sara Meadows and Michael Crossley to mention just a few, it seemed that the tutorial system was much valued by the staff.

As well as talking through issues linked to their studies Teame, considered that the opportunities provided in the tutorials to deal with personal issues was one of the most important aspects of the tutorial system.

One of his international students, a woman, approached him one day and said she wanted to give up the course. She claimed she was not getting anything useful out of her studies and wanted to go home. Teame suspected there was more to her problems than she was saying. He thought it might be the result of a broken relationship with a fellow student. Gently he teased the truth out of her. The woman agreed, at Teame's suggestion, to see a university counsellor. She later withdrew her request to leave and continued the course.

Sometimes international students would have a funding crisis. When money ran short Teame would do his best to help them by seeking support from charities so that they could complete their studies. Among those he helped were Kenyan-Somalis (Somalis by birth but Kenyan nationals) Southern Sudanese and a Mozambican.

On one occasion he dealt with the case of a Malawian student who became ill and had to go to hospital. Teame would visit him regularly. But sadly he died. It fell to Teame to inform the man's wife of his death and arrange for his body to be returned to Malawi for burial. He arranged for another Malawian student to accompany the body back to Blantyre with the expenses paid by the British Council who were sponsoring the student. But first he organised a funeral service at the church he himself attended – Redland Park United Reformed Church in Whiteladies Road – as well as a ceremony in the University Chaplaincy attended by many staff and students.

He raised funds to be sent to the man's wife. But he also sent her money out of his own pocket for a year or so to help pay children's school fees – a not inconsiderable sacrifice on his part. He kept in touch with her for some years afterwards.

The High Commissioner of Malawi at the time wrote to the Bristol University Vice Chancellor expressing thanks for what Teame had done both during the unfortunate man's illness and after he had died. A group of Malawian students also wrote to Teame to offer their thanks.

His commitment to the tutorials meant yet more responsibility being thrust on his shoulders when he was asked to organise all the tutorials for students in the Graduate School. He would allocate students to tutors and manage any ensuing problems as well as conducting his own tutorials. When necessary he would circulate the other tutors with common issues that cropped up and also hold regular sessions to discuss how the system was operating and what needed improving.

Although the personal tutorial system at Bristol was largely successful, Teame felt it was not perfect. There were still issues that slipped through the student welfare net. The international students under Teame's care would still bring up the lack of chances to meet and talk to one or two of their tutors and professors. It may have been that some personal tutors did not put the effort in to draw the students out, or that the students did not feel able to express themselves fully. But, whatever the reasons, Teame decided to attempt to provide a different platform for the students to meet their lecturers and professors.

He established a Student-Staff Forum in addition to the well tried practice of staff-student meetings. It served a number of purposes. The postgraduate students could meet on their own when they would nominate some of their number to represent them at the monthly staff meetings.

But, most importantly, the forum enabled the students to meet together and informally discuss issues that mattered to them in the presence of the tutors and other staff over a cup of coffee or tea. It enabled staff and students to get to know each other better. The relaxed atmosphere with them all sitting around in a circle encouraged the students to say what was on their minds and ask questions. Indirectly they could see that their British tutors were, after all, human beings.

Another reason behind the creation of the Student-Staff Forum was to motivate the students to produce the best essays possible in the three terms. Then at the end of every term a select committee from the forum, chaired by Teame, would choose the most exemplary essays from the various module disciplines which had obtained 'A' grades and deposit them in the department library so that the following year's intake could learn from them.

The forum was well supported by tutors and professors in the department and Teame was grateful for the respect they showed for the idea. The sessions went well. Students would get the chance to ask their tutors about study difficulties they were having. Some would describe the problems they had explaining themselves in English and that they needed time to do so. Teame's role was to be a conduit between the two. He felt it helped produce a stronger student-tutor relationship and helped the students feel valued.

In many ways Teame's administrative and academic involvement in the Graduate School was a continuation of his philosophy which had been honed in his time as Director of the Teacher Training Institute in Asmara when he had built relationships with the student leaders and improved their links with the teaching staff.

During the mid and late 1980s there was a large group of Muslim students in the Graduate School of Education. Many were from Northern Nigeria, Malaysia, Pakistan and the Middle East including Egypt, Libya, Oman, Jordan, and Yemen. During the month of Ramadan, Muslims pray several times a day. Sometimes they would leave their classes to do so.

Teame had allowed them to use his large office to pray in. He provided a set of prayer mats which were laid out when needed by the

Muslim students. The mats would be kept in a corner of the office when not in use. When it was time for the Ramadan prayers Teame would leave the office to give the students privacy.

But before praying the Muslims would, as the tenets of their religion dictate, wash their face, hands and feet. They would use the basins in the department cloakrooms which, not surprisingly, created quite a lot of water spillage over the floor. There were complaints at the mess.

Teame, recognising the problem and the need for the Muslim students to be able to carry out their religious practice, approached the university building department to see if something could be done to provide special facilities for them to wash as part of their religious observance.

He argued that with so many Muslim students it was incumbent on the university to provide the facilities for them. They had recruited them in their countries and encouraged them to study at the university. Their beliefs had to be respected. He believed the cost, a few thousand pounds, was justified.

To the university's credit, Teame's plea was answered. A row of basins, placed low enough for the Muslim students to wash their feet, was installed in one of the men's and women's washrooms. Teame thought it was the first time a British university had taken steps to provide special washing facilities for their Muslim students to use. The Muslim students were delighted and grateful.

There were still some issues over the use of the new wash basins as they were in the same washroom area used by other students and members of staff. Teame encouraged the Muslim students to do their best to keep the area free of spilt water on the floor which did not always happen. One or two members of staff did question the wash basins on grounds of cost but also asking if the university were in a position to meet other special requests from other religious groups such as Buddhists. Admitting that the university's resources may not meet every special request Teame, retorted that such a question was for another day. As far as he was concerned he had done his best to answer a particularly sensitive and urgent need and was relieved the university authorities had supported his view.

(The facilities from that time have since been removed as part of refurbishment but in their place are shower cubicles in both the male and female toilets.)

Teame's care for the students extended to inviting them to his home for meals and the chance to talk more. For homesick students from, for instance, Taiwan or Papua New Guinea to name just two, it was a welcome chance to enjoy the hospitality away from life in a hall of residence. Teblez would provide meals and join Teame in making the students feel at home. It might have been considered above and beyond the call of duty after a busy day. But Teame and Teblez looked upon it not just an extension of his role with the students, but also considered the hospitality was part of their Eritrean tradition of giving a welcome to visitors who otherwise would have spent Christmas or Easter on their own.

A highlight of the year for the department was an end of term party. It had been started by Teame's supervisor Professor Bob Thompson whose duties Teame had taken on. But Teame went a step further and introduced an international flavour with students cooking food from their home countries. There was also national music sometimes on tapes, at other times a student would play an instrument. It was an enjoyable way to end the academic year. So popular was the food that it would sometimes start disappearing before the party had properly got underway.

The academic staff would be asked to contribute or bring a bottle of wine, whilst the secretaries would also prepare desserts and a variety of cakes and cookies. On a number of occasions Teame would invite staff from the British Council in Bristol, the wardens of the Halls of Residence, the University Accommodation Officer, ministers from local churches as well as the Imam from the local Mosque and the priests from the Hindu and Buddhist temples. It was an effective way of bringing together the many different cultures not just in the university but in the surrounding community.

One end of term party became a farewell for Professor Thompson, his old mentor, who had also become a good friend, when he retired in 1985. Teame and some of the international students – elected by their peers – organised the event. Dr Thompson was a popular educator, well known and liked by all the international students, especially the Africans, for his honest comments – based on his long experience of teaching in East and West Africa – on the cause of underdevelopment in what he saw as the 'great, though slumbering, African continent'. The farewell party had been a closely guarded secret. Teame accompanied him into the hall as he discovered to his great surprise that the party was in his honour. There were appreciative speeches from a number of the African students present. The Professor was so overwhelmed that he could not respond for a while.

In 1988, Teame was instrumental in organising another farewell reception for one of Bristol University's most illustrious Chancellors – Professor Dorothy Hodgkin who was shortly to retire. A holder of the Nobel Prize in Chemistry for her work in X-Ray crystallography, Professor Hodgkin was regarded as one of the pioneer scientists in her field. Elected Chancellor of Bristol University in 1970, Teame had the privilege of meeting her several times and admired and respected her.

Apart from her much applauded work as a scientist he, was also struck by her social conscience. She was concerned about social inequalities and the effects of apartheid in South Africa. Teame was particularly appreciative of her part in setting up a Scholarship for students from the developing world. She also established an accommodation block in Bristol, mainly for international students, known as 'Hodgkin House' – Teame had stayed there in his student days. Later, in the 1980s when on the university staff, he served on the Welfare Committee of Hodgkin House as well as being involved in the selection of Hodgkin scholars.

So it was no surprise that Teame wanted to do all he could to mark the retirement of such a luminary. Just a few days before her retirement he organised some very special entertainment at a reception in her honour. He asked a group of South African students to perform traditional dances and songs wearing their tribal costumes. Teame, also in his Eritrean national dress, introduced the group to the assembled guests who included many of the leading members of the university staff. A highlight of the performance was one of the South African students reading a poem in the Xhosa language – famous for its click consonants – much to the delight of Dorothy Hodgkin.

For Teame, his work with the international students was a reversal of roles as he looked back on his own journey as a British Council Scholar to Bristol and the new life he was establishing after the trauma of having to cut ties with his beloved Eritrea and seek asylum in Britain. Now he was giving other international students the chance to improve themselves – although, fortunately for them, they would not have faced the dangers that had forced Teame to leave his own country.

An Eritrean working as a social worker in London, who Teame had got to know, tells of how he became a friend and mentor who helped him in his aspirations to write poetry, even editing some of his work. Another Eritrean student Teame had taken under his wing, worked with him on the Student Staff Forum and described how Teame 'deeply cared for the students' ensuring they had an enjoyable experience as well as being an 'empathetic listener and pragmatic adviser'. A West Indian student described Teame as providing 'a glorious anthem for all immigrants who bring lasting treasures to their adopted homeland in our borderless world.'

Teame has kept up his support for international students even after he retired in 2005. After leaving the University he took three Kenyans studying there under his wing, regularly visiting them, helping them with their dissertations.

Some of the international students who benefited from his teaching and care had their own way of expressing their gratitude. They wrote in appreciation: 'You've been a wonderful, extraordinary teacher. You are our beloved father and brother. You've been there for us. We are proud of you.'

CHAPTER TWENTY-NINE

South-North Conference

Teame's experience in the classrooms of junior schools in Bristol during the Rowntree Trust project, when he introduced children to the mysteries of Africa, had left him convinced that the developing countries and those of the developed world had much to learn from each other. He wanted to change the perception – common in the 1980s – that the North, the developed world, had nothing to learn from the South, the developing countries of Africa, South America and Asia.

His own attitude had changed since his early years as a schoolboy in Eritrea when provincial and cultural loyalties were paramount and little thought was given to the outside world. He now had a wider view which had been influenced by his exposure to life in the developed world both as a student, a refugee and an educator. His experiences had led him to the firm belief that, whilst the world he grew up in might need the support and expertise of developed nations, there was also much that they could learn from the developing countries.

It was a provocative and contentious issue which, among other things, raised the question of the historic attitude of Western powers to the countries they colonised. He wanted to challenge the idea that while the West provided aid, it had nothing to gain from developing countries. It was, he felt, a stereotypical view, although he also

257

perceived that exploitation of valuable mineral resources was a strong
motivation for involvement in the underdeveloped world.

It seemed to him that, in the eyes of the North, the South was
a problem child to be pushed and pulled by its more industrialised
and powerful Northern cousins. But would Northern affluence and
dominance always be so? And what would be the consequences of a
change in the dynamics of power?

There were, he felt, other unanswered questions. Did the North,
for instance, owe the foundation of its science and philosophy to the
work of Muslim and other scholars? Did the 'alternative technologies',
created to fulfil needs in the South, have a use in the North as well?
He reasoned that if the North sought to answer these questions they
might discover that the South, contrary to the pervading belief, might
have something to teach them.

He would wrestle with the issues wondering how he could bring
them to a wider audience. His thoughts would constantly return to
the concept of global citizenship and how education could be used
to promote international understanding.

One night, unable to sleep, he had the clear conviction that he
wanted to organise an international conference where the question of
what the developing countries could contribute to the developed
world could be debated. He would invite distinguished educators from
the United Kingdom and abroad. The conference had to have a global
dimension. He shared the idea with others, including university
colleagues, and to his great delight, found a great deal of support.
Within a few months his germ of an idea had grown to become a
reality. Support grew from around the world. The conference was to
be held just as he had hoped.

It was the summer of 1983 and Teame spent many hours preparing.
He reviewed books seeking likely themes and, more importantly,
speakers from both the South and the North who had something

valuable to share. There followed a series of phone calls, faxes and emails in the ensuing months to the selected speakers on the subjects they would talk about. It meant some delicate negotiations as Teame had to persuade a series of distinguished professors and other experienced professionals to talk about a subject he had chosen for them as he pulled together the conference programme and ensured that all relevant areas were covered.

Organising the conference was a huge and challenging under-taking. But there was an enthusiastic response from the majority of those Teame talked to, although one senior colleague of his did complain that the conference theme was 'prescriptive' in the sense that the 'North' had to learn something from the 'South', which, he felt, 'could not put its own house in order'. There were also others who were concerned that the theme was too wide to be covered in a three-day conference. But the overwhelming majority of those Teame talked to were very much in favour of the conference and its theme.

Teame's perseverance paid off. The conference went ahead. It was to be held on 9-11 January 1984. Having got the backing he needed Teame now was confronted with the huge task of getting it organised. Once again his wife and daughters stepped in to help alongside university colleagues, especially Teame's secretary, Beryl Collins.

It was a hugely stressful time for Teame. The conference had to be publicised to attract delegates. Teblez and all three girls worked in the living room of their home writing out the names of conference delegates to get an idea of numbers. Sometimes they would have trouble deciphering Teame's handwriting after he scribbled names on scraps of paper. Replies to invitations had to be processed. Two university secretaries, Anne Mallitte and Marie Taylor – who had by now become good friends of the Mebrahtu family – proved invaluable in bringing some organisation and efficiency to the operation.

But the main load of organising and planning the conference fell on Teame. He and Teblez played a major part in the hospitality. They ensured guests, some from overseas, were comfortably accommodated. And they entertained some of them in their home – among them Professor Ali Mazrui, a distinguished African academic based in America. It was a busy and challenging time for both of them.

The three-day conference was entitled *Learning from the South: What, Why and How?* It was held at the School of Education at the University of Bristol. Teame and his joint conference organiser, Roy Parker, had assembled an impressive line-up of academics not just those from British Universities but several from Africa and Canada. Among others with an interest in the subject were a medical doctor, a Voluntary Service Overseas (VSO) co-ordinator and a Christian Aid organiser.

There were a hundred and forty delegates in the auditorium representing academia, Non-Governmental Organisations and Aid Agencies. Teame was grateful for the support from Roy Parker who continually encouraged him in his convictions to hold the event and was also instrumental in getting the conference proceedings published by the Bristol Classical Press.

Teame presented the first paper to launch the conference. He had worked hard on preparing what he wanted to say, labouring long into the night as he sought the words to best express the convictions which had led him to be instrumental in calling for such a gathering. As he stood on the platform to give his opening address, looking out at the sea of faces before him, he had a sense of wonderment that the germ of an idea that had set the conference in motion had actually become a reality.

He started off by saying that, in his experience, there was widespread concern and demand by intelligent people of all classes and persuasions for a new view of the global community in general and the South in particular. He expressed the wish that the conference would enrich the experience of those who attended and increase their perception of the realities of the 'strange world in which we live'.

He acknowledged that relationships between countries in the South 'were not as harmonious and co-ordinated' as they could have been. He also accepted the claims of political scientists that conflicts in the South were tending to develop far more swiftly than co-operation – claims that have proved horribly prescient in the light of subsequent events.

He told his audience there was a belief – which he shared – that the resolution of the North-South conflicts must be based on the humility of the North to learn from the South and on the magnanimity of the South to forgive and forget, and to enlist the much-needed support and understanding of the North in its development. The future of both regions was intricately intertwined.

Other speakers took up the theme bringing other insights and arguing that the North learning from the South augured well for both hemispheres. There was general agreement that North-South learning was essential. Justifications for saying so differed between moral, social, cultural, economic and intellectual viewpoints.

Dr Charis Waddy, a distinguished scholar of Islam, put forward qualities that she maintained the North could learn from the people of the Arab nations. These, she said, included hospitality, the discipline of fasting, the principles of Islamic banking, a pattern of family life which accommodated at least three generations, the concept of wholeness of life and the belief in the greatness of God.

A former tutor and later a colleague of Teame's at the School of Education, Nicholas Gillett, argued that the North had 'sold its soul' to material wealth. It had refused to live simply so that others might

simply live. He quoted proverbs from countries in the South to
emphasise his point:

> Hope is the pillar of the world. (Nigeria)
> Wealth comes and goes like the shadow of a palm tree. (Bihar, India)
> Money is the thief of the soul. (Estonia, one of the Baltic States)

Teame's concluding remarks summed up his assessment of the
situation and the changes in attitude he believed were needed: 'I have
implicitly indicated that the North has learned a lot from the South
in areas such as agriculture, spinning and weaving, writing, medicine,
and religious ideas and that learning, either now or in the future, is
also quite possible.'

He added: 'On the other hand I have also implied that, though
possible, learning may be unlikely, as it requires the North not only
to change its lifestyle but also to provide a kind of world leadership
quite different from what it has given thus far.'

Nonetheless, he said, the call to learn from the South, currently an
underdog militarily and technologically, was not in his opinion another
attempt at creating a new mythology. Neither was it an invitation
to engage in a crusade against the North or its conflicting ideologies
(the conference was held during the Cold War). It was made on
the assumption that it might help the North to realise some of the
inherent limitations in its type of 'global leadership' and to try to do
something about them as well.

Shortcomings, he said, included the North's tendency to glorify
power and violence, its inability to transcend the ebb and flow of
national interests; its assumption that it is the salt of the Earth and
that what is good for it is good for the rest of humanity; its lack of
political will (not economic capacity) to change the bases of the
unjust, international politico-economic order; and its refusal to face
the harsh reality of the poverty of its affluence.

He ended by saying that to dismiss the call for learning from the South as myth was to underestimate the past and the future contributions of the South and to delay the progress of mankind.

Thirty plus years on, Teame believes there are still lessons to be learnt from the South. When he considers whether there is better understanding and tolerance between North and South and whether the world is a safer place than in the 1980s, his answer would, inevitably, be no. To a large extent his view is coloured by the many trouble spots of the world and millions of refugees seeking asylum in the North.

His view was substantiated by the findings of the Global Financial Integrity Group of 2015 which declared that the developing world has lost $16.3 trillion – through 'illicit financial flaws and tax havens' – to the North since the 1980s.

Neither would he, with any conviction, claim that the North, and humanity at large, has learnt any lessons in a world where, as he would put it 'the European cattle would have a daily budget of about $2 per head which is a lot more than the $1 per day on which about one billion poor people try to survive.' So, he would add, the trajectory of change was still pointing in the wrong direction, favouring cows over people.

But, being in a profession that builds the generations of the future, Teame believes that despite the dark clouds hanging over a deeply troubled world there can be a new dawn. He is convinced of the resilience of the human spirit, and the potential of education to provide new opportunities.

And he would never discount the transcending power of the world's great religions to change lives and motives for the better if people would only live them as the Prophets intended. He describes himself as an individual 'who prefers to light a candle than curse the darkness'. For him hope, the origin of humanity, dies last.

CHAPTER THIRTY

Extracurricular

Teame carried out a wide range of other activities outside his academic and administrative roles at Bristol University. He was much in demand and this extracurricular work included serving as a specialised consultant and trainer, organising and speaking at conferences and seminars, working with aid programmes, giving talks in schools as well as editing and contributing to educational journals. He was also an external examiner for a number of other universities.

It was a demanding work load on top of his already heavy responsibilities at the university. With his reluctance to say 'No' to invitations for which he felt some empathy, he would often spend weekends and breaks between university terms working with charities, aid organisation and NGOs whose aims he respected. Many of the projects reflected his humanitarian interests. They were able to benefit not just from his academic expertise but also his knowledge and experience of the developing world and asylum seeking. He looked upon this extracurricular work as part of his commitment to bringing an understanding of the needs and aspirations of the underdeveloped world and providing new opportunities for its people. It might have meant further sacrifices in time, creative energy and career advancement but it was a route he was prepared to take.

The 1980s, when Eritrea was still part of Ethiopia, was a period he remembers as one full of both hope and protest. Teame was especially encouraged by the Live Aid fund campaign orchestrated by singer and activist Bob Geldof which encouraged millions of people in the Western World to donate to the relief effort for famine areas in Ethiopia including Eritrea.

Although Teame recognised the irony that around the same time the Mengistu regime were celebrating their tenth anniversary in power by importing crates of whisky. Meanwhile TV screens in the West were showing pictures of Ethiopians reduced by famine to living skeletons. The decade was also marked by concern about nuclear weapons – Teame particularly remembers, and was impressed by, the Greenham Common Women's Peace Camp in Berkshire protesting at nuclear weapons being sited there. (The camp was active for nineteen years and only disbanded in 2000.)

It was amidst this background of protest and action that Teame was struck by the level of interest, mostly from young people, in serving as volunteers in the developing world. Encouraged by their commitment and keen to support them he became involved in the training programme for Voluntary Service Overseas (VSO). He was impressed that young people in the UK were prepared to spend a year or two of their lives helping a Third World country and immersing themselves in different cultures and languages. So he contacted the VSO centre in Birmingham and was accepted to join a team of trainers who ran courses for the volunteers.

He was also invited by the Centre of International Briefing at Farnham in Surrey, to join a team of lecturers delivering talks on aspects of culture and education in developing countries for people going to work in Africa and elsewhere in the developing world. The lectures took place in Farnham Castle, refurbished for the purpose. Teame conducted four briefing sessions there between 1985 and 1995.

He would normally talk for an hour giving the participants – consultants, educationalists and aid agency staff – background about the culture, religion, traditions, language and music of the countries they were planning to work in.

His school talks, for which he was in great demand, would often centre around the issue of cultural diversity in education – a subject close to his heart. One such workshop was at the instigation of a former student colleague, Stuart McFarlane – by then on the staff of the Rolle Teacher Training College in Exmouth to which Teame was invited. He shared Teame's commitment to cultural diversity and became a long standing friend.

Christian Aid was another of his commitments. He felt an affinity with its aims that insisted that the world must be changed to one where everyone can live a life free from poverty and with equality, dignity and freedom for all regardless of faith.

Teame also accepted an invitation to provide his skills as an assessor and trainer for ABANTU for Development (AfD), a non-governmental organisation that seeks to empower African people, especially women, to have a say in the policies and decisions that impact their lives. ABANTU means 'people' in several African languages. The organisation had been set up in 1991 in London by African women who recognised that gender discrimination was a key obstacle to sustainable development and social justice in their countries. AfD had operations in the UK among the African refugees but also in African countries with offices in West, East and Southern Africa.

The invitation probably came about because AfD knew that 'Gender and Development' was a key component of the M.Ed course Teame taught at Bristol University. It was subject he had some empathy with. He had, in fact, supervised fifty M.Ed dissertations on the role of women in national development with students from Latin America, the West Indies, Africa and Asia.

Teame's involvement with AfD's work included joining a team of experienced African consultants to review and rewrite a Training Manual entitled *Engendering the Budget* to make it gender friendly. The manual was prepared for training Permanent Secretaries and other members of staff in the Ministries of Finance and Planning in Africa and was aimed at improving equality.

In 2000, he was involved in evaluating AfD's operation in the UK to ensure that the organisation was proving effective in influencing policies and development programmes for the benefit of African men and women. His report concluded, among other things, that AfD was one of the few Southern NGOs which were totally committed to improving the lot and the place of women in Africa. He acknowledged that another of AfD's qualities was that it believed Africa needed to develop its own solutions to discovering peace and solving conflict. Teame concluded that there was ample evidence AfD was one of the NGOs that had broadened the scope of basic human rights from just civic and political rights to social, economic and women's rights.

AfD's stated commitment, to 'lifting others as we climb', had resonated with Teame who felt it was in line with his own philosophy of life, both as an educator and as a human being. His experience in Eritrea, where his sisters had been victims of the culture of denying the right of education to girls – partly enforced by economics – had left him with a sense of guilt. When he became a teacher, he attempted to rectify the situation by helping his sisters to send their daughters to school. During his travels in the South he had often witnessed girls pleading with their parents to be sent to school – usually to no avail. It had enforced his view that equality of opportunity should be available to everyone. So he had personal as well as professional reasons for wanting to support AfD.

Among the other consultancy roles he fulfilled was one sponsored by the World Bank in Zambia in the early 1990s. The Zambian education authorities, concerned at the lack of management skills among the head teachers of some of their schools, were keen for outside help from an independent source.

Teame was asked to lead a six-strong team of consultants to spend twelve days in the country investigating the problem and coming up with recommendations to solve them. His team was to include three Zambians – academics from the University of Lusaka – as well as an American, a South African and another academic from Britain who had formerly taught in Zambia.

Teame's selection as Team Leader was not surprising. He was well known among other educators in the country having taught many of them who took Master's degree in Bristol and were now head teachers in the country. But they were mostly running schools in the capital city Lusaka and other large towns in the country. It would be in the rural areas where the problems under investigation by the consultancy team were mostly to be found. Many of the rural schools in Zambia, which is a vast country, are isolated and many miles from the larger towns and cities.

Here, many of the teachers, especially those in leadership roles, had not had the kind of training that Teame's students had benefited from. (The University of Lusaka did not run Master's courses at that time, although they do now) So many of the teachers in the rural schools were short on management skills.

Teame divided his team into three groups, with himself leading one of them, and insisted that they spread their investigation among Primary, Middle and Secondary schools so as to get a comprehensive picture of the problems facing them. They set out to identify the kind of training required for the particular needs of staff in the rural areas. The teams sat down with both teachers and heads to ask them their views on the issues they faced.

Perhaps not surprisingly, the views differed. Many of the head teachers, Teame discovered, did not consider there was a problem. But the teachers had another story. They complained they were not given a voice, there was shortage of staff resulting in teacher-pupil ratios of up to 1:60 – high even for rural African schools – and resources like books and writing materials were also in short supply. The country was facing a steep drop in the price of copper – its main export – at the time, which would have had an effect on the problems in the schools Teame and his team were investigating.

As the three teams swapped notes in their regular catch up sessions back in Lusaka they agreed that one of the reasons for the shortage of teachers in the rural schools was the low pay and long hours. In fact they discovered that many of the teachers took second jobs to make ends meet. This was brought home to Teame when he ordered a taxi to take him to a rural school. He discovered that the driver was one of the teachers he had met earlier in another school, who was earning some extra money.

Provision of much needed resources was a major issue. This, the consultants realised, was partly due to the remoteness of some of the schools and the shortage of transport to deliver the urgently needed books and equipment like overhead projectors. Teame came across conflicting views. Ministry officials assured the consultants that lorry loads of what was needed had been despatched. Teachers complained that it never arrived. They were not able to get to the bottom of the issue. There were whispers among some of the teachers that corruption might have been involved, but nothing was proved.

Their investigations completed, Teame assembled his team and together they drew up a list of recommendations. Firstly, they called for more attention to be paid to managing the staff and resources. In particular they highlighted that ways needed to be found to retain and retrain staff through carefully planned and implemented in-service development programmes.

Key among other issues the team highlighted in their report was what they saw as the autocratic manner and way of working adopted by many school directors (head teachers). Teame, from his own experience, knew that such a way of operating was impossible to sustain and that this kind of micromanagement reduced teachers and other staff to cyphers, killed the spirit of delegation and good communication. He blamed the problem partly on school directors not being adequately inducted. And not given clear-cut information from the Education Ministry on what was expected of them.

Teame also served as an External Examiner and Assessor of Course Programmes at other universities. In addition he held vivas for PhD candidates and M.Ed dissertation and worked with the London Institute of Education (part of University College), Birmingham, Manchester, Reading, Oxford Brookes, Glasgow, Wolverhampton, Cardiff and Huddersfield. And finally, Deakin University in Australia which he conducted by post and phone calls. The long list was a tribute to Teame's standing among his peers.

He believed that a robust external examining system played a significant part in enhancing academic and professional standards by, among other things, verifying that the level of degrees awarded were appropriate and comparable to those at other universities.

He saw external examiners as having a 'halo' effect or a 'horn' effect. The 'halo' was when students felt their external examiner was approachable and did not intimidate them, allowing them to talk confidently. But the 'horn' effect was to act like a charging rhino bringing fear into the minds of students and making their minds go blank. Teame aimed to be the former. Although he felt there were some of the latter among other external examiners.

One PhD viva where he was the external examiner was an example of his humane approach. The candidate, a male student from the Far East, completely froze as Teame questioned him on his dissertation.

He broke out in a sweat and could not say a word. Teame looked at the student's supervisor who was also in the room as he pondered how to handle the situation. He felt he had to give him another chance and try and calm the man down and to restore his confidence. He cracked some jokes, told him to take some time to pull himself together. He got him a glass of water and asked him to sit quietly in another part of the room until he was ready to continue. The man did, and after a break of about fifteen minutes, continued the interview and this time his confidence had returned and he acquitted himself well. He got his PhD after undertaking some minor corrections. Later he would write a letter of appreciation to Teame for his consideration.

He was often asked to give talks on third world development and issues surrounding his own African culture. Some of the talks were more challenging than others. One of the most testing was an invitation that he did his best to politely decline. The event was a gathering of Rastafarians – mostly from the West Indies where the religion was founded in 1930 – at the Inkworks centre in the St Paul's area of Bristol. He was asked to talk about Emperor Haile Selassie of Ethiopia. He was reluctant because, firstly, he was Eritrean with a limited knowledge of the Emperor and secondly he was acutely aware that part of the Rastafarian religious belief was the conviction that Haile Selassie was a God, and was worshipped as divine. They called him *Jah*. Although Haile Selassie was generally assumed to have died – albeit in mysterious circumstances – Rastafarians believed he was still very much alive. It was a scenario Teame feared was fraught with difficulties and the possibility of awkward questions.

He tried to persuade the organiser, a West Indian community relations officer, that there would be better people than him to conduct the talk. He had in mind two Ethiopians who were at that time studying in Bristol. But he was told that, in fact, it was they who had recommended him for the task. Reluctantly, he agreed.

On the day of the talk he arrived half an hour early to allow him time to set up his slides. The hall was decorated with the older version of the Ethiopian flag, not the latest one introduced by the new regime which had overthrown Mengistu. And there was reggae music by acclaimed Jamaican musician and singer Bob Marley, a devotee of Rastafarianism, playing in the background.

Such was the interest in his talk that busloads of Rastafarians were arriving from all over the country. It delayed the start by forty-five minutes and by the time he started the hall was packed to overflowing.

Things went smoothly as he went through his slides showing the Emperor's palace in Addis Ababa and other historic parts of the country. He showed pictures of Shashemenie the town in Ethiopia where, in 1948, the Emperor had granted permission for a group of Rastafarians to settle on 500 acres of his private land. He talked about Marcus Garvey, the Jamaican political leader of the mid 1900s, who made the clarion call for the freedom of the black skinned people of Africa to be freed from the shackles of colonisation.

But, the slides over, the meeting was thrown open to the audience. It was the moment Teame had been dreading. First one of the Rastafarians, an elderly gentleman, said he had once been at Kingston Airport in Jamaica and seen *Jah* – the divine form of Emperor Haile Sellasie. The man related how the arrival of *Jah* had been marked by heavy rainfall – which he described as 'divine intervention' – after a drought in the country. Teame thought that it was the man's way of criticising his remarks about the overthrow of the Emperor and his subsequent death.

The next question was the one he had feared most. 'Did Ethiopians in general perceive Haile Sellasie as a God or a human being?' He had expected the question. It was the reason he was so reluctant to accept the invitation in the first place. But now he had to give an answer. The large audience of Rastafarians waited expectantly.

Teame's dilemma was that he did not want to offend the group by suggesting that their beliefs were erroneous. But neither did he wish to compromise his own religious beliefs as a convinced Christian. In the end what he said was a compromise. He said that, in his view, the Emperor was not a God but the head of the Coptic Church, of which he was a member. But he said he could not speak for all Ethiopians. There might well be some who did see the Emperor as God, including the descendants of the Rastafarians who had been allowed to settle in Shashemenie. He knew it was a 'wishy washy' answer but he felt, under the circumstances, it was the best he could do.

He felt more at home when he was sponsored by the British Council to attend forums in Africa to identify likely scholarship candidates for Bristol. He also represented Bristol University to promote it as a destination for potential students.

It was an important event for British universities seeking to attract overseas students. They would send representatives and take stalls in large halls or exhibition centres. One, that Teame attended several times, was in Nairobi in Kenya at the Westgate Mall which, years later in September 2013, was attacked by gunmen who killed sixty-three and injured many others. The Al-Shebaab group based in Somalia claimed responsibility.

The forums attracted large numbers of students anxious for a place at a British university. In Nairobi many of them came from wealthy Asian families prepared and able to pay the course fees and not in need of a scholarship. They had all been well educated in private schools and had good grades. Many of them wanted to study medicine or aeronautical engineering which were not Teame's speciality but he would provide the information on courses that they needed. He was on safer ground with those who chose one of the social sciences including education.

Often the student would arrive at Teame's Bristol University stall with their grandmother keen to see that their grandchild got the best possible education. On one occasion when a seventeen-year-old young man arrived with his grandmother, Teame invited her to sit in on the interview as he questioned the teenager about the courses he might like to take. At the end of the interview he asked the grandmother if she would like to ask a question or make a comment. She asked him if he lived in Bristol. Yes, replied Teame. The grandmother then said: 'I heard Bristol is a racist city.'

Teame was quick to defend the city he now called home. He replied: 'Madam, I cannot speak for the whole of Bristol but I can assure you your grandson will not be subjected to racism if he comes to Bristol University.' Then he held out his arm. 'Do you see my colour?' he asked. And added: 'Do you see my badge as a representative of Bristol University?' Then he said to the grandmother: 'If Bristol was a racist city, do you think I would have the chance to come here and represent the university?' He added that although there might be some racism in some parts of Bristol he could guarantee it would not be at the university. The grandmother was convinced. Her grandson was offered and accepted a place at Bristol.

In fact Teame's African heritage and his experience of seeking asylum was an advantage when talking to the African students and their families. The British Council had chosen wisely when they selected him to work with them at the forums. He was now happy to find himself acting as an ambassador not just for Bristol University but for the city of Bristol as well. It was a remarkable turnaround for an asylum seeker and something he could not have anticipated when he left Eritrea in 1976 with his life in danger.

CHAPTER THIRTY-ONE

Development Education

In the early 1980s the field of Development Education – an approach to learning about global and development issues through recognising the importance of linking people's lives throughout the world – was taking root. Its proponents wanted to challenge national stereotypes and provide people with the skills and confidence to support change towards a more just and sustainable world.

The ideas behind the growing movement for Development Education resonated with Teame. It was closely linked to his own thinking on the need for universities to be development orientated and was related to his area of specialisation which explored the issues facing the developing world seeking solutions through education.

His interest was sparked by a casual invitation from Professor Bob Thompson to be an observer at a meeting of a newly established group of Development Education enthusiasts in Bristol. The Professor, with his background of teaching in Africa, was a strong advocate of the principles of Development Education and was chairing the meeting.

Teame went along after conducting one of his regular sessions of Extra Mural Studies at the University's Wills Memorial Building – a well-known landmark in the city. The sessions were yet another facet of his academic life in addition to his university role. His lecture there was on a not unrelated subject – 'The Causes of Underdevelopment in the Third World'.

Arriving afterwards at the Development Education meeting, in the nearby Cathedral School, Teame needed little convincing of the need for development education. By the end of the evening, he was ready to join their ranks. He quickly became one of its leading members.

He could see that, at its simplest level, Development Education aimed to help individuals or groups to reach their own conclusions about the state of the world instead of being presented with the views of big business corporations who had their own agendas.

As interest in Development Education mushroomed centres were set up around the country including one in Bristol which was established in Old Market. The centre aimed to highlight the issues and offered those interested in the subject free loan of books and other literature.

At its inauguration Teame was invited to give a brief keynote address. Wanting to make a good impression before the invited audience he arrived wearing his best suit and tie to be surprised to find he was sharing the platform with a much more informally dressed Tony Benn, the Labour MP and former Cabinet Minister in the governments of both Harold Wilson and James Callaghan, who was at that time the member for the Bristol South East constituency.

Teame outlined the role of the newly established centre and how it was intended to foster attitudes, behaviours and skills that would encourage Bristolians to get involved in 'the global village' as he described it. The centre would develop a resource centre of artefacts, literature, slides and paintings from the developing world which would help to bring a greater understanding of their background and culture.

Tony Benn took the platform to express his admiration for the centre and how timely he felt it was in providing a different and meaningful form of education for members of the public interested in the state of the planet. He expressed concern about the level of world conflict and the inequalities between the rich and poor world. And he urged the audience to take on board Teame's point made earlier that they should think globally as well as acting locally.

Teame found Tony Benn friendly, relaxed and easy to talk to – a far cry from his public persona as a rabid member of the political left. At this time, in the 1980s, Labour was in Opposition and Benn was a prominent figure on its left wing with the term 'Bennite' used to describe someone who espoused his brand of politics.

After the meeting he sat down with him and they chatted for half an hour over a cup of coffee. Benn was supportive of what Teame had said about the centre and wanted to know all about him, where he came from and what he was doing. He may have been labelled a 'lunatic lefty' by some sections of the press, but Teame was impressed by him, believing him to be a 'very principled man' who had the welfare and interests of the poor at heart.

He developed an ever increasing number of contacts with those of like-minded views around the world. One was Pierre Pradervand, a Swiss philosopher whose book, *The Gentle Art of Blessing*, urged his readers to 'make the conscious choice to bless every person in their lives', instead of lashing out at them or feeling self-pity.

Pradervand had embraced the principles behind Development Education and was one of the guest speakers at a conference in Bristol in April 1983 organised by a colleague of Teame's at Bristol University, Roger Garrett. Teame was among the twelve guest speakers, which also included Pradervand and Ivan Illich, an Austrian with controversial views on education and schooling.

There was a variety of views expressed and issues raised about Development Education and it was clear the concept was open to different interpretations. Questions posed illustrated the multiplicity of views and included: 'What do we mean by development?'

'Does development impinge on social, cultural, political and moral dimensions of society?' 'Is there a causal link between education and development?' 'Is there a place for Development Education in the curricula of both developed and developing nations?' 'Is there a distinction between education and schooling?'

It was that last question which was at the heart of the controversial views expressed by Ivan Illich who gained notoriety in educational and political circles around the world after the publication of his book *Deschooling Society,* a highly radical discourse on education as practised in modern economies and criticising what he regarded as the 'ineffectual nature of institutionalised education'. Teame, like many of the other delegates, was keen to hear his views even if they had some pointed questions to ask about them.

An Austrian by birth, Illich had become a Roman Catholic priest and had worked in one of the poorest neighbourhoods of New York. Later travelling through South America on foot and by bus he founded, in 1961, the Centro Intercultural de Documentación, ostensibly offering language courses to missionaries from North America.

In his *Deschooling Society,* Illich argued that universal education through schooling was not feasible. He wanted to see the system of schooling around the world drastically changed, even destroyed. In its place he wanted to see new ways of learning. One way, he would suggest, was the use of advanced technology to support 'learning webs'. He told the conference that creating a culture of resistance to schools might, in the long run, help to reject what he saw as the 'commodification of education'.

A tall thin man, full of energy, Illich was a person admired by Teame for his great intellect. As he talked to his audience he rarely stood at the podium but instead roamed the platform as if he was trying to get even closer to them.

He maintained that the bond between education and schooling was no longer valid. There was a dysfunction between the two. He avowed that school, in its institutional form, represented a system of rejection for a significant number of youth, especially those who were poor.

To the educators listening to him, most of whom would be working in the kind of conventional education systems Illich railed against and was keen to abolish, this was strong stuff. Those who had read his book would not have been surprised to hear his controversial views. But he was pressed to explain how he thought schools, especially in the developing world, would react to his ideas.

Teame, who had been among those questioning the impact of Illich's revolutionary formula for change, was keen to hear some clarification of his views. He found his reply something of an anti-climax which left his concerns largely unanswered.

In essence Illich responded that creating a resistance to schools might, in the long run, help to reject the commodification of education. Teame understood that to mean Illich wanted to see an end to a school system in the poor underdeveloped world which produced students who were entranced by the glittering lifestyle of the rich world of developed countries.

More than thirty years on, Teame still ponders the questions raised by Illich about how to create a culture of resistance against what he described as 'the massive onslaught of globalisation', at the centre of which lies the modern school system. It is a question which is still open to debate today.

Most radical critics like Illich, knew that the realisation of their dream of de-schooling society depended on a social revolution. Teame was among the educators who, whilst admiring Illich's ideals, took a more pragmatic approach. He recognised that the current school system served the interests of its educators so they would be unlikely to favour change. Also he, like many other educators – especially from the developing world – had placed their faith in formal education. They looked upon it as a cure for social and economic ills and a way of binding the nation state together. So Teame was firmly of the view that schools are here to stay for some time to come.

Teame entitled his own address to the conference 'Curriculum Change for International Awareness'. He wanted to confront what he saw as the barriers to creating the kind of environment in the class-room which would encourage global awareness – a sense of a one world family.

His aim, he said, was to help the younger generation to develop the competence to be able to recognise and reconcile the tensions between their local environment and culture and those of other parts of the world. He talked of his own experience of meeting stereotypical views in the classroom, talking to secondary school children in his time with the Rowntree Project when he toured schools in Bristol and the surrounding counties talking about Africa. Then, he explained how he had dealt with views like 'the Third World is a place of half-naked can-can girls in grass skirts' by congratulating the students on their honesty, before inviting them to further seminars when they could be helped to better understand the realities.

Pierre Pradervand, like Ivan Illich, was an eloquent speaker whose contribution to the conference was eagerly awaited. He explained that in his view Development Education as a concept was intended to educate the inhabitants of the rich North about the problems of their brothers and sisters in the poor South.

Pradervand observed that well intentioned Church Charities and other Aid Agencies had been guilty of what some Development Education exponents described as a 'prostitution of poverty' by presenting images of pot-bellied children, which in his view 'went a little too far'. There had been a shift of focus to embrace issues of social justice, disarmament, ecology and human rights which are all global in nature.

Teame was fascinated and inspired by Pradervand's friendship with a prisoner on Death Row in Texas State Penitentiary for a crime he claimed he did not commit. His correspondence with the prisoner, Roger, is featured in his book *Messages of Life from Death Row*. The two had started corresponding after Pierre had sent Roger a copy of *The Gentle Art of Blessing*, a best seller which explores the power of positive expectations and unconditional love. Inspired by it, as Teame had been, the prisoner, after reading the book, had a spiritual experience which transformed his life of rage and victimhood to one of compassion and forgiveness. As the book relates Roger's favourite hymn was 'Lord do not move my mountain, give me the strength to climb it.'

In fact, as Pierre writes in the book, Roger had been a source of great support to him too. When Pierre was facing a life crisis Roger, from his prison cell, sent him a Post-it note. On it were written the words: 'I am hanging by my right arm by a rope, my left has been tied to my back – and I just hang in there.' Pierre had it stuck on the wall in his office and would look at it every time he was depressed and in need of inspiration.

Although Teame lost touch with Ivan Illich – who died in 2002 – Pierre Pradervand became a close and valued friend. The two men agreed that Development Education would enable people from both sides of the North-South, rich-poor, divide to survive. As Pradervand would say: 'We are all in the same boat.'

CHAPTER THIRTY-TWO

Multicultural

The concept of multicultural education – improving schooling opportunities for ethnic minorities as well as broadening the outlook of all children to raise awareness and understanding of a world outside their own borders – was another subject Teame was passionate about. He had begun to understand the issues during his time with the Rowntree Trust visiting primary and secondary schools, introducing pupils to Africa and the Africans, dealing with their questions as well as discovering the kind of problems faced in the classroom by children from minority ethnic backgrounds.

He wanted to see schools creating Global Citizens – young people with knowledge of the cultures and traditions of other countries and who respected the differences. Stereotypical views such as those he had come across during his Rowntree Trust project – 'all Africans wear grass skirts' for example – would be addressed.

The lack of attainment of ethnic minority children in British schools (this was 1985) was also a major concern to Teame. He wanted to find out why and seek solutions.

As he wrestled with all these issues with a determination to find answers, it became clear to him that there was a need to bring all the interested parties together to thrash out what could be done. Would it be possible to organise a conference he wondered. It would not be easy. There was wide disagreement among educationists as to how to introduce the subject in schools.

He took soundings from fellow academics and others from local education authorities and those responsible for the welfare of ethnic minority children. He was delighted and much encouraged to discover he had considerable support. Before long the idea had taken off and a date had been set for the following January, 1986, at the Churchill Hall in Bristol. Teame had a mixture of emotions. Thankfulness, that his idea was going forward but nervousness about getting it off the ground.

Shortly after the idea was born Teame heard that Lord Michael Swann, chairman of the Committee of Enquiry in the Education of Children from Ethnic Minority Groups, was to speak on his recently published report in Cardiff.

Lord Swann was a former Professor of Natural History at the University of Edinburgh. A member of the original committee of inquiry established in 1979, he had been appointed by Margaret Thatcher's Conservative government to take over the chairmanship after the original report on *West Indian Children in our Schools* had been heavily criticised.

Lord Swann's briefing was only a few days away but, on a whim, Teame decided to attend. He thought that Lord Swann might be the ideal person to give the key-note address at the conference. It might be a long shot but it was worth a try.

On arrival he found the hall in Cardiff packed with university academics, school inspectors and LEA officials. There was clearly a great deal of interest. Lord Swann outlined the report of his committee which highlighted that Britain was a multiracial and multicultural society and there was a primary need to change behaviour and attitudes.

Questions were invited and Teame quickly jumped in asking Lord

Swann if the English and Welsh education system had a global dimension and if so to what extent. Lord Swann replied: 'Yes, but not to the extent that it should.'

Before he could elaborate a coffee break was announced. But Teame, determined to find out more, and emboldened by Lord Swann's courteous manner, went up to him and told him about the Bristol conference on the same theme as his report. Would he consider giving the keynote speech? Much to Teame's surprise Lord Swann said he would consult his diary and let him know.

Teame returned to Bristol hopeful that he had landed his man. A few weeks later he received a letter on House of Lords notepaper. Lord Swann would come to the conference and make the key note speech. Teame was delighted. What he had thought of as a 'long shot' had come off. An important piece in the conference jigsaw was now in place and he could start planning in earnest.

He had six months to pull everything together including finding and recruiting sixteen other main speakers. It was a huge job on top of his already busy life as a lecturer and administrator at the Bristol Graduate School of Education. He was nervous and apprehensive as the realities of what was required became clear.

The three-day conference was to be called *Swann and the Global Dimension: Education for World Citizenship*. Teame, with a combination of diplomacy and persuasion, managed to pull together a distinguished line-up of speakers from the academic world, local education authorities, the BBC Education Department, and the Head of a school with a large number of ethnic minority children. Getting hold of them all and agreeing the themes they would speak on had been no easy task.

When the opening day of the conference arrived Churchill Hall was packed with academics, teachers, post graduate students from twenty-four countries, twenty-three Higher Education Establishments and fifteen schools. The long hours Teame and his team and his secretary, Beryl Collins, had put in, had paid off.

In his keynote address Lord Swann described how wide and complex the brief was and some of the difficulties they had encountered. And he admitted that no member of the committee, including himself, assumed they had got everything right.

As for Teame, he saw the report of the Swann Commission as a watershed moment in the multiculturalism debate. He thought Swann deserved credit for looking into the needs and problems not only of West Indian school children, but those of other less visible minority groups like Cypriots, Ukrainians, Vietnamese, Chinese and the Travelling Community.

He welcomed the report's call for a change in behaviour and attitudes which he recognised was bound to be a slow process requiring government support – something the report had requested. And he agreed, in the light of his own experience, that poorly thought through multicultural education could be counterproductive in confronting racism and negative stereotypes.

Not all delegates were satisfied with Lord Swann's report. Some attacked what they saw as its lack of focus on educational policy and the failure to tackle institutional racism. One critic was a member of the Swann Committee, Trevor Carter, who was one of four West Indian members. He was convinced Lord Swann 'was determined to dilute the racism factor which many blacks felt was the cause of their children's underachievement.'

But, despite the shortcomings picked up by the conference delegates, Teame felt the Swann Report was concerned with laying the foundations for a genuinely pluralist society. He felt it challenged the majority who, as the report outlined, were 'remaining oblivious to the changed and changing nature of British society'.

But, thirty and more years later, how do the arguments and

concerns of the Swann Report fare today? As Teame reflects on the multicultural climate in the 21st century, he sees some progress in providing all children – the majority and the minority populations – with a good education and other positive steps forward too – especially the Race Relations Amendments Act of 2002 which required all public institutions to adopt a Race Equality Policy. That year the government also introduced a Citizenship subject in all Schools policy which involved every student not just those from ethnic groups.

He felt the schools in England and Wales (separate from Scotland which has its own education system) could have done much more to improve their teaching of ethnic minority children by undertaking more research into how prejudice and inherited stereotypes can be tackled at school level.

An inclusive curriculum which reflected the country's ethnic and cultural diversity should be considered, he believed. He sees that as a fundamental change which should be introduced by the State, not left to the schools to deliver. After all, he reasoned, the school on its own was not the great social leveller that many think it to be.

But he considered one of the main contributions of the Bristol conference was to highlight the omission from the Swann Report of 'the global dimension'. He believed many of the problems in Britain, as in other countries, required international solutions. A contribution to the Bristol conference in the penultimate session by Professor Sally Tomlinson from Lancaster University resonated with him. She called for 'greater political awareness and tolerance' and argued that failure to change the entire cultural value base of the British Education system 'would escalate divisions'.

Teame, for his part, understands why some of his academic colleagues preferred to associate themselves with anti-racism rather than multiculturalism. But, he argued, anti-racism is not totally immune from criticism. For instance, in his opinion, it does little to create a genuinely inclusive strategy to address racism – a concept that refuses to accept similarity among human beings. More importantly he feels anti-racism fails to recognise the complex identifiers of many British citizens. In fact, a combination of the two, anti-racism and multi-culturalism, if properly planned and taught would, he believes, bring about a new empathy and sensitivity.

There was wide spread coverage of the debates in press and broad-casting with one station describing the event as an 'eye opener'. Delegates assessed the conference as a 'great success' in evaluation forms. Teame was satisfied that the conference had contributed to the continuing debate on multiculturalism even if there were still answers to be sought.

Three years later, in September 1989, he was to attend a conference in Tallukka, Finland sponsored by the Council of Europe. Delegates came from all over Europe including Malta, Spain, the Netherlands and Italy enabling Teame to gain new perspectives on the issues of multiculturalism.

From the Netherlands he learnt that problems among ethnic minority children there included retarded language development, shortage of sleep due to parents' lifestyle, and social isolation which all led to shorter attention span in classrooms.

He found himself chairing one of the groups when they split up for discussions. His group took on board a contention from Maltese delegates that bilingualism – where they could use their native tongue in lessons – was a positive step. They agreed that it would help ethnic minority pupils not to feel deficient or inadequate, something Teame had seen in some of the schools in Britain that he had visited.

Teame also presented a paper on the educational needs and problems of a small number of Eritrean refugees in London with whom he had been involved. He identified differences between the expectations of parents and children on the one hand and between the expectations and realities of real life on the other.

He also outlined the conflicting perceptions of schooling between parents and their children. The parents, he discovered, were anxious over losing their children fearing that they would move away from their faith, culture and parental influences. Many parents felt that, rightly or wrongly, schooling would encourage their children to challenge parental authority or become disobedient. They also worried that the children would look down on their own language and culture.

But, seen from the children's perspective, Teame perceived that their problems revolved around an inadequate knowledge of Britain and British society. They also had unrealistic expectations of what they might receive from their adopted country. In addition, their command of the English language was limited and they experienced anxiety and insecurity from what they saw as a lack of acceptance.

As he further explored the issues of multiculturalism at Tallukka he was reminded of what he looked upon as the 'great reservoir of talent in British schools' where, in London alone (in the 1980s) children spoke one hundred and forty languages. Creating a positive image of all races, cultures and languages was the rationale behind his argument that any national system of education should contain a global dimension.

In view of the continuing lack of consensus on multiculturalism, Teame would welcome a total rethink of what it actually means. He believes that such a revision of thought might show that 'identity' need not be 'fixed' or 'singular' and could change over time. He remains convinced that a person can hold two or more cultural and national identities. In fact he believes it perfectly feasible for him to perceive himself either as 'British' and 'Eritrean', as well as 'British-

Eritrean' and 'Eritrean-British' at different times. That to him is the true nature of world citizenship which he is convinced could be the answer to many of the conflicts generated within an increasingly multicultural society.

CHAPTER THIRTY-THREE

Zero School

In the summer of 1986, a year after Teame had made the last of his five visits to the schools set up for Eritrean refugees in the Sudan, he got the chance to make good his determination to offer more help to the cause of education among Eritreans caught up in the fight for liberation. This time it was to be the Zero School for the children of displaced Eritreans and liberation fighters which was sited in the liberated part of Eritrea.

His willingness to use his talents as an educator for the benefit of his countrymen and women caught up in the conflict had been well received by those he met in the Sudan camps. They had not held anything against him for his decision to stay out of the Marxist and other ideologies which were behind the liberation struggle. He always maintained he was an educator not a politician.

Osman Saleh, the man responsible for the education system in Liberated Eritrea, who Teame had met during his time in Sudan when he discussed the Zero School, was visiting London holding talks with his namesake, Teame Tewoldeberhan, who looked after the interests of Eritrean refugees in the capital city. It was an opportunity for Osman Saleh to take Teame up on his willingness to help them.

The two men came down to Bristol to talk to Teame about him going out to the Zero School – so called because it was the first in the new Eritrean education system. They came to Teame's Bristol home and sat down for a meal with him and his wife Teblez to discuss what they hoped Teame would be able to offer. Over the meal, Eritrean food prepared by Teblez, Osman Saleh, described why he would appreciate Teame's expertise and assistance.

They especially needed assistance in setting up a curriculum for the Zero School which would be tailored to the needs of Eritrean children and different to the Ethiopian curriculum followed in occupied Eritrea. It would form the template for the new education system in a liberated Eritrea.

Teame, for whom curriculum planning was a speciality, was keen to help and believed that this could be his way of supporting the liberation fight for his homeland. He had always strongly supported the cause of liberation but had never felt he was meant to be a fighter. He believed his most effective way of supporting Eritrea was as an educator. Teblez supported him in his venture to the Zero School even if she was a little nervous at him going so close to the war zone. So Teame agreed to go and they discussed the details of the trip and what was entailed.

It would certainly be a journey not without its dangers. The area of liberated Eritrea, close to the border with Sudan, was regularly patrolled by the Russian MiG jets in service with the Ethiopian Air Force. On the ground, fighting was continuing with casualties on both sides.

Teame was put in touch with the team developing the Curriculum of the Zero School, to further discuss the detail of what was required. At that time many of the team were not trained teachers or educators. One of the team members involved in the discussions with Teame was Tesfamichael Gerahtu. He later came to London to gain a Master's degree and, after independence was finally gained, became Head of the Curriculum Division of the Education Ministry in Asmara. He was also to become Eritrea's Ambassador in London and invited Teame up to the Embassy.

Unlike Teame, he was a politician who, on the one hand was in tune with Teame on the educational needs of Eritrea and was keen to implement his recommendations, but on the other was a convinced Marxist who stayed firm to the party line. So, as Teame would reflect, it was not a straightforward relationship. But it was one that worked as far as his work as an educator was concerned. Both Osman Saleh and Tesfamichael, recognised that, whilst Teame was not 'one of them' ideologically, he could be of considerable assistance to Eritrea and the cause of liberation and was sincere in his desire to help. They clearly felt they could do business with him and Teame had similar confidence in them.

In the run up to his departure, in free moments from his responsibilities at the University, Teame began formulating a curriculum tailored to an education system in liberated Eritrea and working on seminars he would hold with the teachers already working there. He also wondered whether he would meet up with some of his closest relatives – about thirty of them – who had joined the liberation fighters. They included his youngest brother Hagos of whom he had received no news for some time. It would be a challenging time and he had some understandable apprehensions.

Soon afterwards he was on a flight to Khartoum from where he would cross the border from Sudan into liberated Eritrea. He arrived at the airport to be met by members of the ERA, Eritrean Relief Association – an offshoot of the EPLF, the Eritrean People's Liberation Front. To Teame's surprise they had somehow found their way through security and found him in the baggage hall waiting to pick up his luggage. His welcome party asked him to sit on one side as they dealt with the luggage – and the *baksheesh* that travellers were often asked to pay the security staff to get their bags. Soon they were in a truck on their way to the ERA centre in Khartoum in the heat of the Sudanese evening.

He spent some hours discussing his plans with Paulos Tesfagiorgis, head of the ERA schools in the Sudan who Teame had also met when he had earlier visited Sudan. He was updated on the latest situation in Sudan, what he could expect on the journey and when he arrived at the Zero School.

Then he was taken to 'The Garage', a huge compound on the outskirts of Khartoum where the ERA kept vehicles and, sometimes, ancient tanks used in the liberation war. A team of mechanics serviced the fleet of vehicles. There were also stocks of petrol available.

Teame had time for a few hours rest before he was told it was time to leave for the journey across the border into liberated Eritrea. It was 3.00 am. He boarded a land cruiser with a driver and two security guards, armed with pistols hidden beneath their clothing, rather than the Kalashnikovs the liberation fighters normally carried. Teame was given a *jellabiya*, the Sudanese flowing robe, to wear and a headdress. He was told it was important he looked like a local and did not stand out. It was to be a journey fraught with potential dangers.

The night was clear as they set off, with bright moonlight and shining stars. Teame had never seen such a beautiful night sky. They drove through the streets of small towns, free of traffic at that time of night, and along the dusty roads to the border. Teame found the headdress he had been given useful to pull down over his mouth and nose to keep out the dust. They travelled at night, largely to avoid detection by the patrolling MiG jets of the Ethiopian Air Force. But it was also more comfortable in the cool night air than the oppressive heat of the day.

Negotiating the bumpy roads the land cruiser arrived at the border crossing a few hours later. The guards wanted to see Teame's passport.

The ERA had also given him a Visitor's Permit which ensured he was not troubled by local police. Asked why he was going into Eritrea he explained to the border guards that he was a teacher. To his relief, everything went smoothly and they were soon on their way again. He could see the ERA members had a good relationship with the border patrol. The driver spoke good Arabic and got on well with them. He suspected the ERA made this trip regularly.

Now across the border in liberated Eritrea the roads were even bumpier. The Eritreans had built a new road from their camps to the Sudanese border. They called it the 'Road of Hope' which Teame viewed as a great achievement under difficult circumstances. But, as he discovered, it was hardly safe. The road ran over high ground, sometimes escarpments with huge drops on one side. Teame watched nervously as the land cruiser slowly negotiated the tracks looking down on valley floors hundreds of feet below. A car falling down the cliff would be fatal for the occupants.

By 9.00 am they had arrived at a small camp for tea and a chance to answer the call of nature. For Teame it was a cathartic moment. He felt great joy at being in a liberated part of Eritrea for the first time. He was interested to see normal life going on around the camp. Shepherds were out on the hillsides tending their animals. It was a sight which brought back memories of his days in his home village as a young boy. He had the feeling that, one day, the whole country would be liberated. Although he had no idea when it might happen he had always been optimistic that one day it would.

His journey was providing an opportunity not just to help the education system of the country of his birth, but to see how people were living in 'free' Eritrea amidst the dangers of the ongoing war.

They were met by Eritrean 'mothers' who welcomed them with the traditional ululating which was reserved for special occasions and celebrations. It appeared that they had been told 'someone important was coming to see them from Europe' to the embarrassment of Teame, who did not consider himself important at all.

He was impressed and moved to discover that some of the women were former maids to Italian families who had given up their well paid jobs to join the liberation fight. Not only that, they had also sold their bracelets, necklaces, ear rings and other jewellery to raise money for the cause.

The women cooked the visitors a delicious breakfast of *hembasha*, the traditional bread made from wheat which was very thick and filling. Eating it again was a great delight for Teame, as was drinking a cup of Eritrean tea. He felt very much at home hearing his mother tongue, Tigrigna, beautifully spoken by the women. They also provided water for the travellers to wash off the dust of the journey. It was a scarce commodity in the camps and Teame asked if it was all for him. He was assured it was.

The dust from his hands, feet and face was soon washed off leaving him refreshed, with the water drying quickly in the heat of the day.

Refreshed, they were soon on their way again in the land cruiser on the final part of their journey to the Zero School. They travelled down a dry river bed keeping a close look out for the MiGs as it was now daylight. At one point they had a flat tyre which had to be changed. Another time they became stuck in a stream and Teame and the other two travellers had to get out and push the land cruiser clear. Eventually at about 7.00 pm, after a full day's drive, they arrived at Orota, the camp where the Zero School was situated.

They had been the best part of two days traversing the dusty roads from the border. It had been an exhausting journey. The camp was huge. It stood in a river valley in rocky terrain with many acacia trees which provided natural camouflage shielding the camp and its occupants from the marauding MiG jets flying overhead.

The camp accommodated thousands of refugees including about 3,500 children who attended the Zero School. It was a vast enterprise with tunnels set into the hillside to provide all the facilities that were needed – sometimes for several kilometres underground. Branches from the thorny acacia trees would cover the entrances. Even the few stone built huts above ground were camouflaged in the same way. The Zero School had underground facilities including dormitories and eating areas as well as offices. From the sky the camp would have been almost invisible.

Teame noted they had a generator supplying electricity around the camp. There was an underground hospital and a pharmacy, a bakery and pasta making facility and sleeping accommodation for everybody. There were other parts of the camp he was not told about – and did not ask.

Most of the children at the camp were sons and daughters of liberation fighters although there were also many orphans whose parents had died in the fighting or during attacks by Ethiopian forces on Eritrean villages.

Teame was shown to a small stone hut with a bed and told it was his accommodation for the duration of his stay. Like all the rest of the camp it was well covered in acacia branches. He was shocked to hear that it was the bed of the top man himself, Osman Saleh, who had left orders that he be allowed to use it. There was a shower made from buckets with holes in them placed on a platform. Teame was grateful to make use of it. He was careful to carry his own luggage to the hut and draw his own water from the well, not wishing to look as though he was a 'bourgeois'.

He sat down to a meal with others in the camp. It was a collective meal, mainly lentils and dried bread, with everyone dipping into the big plates on the table, and with water to drink. It was standard fare for those in the camps. Residents at the camp were warned not to wear bright clothing which could be spotted from the air by the MiG jets. Teame covered up his white shirt with the scarf covering his head. It brought home the dangers of living in the camps with the liberation war still at its height and the front line not far away.

Teame was impressed with the disciplined manner of the camp residents. They all, both men and women, took their turn in the camp chores of cooking, collecting water and firewood and baking bread. There was gender equality too. With over a third of the liberation fighters being women – some of them were commanders – the old traditions had been abandoned. Women would sit down with the men to eat, and the men would bake and cook which would have been unheard of in their earlier home lives.

Among those in the camp were many highly educated doctors, surgeons, nurses and engineers, including those who had built the Road of Hope.

Teame recognised a number of people in the camp. Among them were some he had met during his visit to the Sudan camps earlier who had now been transferred to Orota. Others were former colleagues or fellow students from his time in Asmara. Another was a fellow student at the American University at Beirut, Tukue Woldeamlak. He had graduated a year before Teame and returned to Eritrea to initially serve as a teacher trainer and ended up becoming a headmaster of one of the biggest secondary schools in Asmara. After falling foul of the Mengistu regime he fled to join the liberation fighters.

Teame was surprised to see him. They greeted each other warmly, his old friend making a joke of his name by pronouncing it in the Ethiopian rather than Eritrean way. He now had a beard and had a leg wound which had become infected. Teame had known him in Beirut as a very smart dresser, in sharp contrast to the drab clothing he and all the other men at the camp wore.

They saw each other regularly during his time in the camp. Sometimes, in the evenings, Teame's former student colleague would come to his hut where Teame would give him his supply of powdered milk which was strictly rationed. It was not something he was used to so he was more than happy to hand it over to his friend who saw it as a great delicacy.

A few days after Teame's arrival, there was a welcome party in his honour. It was an opportunity for the brewing of beer made from rice. But unfortunately the porcupines, which roamed around the camp at night, got to the beer first and there was little left for the party. It didn't, however, stop things going with a swing and Teame discovered the camps had spawned a new dance. He noticed the young people dancing swinging their arms as though they were carrying a Kalashnikov. A sign of the times and apparently now *de rigueur* at dance halls and parties in Eritrea.

It was at this party that he met some of his relatives who had been told of his arrival and travelled to the camp to see him. He had hoped that his brother Hagos and his uncle's son Bereket Ghebremichael, whose family he had lived with in Asmara, might be there. But they weren't and neither was another of his uncle's sons, Tekie Dumtsu. His cousins were like brothers to him. He sadly came to the conclusion that they had probably all died in the fighting. This later proved to be true as none of them came back from the front.

But one who was there was Bereket's brother, Fasil Ghebremichael. He was a liberation fighter too and he came with his partner, a Muslim girl called Julia, who was also a fighter. They had travelled all day to the camp to see Teame, hitching lifts on lorries and sometimes travelling on foot through the rocky hillsides.

Teame was very pleased to discover that at least Fasil was still alive. He had much changed since they last saw each other when he would have been about twelve. He was now in his early twenties. He had a

17 A group of international students from the Graduate School of Education: the Head, Professor Peter Robinson, kneeling second left; Teame back row, extreme right.

18 Drama is introduced in Teame's classes at the GSOE as an aid to learning.

Celebrating Our Cultures...we all smile in the same language.

19 An expression of Teame's philosophy displayed on the door of his office
at the Graduate School of Education.

20 Teame was kept busy on graduation days in Bristol with
requests to pose with his successful students.

21 The Zero School in a liberated part of Eritrea during the liberation war with Ethiopia. Classrooms were camouflaged to hide them from marauding jet fighters.

© Jenny Matthews

22 A teacher takes a class at the Zero School. Teame conducted some of his seminars in similar locations during his time training educators there.

© Jenny Matthews

23 Post-liberation conference in Asmara, planning for the future (Teame extreme left).

24 In-Service programme participants in Asmara displaying the group discussion boards they were encouraged to produce.

25 The In-Service training team entertained at the home of Teame's Uncle Ghebremichael and Auntie Azieb and their son, the famous singer Yemane Ghebremichael.

26 After Yemane's death in 1997, Teame visited his grave in Asmara, along with Yemane's brother Fasil Ghebremichael.

27 Eritrean graduates from the Graduate School of Education in Bristol celebrate back in Asmara.

28 Teame with his father, Mebrahtu Beraky and Aunt Azieb.

29 In an Eritrean restaurant in Asmara, participants in the In-Service programme, with their trainers, celebrate completing one of the Summer courses.

30 Young men conscripted for National Service after independence working on road widening.

31 June 2001, 10th anniversary celebrations of Eritrean independence at the Bristol Graduate School of Education. Teame with the then Eritrean Ambassador, Ghirmay Ghebremariam (left) and Professor Martin Hughes Head of the GSOE.

University of Bristol Library Special Collections. DM2165/68c

32 Celebrations at the 10th anniversary, where many of the Eritreans present were wearing national costume and sharing the celebrations with university staff.

University of Bristol Library Special Collections. DM2165/68c

slab of tobacco in his cheek in the way of the Sudanese which took Teame by surprise and the two laughed as he joked about the lump in his cheek.

Teame had bought a transistor radio with him which he wanted to give to Fasil. But he refused to accept it, explaining that fighters were not allowed any personal possessions. He also turned down Teame's offer of money. Teame was disappointed that he could not help him but understood that he was only obeying the regulations by which the fighters lived by. But he was grateful at least to have seen him again. The next day Fasil and his partner left the camp and went back to the front. Teame was to hear later that he and his Muslim partner both survived the war and returned to Fasil's family home in Asmara.

To his delight Teame was also able to meet three of his nieces. He was driven through the rocky countryside to another camp, called Hishkib, several hours drive away. Two of the nieces, sisters Mulu and Saba Asier, worked in social services in the camps. The other, Jordanos Tecle, was a car mechanic. They had only been told of Teame's arrival that morning so there was an emotional reunion when he arrived. The nieces cried and so did Teame. The three women, now in their twenties, would have been in their teens when Teame last saw them. Like all the other women in the camp they had short hair like men and wore trousers. It was a joyous meeting for the women too as the sisters and Jordanos had not seen each other for some months.

Tea was prepared by the nieces in celebration of Teame's arrival. Others in the camp had heard of his visit. Scores of them had soon congregated around the hut housing Mulu's office, where the tea party was to be held. It was a lively and joyous occasion, with Teame finding former colleagues and acquaintances among the throng, but the huge numbers meant his nieces were hard pressed to provide them all with tea.

They only had Primus stoves to boil the water. Running short of fuel Mulu used some petrol. Unfortunately that caused flames from the stove to leap towards the roof. Mulu tried to beat out the flames with a rag but the rag caught fire as well and soon the acacia branches covering the entrance to the hut were alight too. Mulu received a nasty burn on her arm.

Teame tried to comfort his niece who was by now in tears, more worried that she had put Teame's life in danger than about her arm. Others from the crowd joined forces to try and beat out the flames. Teame was impressed that among them were a number who had lost arms and legs in the war but were still anxious to help.

The fire in the entrance of the hut had by this time trapped a group of about ten, including Teame, inside. The only way out was over a high shelf and through a window. It was too high for Teame to climb so his cousin, Efrem Menghis, pushed him up enabling him to scramble to safety. It was only then that he realised the shelf was full of grenades. They had been left there by the fighters coming to the tea party much in the way that cowboys in the American Wild West would leave their six shooters outside the bar.

Fortunately for Teame, and the rest of the group in the room, the grenades did not go off. Teame scrambled clear, his clothes dirty and smelling of fumes from the fire. The flames were soon put out and fortunately no-one else was injured. Teame was taken to the stream running through the camp to wash himself off. Mulu, meanwhile was being treated for the burn on her arm. When Teame met her years later in Asmara she still had the scar.

None the worse for the experience, Teame wrote a humorous poem in Tigrigna about the incident which caused much amusement. In Tigrigna it went something like, 'Hishkib zbeluki measkeri, zelekiyo bota Hakure mekuri, kbetsehuki zemetsu tebareri. Efrem dea yirkebki, Asa-anberi.' Roughly translated it said, 'What kind of camp are you Hishkib, you are situated in a rock strewn area and you have a strange way of welcoming those who come to visit you! Thanks to Efrem, the brave whale.'

A fighter, a former Catholic priest, Aba Isahak Ghebreyesus, who had taken Teame to the stream, wrote a similarly light hearted poem in response pointing out that Hishkib was not really such an unfriendly place. So the incident was offset with good humour. And Teame was given the nickname 'Hishkib' by those who heard the poem.

It had been an eventful day. Despite the drama of the fire Teame was overjoyed to have seen his nieces and was proud of them for the contribution they were making to the liberation cause. There were tearful farewells as Teame returned to Orota and the Zero School to continue his mission.

The Zero School had been closed down for the duration of his three week stay so that the teachers and administrators could be free to attend Teame's seminars and workshops. But he learnt with great interest how the young students – between three and four thousand of them – were organised into classroom groups, up to sixty strong. There were sessions three times a day starting at 7.00 am to accommodate the huge numbers. Classes would be held under the spread of the acacia trees – and out of site of the MiGs – with children sitting on the ground, or on rocks. Chalk and blackboards were in short supply, as were textbooks where students would often have to share one between many.

Teame noted that the children were a microcosm of Eritrean society. There were Muslims and Christians who came from both the Highland and Lowland areas of Eritrea. One young boy – he couldn't have been more than four or five – seemed to adopt Teame. He would offer to help do his washing as Teame scrubbed his shirts in a bowl of water. But the 'help' turned out to be more of a hindrance as most of the water splashed out of the bowl and then the boy dropped the shirts on the dusty ground to dry meaning they had to be washed all over again. The youngster also told Teame what to do about the 'Ethiopian birds'. It took Teame a while to work out that he was actually talking about the MiG fighters flying overhead. The advice from the boy was to throw himself on the ground and look dead.

Almost all of the nine ethnic groups in Eritrea were represented. Talking to them he was impressed, and surprised, with their expectations. One said he wanted to be a doctor so he could help others and combat diseases. Another wanted to be an engineer. One boy said he wanted to be a pilot so he could fight the Ethiopian MiG jets. Teame was to meet him years afterwards when he was indeed an Eritrean Air Force pilot. Others became doctors as they had hoped.

Teame had spent many hours at home in Bristol preparing his seminars. Osman Saleh had given him a list of areas on which they needed help. He had emphasised that they wanted to create an education system and curriculum which differed from the Ethiopian model which schools in Eritrea were subject to under the Mengistu administration.

They had already made a start with the Zero School introducing lessons which included more vocational subjects like arts and crafts alongside the more traditional academic subjects. There was even a chicken farm which the children ran. This was in contrast to the Ethiopian system which they saw as exclusively academic.

They wanted stronger links between schools and society at large with parents' committees and associations – something Teame sagely observed could be a way of bringing government influence to bear by appointing their own supporters. Strengthening links between teachers and pupils was also high on the agenda.

So Osman Saleh and his team knew what they wanted to achieve. But, where they realised they needed Teame's help, was in creating a curriculum and teacher education which would bring about their vision for a new education system.

He was asked to provide seminars on subjects which included creating an elementary school curriculum, explaining the issues involved in technical and vocational education, education for self-reliance, and equal opportunities. He was also asked to talk about what was involved in setting up a successful school, the professional development of teachers, assessment and evaluation and setting up exams.

'Education for self-reliance' was one of Teame's favourite hobby horses, so he had no reservation in encouraging them to follow that path. Although he was grateful that he was given the freedom to teach what he felt was necessary and was under no pressure to include subjects he might have thought irrelevant.

Although there were teachers in the Zero School who had been trained – Teame had known some of them as colleagues or fellow student teachers – there were a great many who had no training at all. So Teame had to go back to basics and include in his seminars basic subjects like Planning a Lesson and Managing a Classroom.

With such a huge number of pupils there were a great many teachers. So Teame's seminars, which took place on the rocky ground beneath the branches of the acacia trees. Some seminars would attract as many as four hundred participants. He would liven up his lectures with discussions taking into consideration the fact that some of the seminarists had to sit on the branches of the trees. He also showed videos using a projector and screen which he had brought with him. He gave it to them when he left.

There would also be workshops with Teame setting the teachers projects to complete – like planning a lesson, or taking class on a chosen subject – something as simple as talking about the rocks on the ground and the terrain.

During one seminar he asked the participants to write or talk about the subject 'Have you heard?' He wanted to give them the opportunity to express themselves in writing, pictures or verbally. It was a chance to find out what they were thinking in the midst of the kind of traumas inflicted by war but also what they had gained from his lessons. Teame was particularly moved by a poem from one of the students. It lauded the 'extraordinary work being done in the valley of Arareb beneath the big tree' – a reference to the enormous tree the audience sat upon and beneath as Teame took his classes. The poem went on to describe how the 'big hall was flowing with happiness'. And the cause of it was, 'Brother Teame who is happy to visit his Fatherland and meet with his brothers and sisters.' He was, said the poem, educating the youth for national development and instilling in them the right values so that they 'could flower and blossom to achieve their national responsibility'.

It ended with the Marxist war cry: 'Victory to the masses.' Here is the poem as it was written in Tigrigna:

Tsehay mes bekeket berhana muketa
Gobotat teshefinom bgme zaezaeta
Ab ewan qurri ewan asahayta
Ab ewan eto eto tedereb koberta
Semiikado were kunetat Orota ?

Nabta tsebab sinchero nab ketema Ararb
Nabta tqa baska nabta Abbay ghereb
Beftnet kisguma kigsgsa aegar
Aeyenti kemaadwa aedaw enkwirwer
Aezan ktsenatewa melhas enketmeder
Semiikado were serhat mestenker?

Eti behtew kebabi weg'ee tekiuwo
Eti sefih adarash hagos werisiwo

Sehaqn qumnegern girmayu aezizwo
Semiikado were mekniat zkonwo?

Btsayna Teame kab sidet metsiom
Merietom regitsom kindey des eluwom
Nehna'wn des eluna kemti des zbelom
Mes ahwatom terakibom beti fehshew getsom

Hizomwo zmetsu bezuh qum neger
Meseltan ziegatat nEbiet nay hager
Mequsquas htsanat begubue keAbyu
Tsamaom keAgb Ambibom keferyu.

Awet Nhafash!

There were to be further seminar visits over the next two years. Teame had been unsure how to pitch his seminars when he first arrived as he had not been able to assess the levels his students had reached. But in subsequent visits he was able to better plan his lectures to suit their needs by including more advanced themes.

In 1987 he was met by a new Head of the Education Department, Ato Beraki Gebresellasie, a friendly and affable man with whom he quickly established a rapport. A former teacher in Ethiopia, he would attend the lectures, dismissing Teame's concern that he might be wasting his time by saying it was his opportunity to learn. Teame admired his modesty.

The two men had a shared love of Eritrean coffee prepared in the traditional way – by Beraki's partner Mehret Iyob, also a teacher – which meant boiling the water three times. The process would take over an hour, sometimes longer, and was considered a social occasion with time for much talking. It resulted in a strong friendship.

In this second visit to Orota and the Zero School, Teame decided that he would not use the land cruiser put at his disposal to get him to his seminars, which took place several kilometres from his living accommodation. Planning them was an uncertain business as they sometimes had to abandon them if the MiGs were patrolling overhead on that day. Instead of driving, Teame walked accompanied by Aynalem Marcos, a teacher at the school, who guided him through the countryside. He proved an amiable companion, pulling Teame's leg when he sat down to rest during the long walk and telling him the rock he was sitting on would be named after him.

Walking back from the seminars was another experience which Teame thoroughly enjoyed. He would be accompanied this time by the entire seminar group which often numbered four hundred. They would traverse the dry river beds and mountain tracks in a long line and Teame would chat with them as they went. His students would come up to him and ask questions or give him feedback on the seminars. He was kept busy the whole way back to the small hut where he was living. There he would join Beraki, who would have been at the seminar, at his home and enjoy another of those long Eritrean coffee sessions in the cool of the evening.

Teame returned once again in 1988 to find that most of the previous participants were still there. This time there was yet another Head of Department – Ato Andeberhan Woldegiorgis – who proved a very different character to the affable Beraki. He was very formal and kept very much to himself. Educated in America, he was highly qualified. But Teame thought he was much more of a self-serving politician than Beraki. Both men were given high office after Liberation in 1991 – Andeberhan becoming president of Asmara University and Beraki, Minister of Education. After the Badme war between 1998 and 2000, Beraki joined the G15 who were arrested by the government, but Andeberhan escaped arrest. Teame understands that Andeberhan is now running an opposition group from a base in Europe.

Before he left the Zero School for the last time Teame gave a partly tongue in cheek speech to his seminarists, imploring them to move closer to Asmara if he were ever to return, as the diarrhoea he had suffered from had meant frequent trips behind bushes. There was a serious side to it. It was his way of urging them to finish the war and win independence because that was the only way he could go back to Asmara. His listeners got the point and enthusiastically replied: 'Yes, we will do that!'

It had been an exhausting time for Teame who wondered afterwards if he had tried to cram too much into such a short time. His health had suffered. As well as the diarrhoea he had also caught malaria and had to have treatment in the camp clinic. In addition the dusty journey triggered the asthma which has troubled him ever since. He was treated by the so-called 'Barefoot doctors' – liberation fighters who were not actually doctors but had some medical knowledge – who served as medics and carried their equipment in a metal box as they moved around the territory.

But he did not begrudge the efforts he had to make, or the effect on his health. He looked upon it as his contribution to the liberation cause and was glad to have seen his countrymen and women living and working in a liberated part of Eritrea. His visits were the first by an academic from a Western university and it inspired others to follow although none spent as much time there as he did.

His work was welcomed and appreciated by the Zero School 'fighter/teachers' and was to provide the basis for a new Eritrean curriculum which was developed over the ensuing years. Years later he would meet some of the Zero School teachers who proudly told him that they still carried the tiny notebooks in which they had written down the essence of his seminars and were continuing to use them as guidelines in their jobs after liberation.

CHAPTER THIRTY-FOUR

Working with Refugees

As both an academic and someone who has experienced the trauma of seeking asylum, Teame was well placed to understand both the problems facing refugees in the UK education system and the issues of living in a strange country faced by them and their families. He would remember the heart-searching and the agonising decision he had been faced with when he applied for asylum. The feelings of loss and the uncertainty about his and his family's future.

So he takes a great interest in the plight of those who, like him, have been forced to find safe haven. He has become not just a mentor to refugee communities but also an acknowledged expert on refugee studies.

His strong conviction that education is the key to many of life's ills is laced with a desire to seek ways of negotiating the hurdles that refugees have to face in the complex new world in which they find themselves. His efforts embrace the education difficulties refugee children often face in schools, something he witnessed in his time with the Rowntree Trust, issues relating to the change in culture and the mental health problems which are not uncommon among refugees.

He sees refugees as people fleeing from conflict in their own country whose lives are at risk, as opposed to economic migrants looking for a better life. Refugees leave home at short notice with only the possessions they can carry, he points out. They have no choice. But, he perceives, there is another difference. The refugees, at least initially, see their flight to a new country as temporary and hope to go back if things improve. It doesn't always work out that way – Teame himself is now a well established and loyal British citizen even if his heart is still in Eritrea. But he has witnessed the mixed emotions experienced by refugees and found himself involved in helping them, and the relevant agencies, to identify the problems and find solutions.

He has studied the causes of the refugee crisis and believes that there are many reasons for it and they differ from time to time and place to place (witness the crisis in Syria, and other countries including his own Eritrea, which came to a head in 2015 resulting in a flood of refugees into Europe and forcing a rethinking of immigration policy by European countries). But he has no doubt that historically one root cause is the process of colonisation by European powers with Africa being described as the 'Dark Continent'. It resulted in artificial boundaries being created with no thought of the different ethnic groups that were brought together or divided up. Then, when power was finally relinquished, political leaders who had fought for independence took over. In some cases, he noted, it resulted in despotic regimes with leaders holding on to power and presiding over oppressive one-party states which have added to the flood of refugees.

As Teame sees it 'intolerant regimes' have created instability which in turn have led to fear, the fear has led to hate; hate to war and war to more war and finally to the displacement and migration of people. So 'insane leadership' is a root cause but the ex-colonialists have much to answer for as well, he believes.

In talking to refugees Teame would often find that the forced departure from their homeland, leaving behind family and traditions they had known since childhood, had left them with mixed emotions.

The hope of freedom, safety, and a new life on the one hand, and despair at what they had left behind on the other.

From his own experience he knew that the refugee's state of mind was not a happy one. It was characterised by a feeling of restlessness. In their new host country they were thankful that the threat to their lives was over. But their minds would constantly return to the life they had left behind. The traditional culture where the pace of life was slower and where they had self-esteem. They instinctively wanted to go back to their roots, the place where they would want to be buried when they died. So, unlike many economic migrants who are future-orientated and want to settle permanently in a new country, the refugees are torn between two worlds as they are past-orientated.

Teame understood their feelings, but knew – again from his own experience – that they would have to come to terms with the fact that life, and the world, do not stay the same. He would devote many hours endeavouring to help members of refugee communities assimilate themselves into their new surroundings by both personal conversations as well as working with refugee organisations and local authority agencies.

His work with refugees embraced the professional as well as the personal. Professionally, he was involved in refugee education which ranged from advising individual Eritreans, Ethiopians and Somalis in Bristol, to contributing to professional journals such as the *Journal of Refugee Studies* in Oxford.

He was also asked to serve as a member of the Middle East and African Committee of Christian Aid and on the group providing educational assistance to refugees of the World University Service in the UK. In Bristol he was a member of the local Refugee Council. And he was a Board Member of the Conflict Resolution Organisation based in Birmingham.

Moreover, he served as an Executive Editor of the *International Journal of Educational Development* which published refugee-related articles and was also a head trainer of a Training Workshop for refugee communities in Oxford, sponsored by Abantu for Development. So his services were much in demand. Sometimes it was hard to juggle the responsibilities of his academic and administrative roles at the Graduate School of Education with his work with refugees.

His involvement with such a huge variety of organisations dealing with different aspects of the refugee situation brought him a great deal of satisfaction, even joy, but there were also some difficult and frustrating moments. One of them came as a result of his chairmanship of a group called ERED-UK a non-profit making charity set up by a small group of like-minded Eritrean educators in the UK. Their aim was to provide a platform for discussion on educational matters involving Eritrean refugees and also to raise funds for the Eritrean refugee schools in Sudan which Teame had visited earlier.

The group's work for the cause of Eritrean refugees brought them to the notice of other Eritrean educators in other parts of Europe including Sweden. One Eritrean-Swedish educator, Dr Bereket Yebio from Lund University came all the way to Bristol to meet Teame and exchange ideas. He was to go out to help at the Zero School in liberated Eritrea as Teame had done a few years earlier.

The ERED-UK group – which included Dr Maknun Gemaladin, Giorgio Fessehaye, Berhane Tewolde and Bereket Woldeselasie – prided themselves in being non-political. They stayed clear of the various wings of Eritrean politics including the EPLF – the Eritrean Peoples' Liberation Front. As a result they found themselves in bad odour with members of the EPLF in London, some of whom rang Teame to complain that they should be working under the EPLF umbrella not acting independently.

Teame suspected it was a calculated move to force them to join one of the political wings. His fears were confirmed when he and an Eritrean friend decided to attend an occasion in London when British journalists were to be briefed on the situation in Eritrea. Arriving at the venue late after driving up to London following a day's work at the university, Teame and his friend were accosted by a young Eritrean who demanded to know if they were members of the organised group – a euphemism for card carrying members of the EPLF. Teame and his friend were angered by the young man's attitude and replied that they had merely come to support the cause of Eritrean independence and it should be immaterial what political affiliations, if any, that they had.

He experienced something similar when he became involved in setting up an Eritrean Civic Communities Association working with an older Geneva based Eritrean, Ato Ghebrekidan Alula, to draw up a constitution. The two were helped by a former Air Force General, Merkorios Haile, who was then living in London, and an Eritrean engineer, Dr Kesette Ghebrekidan. The constitution they produced was sent out to Eritrean communities throughout Europe with the aim of fulfilling a desire for ex-patriot Eritreans to set up their own civic societies. Several Societies were set up but they were quickly taken over by the EPLF. Teame suspected that they were hijacked in order to kill off the idea of establishing a non-political platform. General Merkorios Haile later set up his own independent group in London.

These experiences made Teame even more determined to remain independent and stay clear of politics. He would continue to affirm that his best service to Eritrea was as an educator and he would maintain his academic independence – although he would not have wanted that to be seen as some grievance he harboured against the EPLF or its ideology, which was not the case. Rather it was out of his long-held conviction that academics better serve themselves and their clientele when their integrity is not compromised by politics.

In 1993, he was invited to run a day's workshop in the Enfield borough of London on the theme, 'Working with Children from Refugee Communities in the UK'. Word of his work with refugees had clearly reached the workshop organisers who were a group of educational psychologists. They might have heard of his work with the Rowntree Project in West of England schools. But they clearly felt that his background as an African and as a refugee himself, as well as an experienced educator, would be of great value to them. Enfield was a borough with many refugee children from Africa, Latin America and Asia. In fact London, at that time, was host to ethnic communities speaking a hundred and forty or so different languages.

Teame spent many hours preparing for the workshop. He began by highlighting the complex nature of the 'Refugee' theme, especially in view of the massive migration of people not only from one country to another, but also from one continent to another. He then went on to outline the size of the refugee problem and describing it as a puzzle where the questions and the answers were constantly changing. The demarcation lines between causes and effects, actions and reactions, were also blurred.

Aware that his audience of about sixty educational psychologists, psychotherapists and counsellors were particularly interested in the state of mind of refugees, he told them that from his own experience they could see life swinging like a pendulum between hope and despair. He went on to identify some of the hurdles the refugees had to negotiate and the variety of psychological, emotional and social traumas they encountered.

He talked of how children who had gone through the harrowing experiences, first of having to leave their home, then the traumas of the journey to safety, followed by the complex business of settling into a new country with different traditions and a new language. He told them of the experiences related to him by refugee children of seeing people die in front of them and of witnessing corpses in a rubber dinghy. These children, he said, could not be expected to learn in their new schools without psychotherapeutic intervention. Studies had shown that they would soon get over any physical scars they might receive but the overwhelming majority of them would find it difficult to overcome the emotional and mental scars. He said their problems were sometimes compounded by family break ups, caused by the traumas of upheaval to a new culture, leading some of the children to self-isolation which in turn led to disillusionment, displaced aggression and eventually loss of self-esteem.

Refugee children would, he said, often find themselves taking on responsibilities which no child of their age should have to face. With many parents having no formal education, or a limited one, few of them spoke good English. So their children, whose own English might not be perfect, would find themselves interpreting conversations, even telling their parents what was on the TV news. They would sometimes accompany them to interviews acting as interpreters. The parent's lack of education also meant they could not help or encourage their children with homework.

Another related problem, he told his audience, was the conflict created in the child's mind by their parent's talk of returning when the children are putting down roots in their new country and immersing themselves in the local culture. Teame pointed out that the parents would often, in time, choose to stay if only to remain close to their children.

There were also Teame said 'unrecognised and unadmitted' problems affecting many refugees in their schools. Chief among them was the stereotyping and labelling that they were subject to. He said that teachers had a general tendency to pre-judge students and to subject them, however unintentionally, to stereotypical views about their intelligence, ability and even common sense simply because of their limited command of English, their accent or the colour of their skin. He added that being forced to speak in a foreign language, especially for the first time was extremely frustrating – a process described by one refugee as 'preventing his inner most soul from breathing'.

He backed this up with quotes from pupils from ethnic communities. These included a Pakistani boy who was bullied, called a 'Paki' and chased from one building to the next, a fifteen-year-old black girl who said that black children are not less intelligent than white but claimed the school system doesn't care for their needs. Another girl, from an inner-city comprehensive, described the low expectations her own teachers had of her and how surprised they were when she did so well in her 'O' and 'A' levels exams.

Copies of these and other quotations from refugee pupils were displayed on the walls of the hall where the workshop took place. Teame used the words of the young refugees to make the point that there was a problem and budgets needed to be found to resolve it.

Teame was impressed with the quality of his audience. He felt the psychiatrists, psychotherapists, and counsellors attending the workshop were well equipped for the job in hand and understood the core values required which he saw as integrity, impartiality, justice and respect for the autonomy of the client. But he had some suggestions to pass on as well.

He felt that there was a need for research into all aspects of the education and well-being of refugee and ethnic community children in the UK. This, he said, was necessary in view of the disproportionate number of black men, mainly West Indians, in prisons and mental institutions. There were also many ethnic minority and refugee children in schools for children with learning difficulties.

He asked: 'Was there a divergence between the Western concept of mental health and the life experiences of the ethnic community?' Teame said he considered psychological counsellors needed to improve the school/home relationship to find out more about home backgrounds. He said it would help if the training and practice of counsellors and psychotherapists was looked at from a cultural perspective that took into account the background of the student. But in the long run he considered that what humanity needed was not only a wider training in psychiatry, but a vision of a reconciled world. One that was not divided into 'developed' and 'developing' and 'minority' and 'majority' camps.

Government officials needed to be more sensitive to the complex nature of the educational needs of refugee children and should encourage the educators and psychologists to treat this area with great concern. After all, working with children from ethnic minorities should not be perceived solely as a 'minority' issue.

Refugee communities should also be encouraged and empowered to handle some of their problems themselves. They should not depend on government help and charities every time assistance was needed.

Teame would often find himself not just dealing with academic issues concerning refugees but handling some personal ones too. His standing within the Eritrean communities in the UK was such that he was seen as an Elder – someone who under the Eritrean culture was a wise man who could be turned to when there was a problem to be solved or arbitration to be carried out.

One of the consequences of the trust placed upon him was receiving telephone calls from Eritrean fathers of prospective brides – who for a variety of reasons could not attend the wedding in Britain – asking Teame to give away their daughters. It was no mean request. Eritrean weddings are elaborate affairs which took a lot of organising. But

Teame, not wishing to disappoint the fathers who were distraught at missing the ceremony, took on the responsibilities and did his best to fulfil the role of 'surrogate father' – travelling to places as far away as Manchester and Birmingham.

He was also asked to help with the marital problems of Eritrean couples. He explained that he was not a trained marriage counsellor but he would do what he could. Twice he found himself called in to try and help couples living in London. It meant four or five trips to the capital city to talk to them and try and help find a solution to their problems.

He would talk to the individuals involved separately to get to the bottom of their problems. In both cases he felt that their removal them from the traditional family structure back in Eritrea was largely to blame for their problems. One of the wives complained that her husband did not communicate with her and that he was too 'controlling'. The husband said she defied his authority. It was, thought Teame, a question of acquired British values clashing with latent Eritrean values. Back in Eritrea there would be a mechanism for dealing with issues like this. Other members of the family would be consulted, advice would be given and comparatively minor disputes would be amicably resolved.

He was successful in saving the marriage of one of the couples. They stayed together and went on to have children. But the other couple went their separate ways. It had been a time-consuming process for Teame. He had done his best but he knew that the issues among the families – largely triggered by a new-found independence, especially for women and children, and a different culture – were not uncommon among the refugee communities and it was not always possible to resolve them.

Another time he was asked by a Somali family in Bristol to help their fourteen-year-old son who was proving a troublesome pupil at his school – the same school that one of Teame's daughters was attending. The boy had been missing lessons and was constantly getting into fights with both white and West Indian children.

His father came to Teame's house and asked for his help saying his son would be expelled if he did not mend his ways. Teame went to see the headmaster whom he knew from previous school visits in connection with his daughter. The headmaster appreciated Teame's intervention, but felt that the young man was influenced by the wrong company.

He attempted to resolve the situation, talking to the boy to try and discover what was really behind his behaviour. What emerged was a similar story in some respects to that of the young married couples he had been asked to help. It was a question of the change of culture and, in this case, the difference in attitude between child and parent. The young man seemed to have no respect for his father who was semi-literate. He took no notice of his father's protestations for him to behave.

The father, who was brought up in the traditional authoritarian Somali culture, wanted to resort to physical punishment but Teame advised him against it. When he spoke to the boy on his own he discovered that he was going to report his father to the police if he laid a finger on him. The boy eventually agreed to improve his behaviour at school. But Teame recognised that there were deep issues of unresolved anger and bitterness which were preventing the boy taking advantage of the educational opportunities at school. He felt he had done all he could. But it was an example of the kind of problems which some refugee children faced.

But the most serious and emotionally draining cases he had to deal with involved the deaths of two Eritrean men. Both of them had committed suicide. It fell to Teame to handle the aftermath of the tragedies.

The first was a young man in his twenties who was living at Methodist International House in the Clifton area of Bristol which accommodated foreign students. He was taking an intensive English language course with the hope of improving his 'A' level results and getting a college course. Teame was a member of the Welfare Committee at MIH. He received a phone call from the warden telling him the young man had been found dead. He had hung himself inside a cupboard in his room.

Teame had the painful experience of going to the room and observing the scene after police and paramedics arrived to take the body away. He informed the Eritrean Community Association in London and got in touch with the man's friends in Manchester and Birmingham to give them the sad news and also give them an opportunity to come to the funeral.

He also wrote to the man's parents in Eritrea with a letter of condolence composed in the traditional way in Tigrigna. It was a difficult time. Neither Teame or any of his friends had seen it coming and it was a shock. But Teame wondered what had been going through the poor man's mind that he lost the will to live.

There was a further issue that Teame had to deal with. He was unable to persuade any of the local Imams to perform the traditional funeral rights because the man had committed suicide. He was at a loss to know what to do. He explained his predicament to a Pakistani who ran a local fish and chip shop. The man, himself a Muslim, agreed to help. He assumed Teame, who spoke to him in Arabic, was a fellow Muslim and Teame thought it diplomatic not to tell him he was actually a Christian.

But the Pakistani, a compassionate man, went with Teame to the funeral home where the body was kept, and carried out the traditional Muslim funeral rights saying the appropriate prayers and embalming the body.

The man was buried in a local cemetery and Teame ordered a head stone with his name in Arabic, Tigrigna and English. More than a hundred of his friends came to a funeral wake at the Victoria Methodist Church hall where Teame's wife, Teblez, Woizero Assefash Ghebrekidan, a senior nurse, and a group of Eritrean ladies from London (who brought additional food with them) served the refreshments. A collection among those present produced enough to pay the funeral costs and send some money to the man's parents in Eritrea which was sent with a statement from the coroner explaining the circumstances of their son's unfortunate death.

It was a distressing occasion. But it was followed by another. This time it involved an Eritrean man in his thirties who had come to Bristol from London. He was introduced to Teame by a West Indian woman who assisted refugees that she met through local church groups. He was working as a waiter at the Marriott Hotel whilst attending college. Getting to know him better, and inviting him round to his home for meals, Teame discovered the man was a distant relative and he knew his father. The two men got to know each other well and Teame found out his fellow Eritrean had fallen out with the EPLF and so was unable to return to the country after independence to visit his aged mother – a big blow as he was the eldest son.

Later Teame heard that he had been admitted to a mental hospital. He and Teblez visited him several times and were told he was not co-operating with staff on taking his medication claiming it made him 'puffed out'. Things got worse when he absconded from the hospital and had to be detained by police. He absconded again shortly afterwards. Later he was sent to a rehabilitation centre where he seemed to improve and was able to leave and live in a flat in the Old Market district of Bristol. But things became bizarre when he joined an Evangelical church and began claiming that he was being tempted by Satan. The story was to end in tragedy. He was found dead in his flat and, like his fellow Eritrean, had committed suicide.

Teame, once again, began the sad process of dealing with relatives and what was to happen to the body. The man's sister flew in from Rome. He took her to the flat where her brother's body had been found which she, inevitably, found very distressing. Teame too was distressed to read the dead man's diary where he had written of his torment and 'battles with Satan'. He felt guilty that he had not asked him the true nature of his anguish and not invited him to spend the nights at his home rather than on his own in the flat.

But his immediate problem was to arrange for the body to be sent back to Eritrea for a traditional burial. He also dealt with all his affairs to avoid the man's sister, who was still in Bristol, having to do so. It meant shutting down his bank account and cancelling the letting agreement on his flat. He had feared that the man's opposition to the current regime would hold up the paper work needed from the Eritrean Embassy in London. But he need not have worried. They responded without delay and went out of their way to help both Teame and the man's sister deal with all the official business.

Teame wrote a eulogy in Tigrigna for the man which was read at his funeral service before a congregation of hundreds of friends and relatives in Asmara. He thought it was the least he could do for a young, brilliant and articulate fellow Eritrean who came to such a sad end.

He could not be sure what was really in the minds of the two unfortunate men. But he did wonder whether the 'mental health problems' they both went through could, at least in part, be the result of the loneliness and isolation that many refugees feel in a strange country rather than the 'depression' that might be diagnosed in Western medical circles.

It is interesting to note that another Eritrean man who was committed to a mental ward in Bath and was visited by Teame, was later released and returned to Eritrea where he recovered from his 'depression' or, as his family described it, his 'loneliness'. In his case anyway a return to the traditional treatments of his homeland and the closeness of a family network seems to have achieved what Western medicine could not.

He felt the two cases, in a sense, illustrated how unpredictable the refugee mind-set is or could be, especially when challenged by the uncertainties of their new life.

CHAPTER THIRTY-FIVE

Community

Ever since the day he was accepted as a refugee and began a new life in Britain, Teame had wanted to pay something back to the country and the community where he set up home with his family. Not only did he not want to claim state benefits – and never did, preferring to find ways of earning a living – he also immersed himself in local life and over the years became involved in many community activities which included serving as a Magistrate, becoming an Elder at his local church, looking after elderly neighbours, raising money for charities and supporting his wife Teblez in her commitment to caring for the homeless.

The idea of public service and helping others is deeply ingrained in him. It had manifested itself in his time as a teacher and senior academic in Asmara. Then he had often gone out of his way to help those in need. So it would have seemed to him a natural progression to continue this sense of duty in serving the community in his new homeland.

When you take into account his heavy work load at the Graduate School of Education, and his many extra-curricular activities, one might wonder how he found the time to engage in so much work in the community. But find it he did, no doubt with the help of a very understanding wife. Teblez has supported him in many of his community ventures and provided a welcoming home for their multitude of visitors.

At the heart of Teame's and Teblez's approach to life in Britain was a spirit of good neighbourliness. There was a strong element of give and take with those they met in the community and being prepared to make concessions if a disagreement or misunderstanding arose. Their neighbourly attitude was influenced by the culture in which they were brought up in Eritrea where respect for elders and a willingness to help others was deeply ingrained. But there was more to it than that. The two of them demonstrated a care for people and a willingness to go the extra mile for those who needed help which went far beyond the dictates of culture. There was an element of wanting to be useful citizens in the country that had given them a new life. Their strong Christian faith would have played its part too. But it was also a question of the kind of people they were which had nothing to do with background, culture or ethnicity.

Teame would admit to being a born optimist – something his neighbours would sometimes pull his leg about. He would see hope in every situation and empathised with the words of John Donne, whose iconic poem 'No man is an Island' he had discovered during his English literature studies at the American University at Beirut:

> No man is an island
> Entire of itself,
> Every man is a piece of the continent,
> A part of the main.
> If a clod be washed away by the sea,
> Europe is the less.
> As well as if a promontory were.
> As well as if a manor of thy friend's
> Or of thine own were:

> Any man's death diminishes me,
> Because I am involved in mankind,
> And therefore never send to know
> For whom the bell tolls;
> It tolls for thee.

He firmly believes that there has to be a bigger purpose in life than living purely for oneself and that life becomes more meaningful if you have a bigger goal that impacts on community or society.

The invitation to join the Bristol Magistrates bench came as a surprise. To this day he has no idea who recommended him. But one morning in 1984 a letter arrived in the post asking if he would like to apply to become a magistrate. There were a sheaf of forms to fill in and leaflets about what was entailed.

Teame felt honoured to have been asked although he knew little of British law and even less about what a magistrate actually did. But he was intrigued by the opportunity and quickly decided that he would like to pursue it. So he filled in the forms, making clear his lack of knowledge of the legal system, but stating he would be very happy to serve his second country, now his home, in this way.

He was called for an initial interview. It went on for about an hour and Teame faced questions about his background and work at the university. He realised from the line of questioning that the panel were keen to discover his potential as a magistrate, his personality, ability to make decisions and to be part of a team of others sitting on the Bench.

The panel wanted to know if Teame was prepared to 'pay allegiance to the Crown'. He replied that he would have no problem with that because he had great respect for the rule of law. He drew smiles from some members of the panel when he remarked that he preferred the British legal system to that of some countries where presidents managed to stay in power by changing the law to suit themselves.

He thought things had gone well and was told he would hear from them shortly if they wished to call him in for a further interview. A few weeks later a second letter arrived asking him to come in again. This time the panel were interested in the practicalities of becoming a magistrate. How well could he justify his arguments, was he consistent in his thinking, how did he decide between right and wrong? Teame's answers must have been satisfactory because a few weeks later he got another letter informing him that he had been accepted as a magistrate. He was now a Justice of the Peace, a JP, in his adopted country and was asked to begin training sessions to prepare him for his new role.

It was a big moment not just in Teame's life but in the history of the Bristol Bench of Magistrates. Teame was the first black African person to be asked to serve on the Bench – although others would soon follow. Teame understood that, apart from any other qualities that he might possess, his appointment was also part of moves to enlarge the representation on the Bench to include more black and ethnic minority JPs. They also wanted to find additional younger people –Teame, now in his mid-forties, would qualify on that score – as well as increase the number of women magistrates. It was a process of change that Teame thought was commendable, and he felt privileged to be part of it.

On his first day as a magistrate he arrived wearing a smart suit and tie. It was a new experience to walk into court with the other two magistrates and see everyone stand up as they walked in. It took a little time to get used to being called 'Your Worship'.

It was a long way from his brushes with the law in Asmara when as a teenage demonstrator he had ended up in prison. Or, when as a newly married man, he had found himself being asked to help villagers from the Highland area his family came from. They were often in dispute with neighbouring villages over issues like land rights. He remembered how the Village Elders, sometimes including his father, would come and stay at his house before a case. And he would be embarrassed when they expected him to intervene with the judge before the court hearing. Sometimes, to Teame's great discomfort, they would urge him to take a box of home-made butter to the judge's house to 'encourage' him to treat their case favourably. He usually managed to avoid doing so. But, to the villagers, it was the way things were done. They couldn't understand Teame's reluctance to get involved.

The regular attendances on the Bench, fitting in with his work load elsewhere, introduced Teame to a new world very different to those he experienced in Asmara. He had undergone the obligatory new magistrate training programme which had introduced him to the legal system, the sentencing policies, and taken him into bail hostels and visiting community service projects. It enhanced his understanding and respect for the rule of law which he firmly believed was necessary in a well ordered society. His view was: 'If you respect the law, you respect humanity.'

He sat with two other JPs, one the chairman, on the Bench in the Adult Court dealing with cases of petty crime, assault, driving offences and fraud. Many of the cases involved young men who had a problem with drink or drugs. He rejoiced when some of them successfully underwent a rehabilitation programme and turned their lives around. But it didn't always happen. He was saddened to see others re-offending and turning up before the Bench again. For some of them, he considered, prison was the place where they felt secure because outside it their lives had no structure. Many of them came from broken homes with no role models in their lives.

The defendants were a mixture of black and white. Sometimes they would be Somalis who, in the 1980s, were beginning to settle in Bristol. On seeing a fellow black face on the bench, Teame would often find the Somali and West Indian defendants keeping their eyes on him. He suspected they thought he, as a fellow African, would look favourably on their case. Teame would make a point of not meeting their eyes. He would look away or hold his hand in front of his face. There was no way he would have been anything other than totally impartial to any defendant whatever their background or colour. In any case he was just one of three magistrates. But he understood that it was a not dissimilar situation to the one he experienced in Asmara with the villagers who expected special treatment from the court. It was a cultural thing that, he believed, had no place in a British court.

After he had been a magistrate for several years he, and other black and ethnic minority JPs from other parts of the country, were interviewed by a Bristol University law professor interested in their experiences on the Bench. He wanted to know if they felt they were adequately catered for. Teame's answer was Yes and No. Although the very fact of their appointment was a positive and welcome move, he also told the professor that there was a need for more ethnic minority people to put their names forward. He said that, in particular, he would like to see more West Indians and Somalis on the Bench. They should be encouraged, he said, to come forward by ensuring they were made aware of the opportunities.

As a magistrate he would get letters and circulars from the Lord Chancellor's Department on all sorts of issues. He was intrigued one day to receive a letter instructing local magistrates not to use the JP suffix after their names in anything other than official correspondence. Apparently some JPs were using it in 'inappropriate' ways such as enhancing a business venture. The instruction had a mixed reaction amongst Teame's colleagues on the Bench. Some agreed with it but others thought it was wrong that all magistrates were being tarnished and that only those who abused the system should be targeted. As for Teame, he had no business interests or reasons to gain favours from anybody, and he was far too modest to want to put JP after his name.

During thirty-plus years of living in the same terraced house in North Bristol – where they brought up their three daughters – Teame and Teblez played a full part in community activities. It was a cosmopolitan area. The street they lived in has a vibrant mixture of nationalities. As well as British born families, young couples as well as pensioners, there were Japanese, South Americans, Chinese and Indians – most of them, like the Mebrahtus, making a new life in Britain. Among them were doctors, lawyers, academics, musicians and businessmen. There were many families with children under ten.

The Mebrahtus enjoyed the friendly atmosphere. Every few years there would be street parties with the road closed off, food prepared by residents and eaten on tables laid end-to-end. There would be games for children, music and decorations hanging from lamp posts. There were stalls selling second hand goods for charity. And Teame would find himself playing a leading part in the organisation. But he and Teblez relished the community spirit it engendered and were delighted to be part of it along with their own three children. Christmas Eve would be another opportunity to invite the neighbours into their home.

They became the longest serving residents in their street and would make a point of welcoming newcomers with an invitation to their home for tea. Sometimes they would look in on elderly or sick neighbours, on occasion accompanying them to hospital appointments or the dentists. Once Teame frightened off two intruders who were pestering his elderly next door neighbour on a winter's evening. They ran off when Teame confronted them.

Teame and Teblez had gone out of their way to befriend the neighbour, who was by his own admission 'anti-social' and not keen in getting to know others in the street. But after several attempts to invite him to tea he eventually came. They discovered that his 'anti-social' attitude was really because of a condition that gave him shaky hands and he was worried about dropping his tea cup. Assured that this was not a problem to the Mebrahtus, a firm friendship resulted. He presented Teame with an African stick which a relative, who had been stationed there, had given him. The man said Teame 'was the most deserving person to have it'. The stick is still a treasured possession in the Mebrahtu household.

On another occasion this elderly neighbour did something that brought delight to Teblez. There is a beautiful flowering tree in the Mebrahtu's back garden which Teblez would admire. But one year it blossomed while she was away in Eritrea renovating the family home. When she returned she found her neighbour had taken a picture of the tree in all its glory. She was very touched by the man's thoughtful action. It was sign of the friendship and trust that had developed between them.

Teblez spent many hours with a woman who was suffering from dementia and whose husband was in need of respite. They became good friends. Teblez and Teame also became close to another neighbour who was diagnosed with cancer. They took her to the hospital for her chemotherapy. In return, a shrewd judge of a bargain, she would give them tips on the cheapest shops to go to and who were the most reliable builders.

Such was the confidence that neighbours had in them that some entrusted them with their spare house keys for the occasions when they locked themselves out or lost them. But it worked both ways with Teame being helped by a neighbour to get back into his house when he was the one who locked himself out.

Another neighbour they befriended was Dr Sally Masheder, a GP in Bristol. She organised occasions in her home when Teame would be asked to talk about Eritrea or some other subject connected to the Developing World. When Teame's youngest daughter, Zeb, decided to study medicine Dr Masheder gave Zeb her used medical textbooks.

For fifteen years – on the 14th day of every month – they have made regular visits to a centre for the homeless in Easton, Bristol taking food for up to thirty people which Teblez would prepare. They felt it was important to care for those less fortunate than themselves. But it was an eye-opener to Teame and Teblez seeing so many homeless and vulnerable people in a country which, compared with the developing world, was very affluent. Teame noted from how quickly the food – delivered by them as well as others – was demolished that the people they were helping must have been very hungry. They were impressed at the work being carried out at the centre which accommodated the needs of up to a hundred homeless people a day. Teame was interested to see that some of them were obviously refugees.

For a number of years Teame also supported Teblez in the Soup Run, a church sponsored initiative, which provides a hot drink and sandwiches to homeless people living on the streets. For many of them it might be their only meal of the day and the soup run volunteers would get a grateful welcome. Sometimes they would have to search for them in the dark and dingy buildings and street corners where the homeless congregated with their sleeping bags, few possessions and, on occasions, accompanied by a little dog. Teblez had to give up after an illness but after she recovered she started working with a similar project, cooking food for the homeless, again in the Easton area of the city. She continues volunteering there once a month.

The couple raised money for a number of local charities and were frequent visitors to charity shops in the busy main road near where they lived, donating their old clothes and books.

Their upbringing in the Coptic Christian Church did not stop them from joining a non-denominational church in Bristol – the United

Reformed Church. It was largely due to a meeting with the Minister at the time, Rev Cyril Grant, a charismatic clergyman renowned for his eloquent sermons full of spirituality, wisdom and humour. He would sometimes put on different hats to make a point in his talks from the pulpit. As he ended his days in his late nineties in a local care home, Teame and Teblez would regularly visit him. He had always told his congregation that they should look after the lonely, the isolated and the aged. The Mebrahtus wanted to offer that service to the man who had become a good friend and spiritual mentor and they did so until he died.

Teame became an Elder in the Redland Park United Reformed Church playing a full part in the life of the church, serving at communion, taking and counting collections, serving coffee along with Teblez at the end of the services, and writing articles for the church magazine. He would also attend the monthly Elders' meetings and undertake pastoral care – visiting church members in their homes. A much valued member of the church community he has made many friends there including fellow Elder and another educator, Les Fry, who credits him with enriching his understanding of a wider world. He received great support from Teame when he spent six months as a VSO teaching volunteer on Pemba Island in the Indian Ocean off the Tanzanian coast.

But whilst embracing the local community as their own, Teame and Teblez have never forgotten, or neglected, their countrymen and women now adapting to living in Britain and the challenges that can bring. They have entertained many of them in their home and taken long phone calls when help or advice was needed.

In the event of a death they might help with the traditional Eritrean ceremony of mourning. Teame and Teblez can spend the whole day at a funeral comforting and looking after relatives and friends some of whom might have travelled from far afield to be there. It can be an exhausting business for two people who have had their share of ill health, but they willingly carry out what is required by the traditions of their Eritrean heritage.

Sometimes it has fallen to Teame to break the sad news to the family back in Eritrea or some other part of the world. He has on occasions liaised with the Eritrean Embassy to arrange for the body to be returned to Eritrea for burial thereby relieving the family from the distress of having to deal with it.

Family has always been important to the Mebrahtus. It could be said that the deep traditions of Eritrean family life – supporting each other and reaching out to those around them as part of a wider family – has helped them to better integrate into the community.

As they grew up and left home to take up careers elsewhere the Mebrahtu daughters have become a great support for their parents. There have been phone calls and visits when both Teame and Teblez have been ill. The three sisters always try to come to the Mebrahtu home in Bristol at Christmas and attend church together as well as meeting up with other friends. They are a close knit family who ring each other on a daily basis. Teame and Teblez are immensely proud of their daughters, both for their thought for others, and for how they have made their way in the world. Aida is a lawyer, Esther a development consultant and a business woman and Zeb a doctor. One good friend describes them as 'the three pillars of state'.

As for Teame, he was a long way from his roots in Eritrea, but embracing his new country and playing a full and active part in the life of the community was part and parcel of his philosophy. He would admit, though, that it was not always easy to be admitted into the fraternity of the 'Anglophiles' some of whom perceived themselves 'a cut above the rest'.

The colour of his skin was not normally associated with *Anglos*. He wondered whether that perception might have been behind the question from one group of new neighbours. They asked him how he would describe his identity.

Teame repeated the words that he would use when talking to his students about multiculturalism and identity (see Chapter 32). He told his neighbour he was 'British-Eritrean' or 'Eritrean-British' or 'British' depending where he found himself and what service he might be providing. His view was that in a highly globalised world, it was possible to be born in one community and then live and die in another half way across the world, in between acquiring a multiplicity of identities. In fact questions of 'identity' did not concern him as he genuinely believed that one should have loyalty to the country in which one lives. Perhaps that was what made him such a good neighbour.

CHAPTER THIRTY-SIX

Independence Beckons

The Mengistu regime was losing its grip on power in the late 1980s as the Tigray Peoples' Liberation Front were joined by other rebel groups. Over the next few years, with the assistance of the Eritrean Peoples' Liberation Front with whom they were allied, they took over large parts of the country. This strengthened the hand of both the Ethiopian rebels and the Eritrean liberation fighters. With Mengistu's army on the verge of defeat and in disarray – he fled the country in 1991 and was granted asylum in Zimbabwe – the door would soon be opened for the EPLF to advance into Asmara bringing Eritrea's thirty-year bloody struggle for liberation to an end.

The Eritrean liberation army had already shown their mettle against the Russian backed Mengistu forces by holding on to their last fortress of Nacfa despite repeated attempts to defeat them and promises from Mengistu that he would celebrate a crowning victory. But the Eritrean's finest hour came in 1989 when they humiliated the Ethiopian Army by crushing their Nadew Command, which included three combat divisions. Three Soviet military advisers were captured and a fourth died in the fighting. It was a victory hailed by British historian and journalist Basil Davidson as the most significant victory for any liberation movement since the Vietnamese victory at Dien Bien Phu.

Eritreans had long-awaited this moment and preparations for its arrival had been going on for some time – the professional development workshops at the Zero School was one example. Another was a one-day conference in London in 1990 organised by the Research and Information Centre of Eritrea (RICE) at which Teame was invited to participate by the Co-ordinator, Dr Berhane Woldemichael. With liberation now a certainty and hopes of a better future running high, Teame chaired a panel discussion reflecting on Eritrea's postwar economic recovery and rehabilitation. Panelists included Professors Asmerom Legesse, John Markakis and Lionel Cliffe.

The following year, 1991, Teame found himself involved in another event as the plans for a liberated Eritrea gathered momentum. This time it was at Bologna in Italy. Bologna had, throughout the years of the liberation conflict, been a meeting point for Eritreans. The old colonial links from the days of the Italian occupation were still strong. There was an annual Festival there – since the 1970s organised mainly by the EPLF – which attracted ex-patriot Eritreans from all around the world. As well as promoting the political aims of the EPLF it celebrated the country's cultures, and traditional food. It was also an important fund raiser for the liberation cause.

So it was no surprise at this historic moment for Eritrea that Bologna was chosen as the venue for a Festival where plans would be made for the rehabilitation of the country which had been devastated by the war. Its industry and agriculture were badly hit, 50,000 homes destroyed and the education system was in need of a major rethink after years of imposed Ethiopian teaching and the suppression of traditional Eritrean culture. Not the least was the ban on the Tigrigna and Arabic languages which were the medium of instruction since the British Administration in 1941.

Teame had received a call from Ato Amdemichael Kahsay, an EPLF official in Paris asking him to address the festival on the role of higher education in the new free Eritrea. He would be one of a number of speakers addressing issues faced by the liberated country which would also include an engineer talking about how the country would build new homes to replace those destroyed, and an expert on Basic Public Health amongst others.

He readily accepted the invitation considering it an honour and hastily cancelled other plans, which included a trip to America. He decided that at such an important event for Eritrea he would like to take his wife Teblez and his three daughters as well. He told the organisers he would be happy to pay his own travel expenses but asked them to provide some basic accommodation for him and his family.

The Festival, organised by the EPLF and the Eritrean community in Italy, was an enormous event which attracted 10,000 Eritreans from all over the world. Teame thought that arriving with his family at Bologna airport was just like going back to Asmara, such was the atmosphere as hundreds of Eritreans flew in from different parts of the world. They greeted each other loudly and with much laughter as well as tears as they met friends they had not seen for years or known whether they had survived the liberation war.

He was also struck by the sense of anticipation among his compatriots as they looked forward to a final victory in the liberation struggle and the dawn of a new era. They were keen to go back to Eritrea and see the family and friends they had been cut off from for so many years.

Teame noted that amidst the huge crowds were representatives of all the ethnic groups of Eritrea as well as the principal religions – Muslim and all three Christian denominations, Catholic, Protestant and Coptic. There was a wide age range from small children to octogenarians. Many were wearing traditional Eritrean costumes – of which there were many different types representing the nine regions of the country at that time. They have since been reduced to six military administrative regions.

With many of the Eritreans having fled the war zone to live in other countries, the children who accompanied them to the festival were more familiar with the languages of their host countries than the Tigrigna or Arabic of their parents. Teame was amused to hear some of them greeting others in German, Swedish, French or English to be met with blank stares.

With the exception of the few who stayed in hotels most of the visitors were put up in a tented camp set up in a city park. There were communal facilities including showers and toilets which were regularly cleaned by young Eritrean volunteers who also emptied waste bins and acted as security guards.

As Teame walked around the crowded stalls set up around the festival site, it brought home more memories of the country of his birth. The smell of Eritrean cooking, precious remaining copies of the Tigrigna and Arabic books which the Ethiopian Army had banned and mostly burnt, the sound of Eritrean music, even the twigs which many rural Eritreans used to clean their teeth.

There were happy reunions with former colleagues and classmates he had not seen or heard of for years. One of them, a fellow student at the Asmara Teacher Training College, Ato Ady Ghebre was selling computer equipment on a stall. He also met up with two he had known at secondary school – one of them had been in prison with him after they joined the student demonstration. Another had been beaten by Teame and friends for refusing to join the demonstration. But such differences were forgotten in their delight at seeing each other again.

Whilst talking to these two fellow students Teame was hailed by another Eritrean who recognised him. He had been a pupil in one of the schools in Asmara where Teame supervised student teachers and he described how their teachers would urge them to behave themselves because Teame was 'too strict'. But his strictness did not seem to have inflicted any long term damage as Teame noted with, some satisfaction, how skilful and knowledgeable the young man was in the art of street trading at the festival.

He met many other old friends and acquaintances. Among them Dr Kidanemariam Zerezghi, a close family friend, who he had not seen for twenty years. He was working at the UN office in Austria at the time but returned to Eritrea after independence. Teame also met a former classmate at Dekemhare Middle School, Ato Ghebretensae Kelati, and Dr Woldeab Isahak who later became President of Asmara University.

Another that he was delighted to see again was an Englishman, Paul Highfield, who had been a volunteer teacher of English at the Zero School. He was called Paul *Laelay Adi* (the Tigrigna for Highfield) by the Eritreans. Paul had often shared Teame's evening meals during their time there and he had a good command of Tigrigna. In fact such was his facility in the language – an unusual accomplishment for a Briton – that he gave a ten minute talk at one of the festival seminars which resulted in loud applause.

One of his most treasured meetings was with the man described as one of the 'fathers of Eritrean Independence', Ato Woldeab Wolde-mariam. Then in his eighties, he was staying with his wife in the same hotel as Teame. He was a man who both Teame and Teblez had known in Asmara and had admired his determination to stand for the Eritrea for Eritreans Party during the struggle for liberation. It had resulted in numerous attempts on his life. Ato Woldeab, a journalist, had written textbooks, which Teame had read at elementary school, and he had tried to reconcile the two rival liberation groups in the 1970s.

A humble man with a deep Christian faith, Teame remembered him addressing both him and his wife as 'thou' in Tigrigna – a sign of respect and, considering they were both younger than Ato Woldeab's own children, an unusual honour. The two of them had breakfast one morning with the great man and appreciated the chance to reminisce and talk of their hopes for the new Eritrea. Ato Woldeab received warm and rapturous applause when he addressed one of the most crowded plenary sessions and urged delegates to work together to safeguard a free Eritrea. He never gave up his tenacious support of a liberated and united country.

For some of the other Fathers of the Revolution – the generals whose famous victory over the Ethiopian Nadew Command in 1989 had been a decisive moment in the liberation struggle – the Festival was an opportunity to celebrate that historic moment and the subsequent liberation success. There were films of the battle and the generals outlined their battle winning strategy. There were scenes of great euphoria as the celebrations continued.

Teame's seminar, on the third day of the festival, was attended by a packed audience of not just educationists – although there were many there – but also members of the military, including some high ranking officers in the liberation army and top officials of the EPLF. He started off by saying how lucky they were to be seeing a whiff of freedom in their beloved Eritrea as a result of 'the immense sacrifice paid by our fathers, mothers, brothers, sisters and daughters over the last 30 years.' He also said that they should all rejoice at the near dissolution of the unholy marriage with Ethiopia.

Teame explained that it would be difficult to foresee the kind of education Eritrea would need after liberation. He said there needed to be systematic consultations directed by a National Committee of Education to discuss the complex issues involved with the diverse ethnic groups.

What kind of education model did they want? he asked. To answer that question, he said, they would have to decide what percentage of the national budget would be allocated to every strand of education from primary and secondary to tertiary levels. They would also have to decide whether basic education (up to Grade 8) would be free and whether the new country would have the means to provide Higher Education free of charge too.

Moreover, he said, Eritrea and the Eritreans would have to agree on how to mix their secondary education between academic and vocational courses. They would also have to formulate education policies that enhanced plans for national development, but which were also endorsed by the people.

He warned that the new government would have to make a choice on the model of university it wanted to set up. For example 'centres of excellence' or 'development oriented' types.

He dealt with the issue of Eritreans returning to the country to teach after independence asking what kind of reintegration courses would be run to familiarise them with the newly liberated country. As a country which had gone through the experience of war, Eritrea was bound to have many teachers and students who had suffered from physical and mental traumas. There would be a need for Guidance and Counselling services. Teame also reasoned that the new curriculum should reflect some aspects of the culture, languages, values and names of the nine ethnic groups.

He added that education provided in a free and liberated Eritrea should encourage students to understand human rights. The days of 'whoever reigns is our king' were over. And he shared his vision of what he felt the education system could become with well trained teachers. One that produced 'well rounded citizens' who were trust-worthy, humble, empathetic, tolerant and had integrity.

He talked of the need to challenge the 'Diploma Disease' which could result in students avoiding vocational courses to concentrate on academic qualifications in the hope of getting white-collar jobs. The result was, in many cases, a rise in the numbers of the unemployed as well as the unemployable.

There should be greater opportunities for adults and especially women to cater for the urgent needs of returning refugees. And the status of teachers should be improved with particular attention paid to rewarding good classroom teachers to keep them teaching rather than moving into administration.

And he had a word for the post referendum political leaders too. The country needed leaders, he said, 'dedicated to the service of their people'. He warned about the dangers of sycophants trying to influence policies and damaging relationships with the population. Ex-patriots planning to return should ask themselves what they could contribute to a country devastated by war, he added.

There was another word of warning. They needed to realise how closely 'national euphoria' could be followed by 'individual despair'. He added: 'Being aware of this let us all protect with our educational sword the little Eritrean chick so that it grows and prospers in its own land in peace.'

They were strong words. Teame had not pulled his punches. He had poured into his presentation his philosophy of education which had the welfare of the students and the development of the country at its heart. He had not shied away from addressing potential conflicts of politics and an independent system of education – something he had strong views about.

At the end of his address Teame invited questions. One was rather pointed. The questioner asked: 'Why did you not participate in previous Bologna festivals considering you had so much to offer?'

Teame explained his absences at other Festivals by pointing out he had, for the previous few years, been spending time at the Zero School helping to train teachers for a liberated Eritrea. He also mentioned the last time he had been in Bologna – which was whilst he was a student in Beirut in 1963 when he went as President of the Ethiopian Students Association of the Middle East. He related that while attending the conference there he had covertly distributed anti-annexation pamphlets. And he also told the story of his time in prison as a teenage demonstrator when he attacked the Haile Selassie Secondary School in Asmara and was arrested.

These revelations would have gone a long way towards convincing the audience that he had worked, in his own way, for the liberation cause. It would certainly have added to his credibility with those – especially liberation fighters – who did not know him.

If there were any detractors from his ideas in the audience they showed no sign of it. In fact Teame felt they seemed warmly appreciative of his words. When he suggested they end the session singing the old school song, which he had himself sung as a schoolboy, they all joined in. So together they all rose from their seats and sang: '*Dleyuwa ntemherti mealti msleyti, nsa eya abay habti*,' 'Search for education day and night as it is the greatest gift and wealth.'

As the festival drew to a close Teame had an experience which he considered illustrated the kind of problems of the human kind that a free Eritrea could face. It all started with an urgent summons.

At the end of the seminar session one day, Teame had taken his wife and three daughters to one of the marquees to enjoy a meal of the delicious Eritrean food prepared by the 'Mamas', the Eritrean women working as cooks and maids in Bologna and other Italian cities, who had volunteered their services to the festival. There was a jovial atmosphere full of animated conversations and the spicy smell of good food.

After queuing to collect plates of food for himself and his family, and just as he had started eating, a man rushed up to Teame and demanded that he follow him straight away because he 'was wanted'. Teame asked for five minutes to finish his meal. But the man insisted he come straight away. So leaving his plate with Teblez he followed the man.

He was taken to another marquee where all became clear. It was a simple request for Teame to check over the English of a press release from a top EPLF official which was shortly to be handed out to the assembled media. Teame soon did as he was asked and returned to his family.

When he got back he discovered someone else had demolished his tasty meal. But he was also surprised by the reaction of a senior Eritrean colleague who had witnessed his sudden summons. The man was angry that he had accepted. He claimed Teame was being exploited. But Teame realised that what was really behind the man's furious reaction was anger that he had not been chosen.

It was, he believed, a sign of the kind of jealousy and jockeying for position that the soon to be free Eritrea was likely to face. He hoped he was wrong. But he could see that such attitudes would be a considerable obstacle to cementing the kind of relationships which would be a vital ingredient in building a new nation.

Teame felt he had done all he could to fulfil his brief to lay out how a Free Eritrea should develop its education system. But he also knew there was much more work to be done before theory became reality. It would not be long before he would be invited to a free and liberated Eritrea to take his ideas further.

CHAPTER THIRTY-SEVEN

Independence

In 1990 the Eritrean Liberation army of the EPLF had liberated the strategic port city of Massawa on the Red Sea. They suffered heavy casualties in the battle but it was another key victory in their thirty-year struggle for an independent Eritrea. Within a year the victorious liberation fighters were finally able to march into the Eritrean capital Asmara to be welcomed by cheering crowds. Effectively they now had control of the whole country. Eritrean villagers had played their part, sometimes at great risk, by providing the fighters with food and water.

The long held hopes of liberation had finally become reality. There was a UN resolution for a referendum in which the Eritreans could vote for the future direction of their liberated country. In the meantime a Provisional Government ran the country.

The protracted war had cost thousands of lives – an estimated 60,000 EPLF fighters and 75,000 Ethiopian troops – with thousands more disabled in the fighting and 90,000 civilian casualties. A million people were displaced, becoming refugees. It had been a bitter war with atrocities which included a hundred and ten people in the village of Wokiduba massacred by Ethiopian soldiers and Eritrean students suspected of supporting the liberation fighters hanged in front of their parents who were forced to cut down their bodies.

The struggle for independence had not only involved the EPLF in conflict with Mengistu's Ethiopian forces, but also with the ELF, the Eritrean Liberation Front, who had started the liberation struggle and held some of the liberated areas near the border with Ethiopia. In what was a battle for control of the liberation movement the EPLF, aided by the Tigray People's Liberation Front who held territory on the other side of the border, jointly attacked the ELF fighters in a pincer movement forcing them to flee over the border to Sudan leaving many thousands of dead and injured.

The power struggle, won by the EPLF, had caused deep division among Eritreans with members of the same family sometimes supporting different sides. The divisions simmered on over the remaining years of the liberation struggle. Teame hoped they would not hinder the development of a now liberated Eritrea which, he strongly believed, needed a united front to face the challenges of rebuilding a country shattered by war.

But as he rejoiced with his countrymen and women, Teame had noted with some pride that despite the horrors of the war the victorious EPLF and the civilian population ensured the safe return of thousands of Ethiopian prisoners – soldiers from the forces who had terrorised the Eritrean population. The prisoners were given food and water as they were repatriated. Teame hoped it was a sign of the new country putting the past aside and moving into a new and peaceful era.

News of the final liberation of Asmara, which signalled the end of the country's long struggle for freedom, was greeted with a sense of both joy and relief in the Mebrahtu household in Bristol.

Teame marvelled that his comparatively tiny country had been victorious over the might of the Ethiopian military machine – among the strongest in Africa at that time. It had been backed by two superpowers. First by the Americans during the reign of

Emperor Haile Selassie and later, during the Mengistu regime, by the Russians.

Once the news was flashed on TV screens and radio bulletins around the world, Teame's telephone never stopped ringing with calls from Eritrean relatives and friends not just in Europe but from Canada, America, the Middle East, Africa and Australia. They would share their joy at the news of liberation and their hopes for the future. The calls went on through the night with the time difference being so great among the continents.

And how did the Mebrahtus celebrate the occasion? Teame asked his three daughters what they would like for a celebratory meal. The answer from the girls – now firmly Westernised – was Kentucky Fried Chicken. Teame duly went to the local KFC and brought the meal for all the family to enjoy around the kitchen table at home. It was a moment they would never forget.

Teame, and all other Eritreans, had to wait another two years before the military victory officially led to independence. In April 1993 the UN sanctioned referendum was held. Every Eritrean got the chance to cast their vote. That included those, like Teame and Teblez, who lived in other countries. Voting centres were set up in London and other cities. Teame and Teblez both cast their votes in London.

The poll was organised by the EPLF and once a vote had been cast the voters were given a card confirming that they had been to the polls. Not surprisingly there was an almost unanimous vote – 99.8% – in favour of an independent Eritrea.

Along with thousands of other ex-patriot Eritreans from the diaspora around the world, Teame decided to go to Asmara to witness the Independence Day celebrations and join in the euphoria of such a historic moment. His polling card confirming he had voted served as identification along with his British passport when he arrived at

Asmara airport. Eritrean passports had not yet been issued. Many other Eritreans who could not make the trip sent congratulatory telegrams and began raising funds for the orphans and disabled veterans of the war.

The streets of the city were packed with a heaving, cheering, dancing crowd – both men and women. As Teame joined them he found the throng so dense that he just had to allow himself to be pulled in whatever direction it was going. It was in sharp contrast to the days of the Dergue and the Mengistu regime when there was a curfew from 8.00 pm and the streets were deserted.

Teame, not usually one for being too demonstrative, couldn't stop himself from joining in the frenzied dances. He remembers closing his eyes and letting his body be gripped by the pulsating rhythms and melodies. Whatever happened in the future the crowd were convinced it would be a better one than under the grip of Mengistu's Dergue and its Red Terror death squads.

He remembers the day as being one where people were full of hope and confidence. The festivities went on throughout the night and as the cold evening air encroached many in the celebrating crowd covered their shoulders in the traditional Eritrean shawls.

Earlier in the day there had been a huge ceremony at the Bahti Meskererm Square in Asmara. Teame was among the 100,000 joyful Eritreans who were there. The event was also attended by UN officials and other dignitaries from around the world as well as the Prime Minister of the post-Mengistu Ethiopian government, Ato Meles Zenawi. Teame remembers him congratulating Eritrea and the Eritreans for their determined fight for liberation and pledging his personal and official support for a Free Eritrea. But there were words of caution too. He urged them to 'stop scratching old wounds' and to look towards building a peaceful and neighbourly future between their two countries. It was reference to the simmering border war. As events were later to prove his warning was not heeded by the new Eritrean government.

But at the moment of celebration there were thoughts only of independence. The party went on for several days not just in Asmara but in the towns and villages across the country. A new National Holiday was announced. The now free radio service broadcast patriotic songs and dramas. There was a new national flag. And there was a salvo of gun shots in honour of the freedom fighters who died in the struggle along with thousands of other unsung heroes who made independence possible.

The overall feeling among the crowds, Teame perceived, was that rightly or wrongly they had finally served the punishment for wanting to be free. As he saw it, the curse that the Eritrean people had been subjected to was finally lifted from their conscience and replaced by an inner peace however temporary it might be.

He considered the new Independence Day would be viewed by many Eritreans as a deliverance from the yoke of oppression. But he also saw it as a declaration of the qualities of honour, courage, resilience and selflessness that he believed characterised his country-men and women. He was reminded of Mahatma Gandhi's description of freedom as being 'a breath of life that every man would be happy to pay in order to live'.

The hailing of the freedom fighters as 'the lions of Africa' by a number of other African countries including Kenya and Tanzania was a welcome recognition. But he also ruefully noted that they did not lift a finger to assist in Eritrea's hour of need.

As he was swept along in the vast crowds he wondered about the fate during the war of his many friends and relatives. In a crowded bar he was hailed by two residents from his home village of Adi Ghehad whom he had not seen for many years and did not instantly recognise although they clearly knew who he was.

They called out 'Teame' to him as he made his way through the crowd. Realising who they were Teame greeted them warmly giving them both an Eritrean embrace. One of them he had last seen in Addis Ababa when he was driving a road tarmacing machine. The other was the director of the school at Adi Ghehad which had now been established in the village. He had been a child of four when Teame had last seen him. Teame had wanted to establish a school at Adi Ghehad when he was working in Asmara years earlier but did not have the funds. He was delighted there was one there now.

They spent the evening talking and reminiscing, Teame sitting with one on each side of him. They didn't want to let him go. Teame bought drinks not only for them but any others nearby whose glasses were empty. There was an air of jubilation. He was interested to see Christians and Muslims celebrating together – the Muslims buying alcoholic drinks for the Christians, who would buy soft drinks for their Muslim brothers.

The following day he met up with many of his extended family at the house of his brother Anghesom in Asmara. Among them were his sisters from Adi Ghehad who by now had children of their own. Some of them were teenagers who had been fighters in the liberation war. It was a wonderful time of reunion and celebration. But also one of sadness as he discovered at least forty of his relatives did not come back from the fighting and were presumed dead – one of them his own brother Hagos. Others had suffered lost limbs or eyes.

One of the saddest stories was that of one of his uncles Berhane Dumtsu, who lived in Massawa and was a port worker. He had lost four of his five sons along with a brilliant younger brother, Tekie Dumtsu, in the war. Another uncle had lost his son Bereket, a bright student who Teame had great hopes for. But one who did come back was Bereket's brother, Fasil Ghebremichael, who he had met at the Zero School camp a few years earlier. Others of his nephews and nieces who also made it safely back included Efrem Menghis as well as Mulu and Saba Asier – who he had also last seen at the Zero School along with Jordanos Tecle.

Teame spent many hours talking to the family members about their experiences during the Liberation War. They discussed how risky and dangerous it was and the bravery of fighters and others who had seen some of the atrocities. Teame did his best to console those who had lost relatives telling them they did not die in vain. They had given them all freedom.

He knew most of his relatives, especially those from the village, were short of money having just come through a war so had come prepared with as much extra funds as he could afford – with help from his wife and daughters – to buy them some necessities.

There were dresses for his sisters and he took his brother Anghesom's advice on who else to help and what they needed. With such a large group he did not want to offend anyone who might have been missed out.

Another of his relatives he tried to help was the son of his maternal uncle who had sustained a head injury during the war and had come back traumatised and in need of psychological treatment. His uncle pleaded with him to help. There was only one psychiatric unit in Asmara and it had just one doctor.

The father was desperate and Teame agreed to take the traumatised young man to the hospital although he had no appointment. He was difficult to control because of his head injury, dodging out in front of traffic and having to be pulled back. When he got to the hospital Teame was relieved to discover that he knew the doctor in charge who offered some medication for the young man to calm him down although it would not cure him. But he said that he could not find him a bed in the hospital. Teame realised there was nothing more he could do. But at least he had done his best.

A day or two later Teame went to his home village of Adi Ghehad where his father was still living. It was the first time he had seen him for nineteen years. His father welcomed him joyfully saying: 'My eldest son, you are alive and back! May the Good Lord be praised for giving me the opportunity to see you.' He added, 'From now on I am ready for death as Adam was.'

Teame was shocked to see Mebrahtu Beraky looking so weak and obviously in poor health. He had lost all his hair and his eyesight was affected by cataracts – although that condition was rectified a few months later thanks to the generosity of a close relative of Teame's, Fessehaizon Ghebremedhin, who paid for an operation. He did not at first get an opportunity to talk further with his father who, despite his poor health, was busy slaughtering a goat to feed the enormous crowd of well-wishers.

The whole village turned out to welcome him. The women gave the traditional ululating greeting and some of the villagers arrived bearing gifts of chickens and eggs, and home brewed *suwa* beer.

One of the eldest villagers made a speech welcoming Teame back 'to his roots' and, like Teame's father, praising the Lord. But he then went on politely and poetically, scratching his head as he did so, to put forward the villager's expectations from someone now living in Britain. Would there be any chance, he asked, of a taste of what people in that far off part of the world called whisky before the villagers had to collect their animals and take them to their sheds for the night.

It was the cue for Teame to present them with the two bottles of whisky he had brought with him for the occasion knowing that it was a tradition with which he was expected to comply. He said they deserved more and apologised he couldn't squeeze extra bottles into his suitcase on the flight from London.

The whisky was poured into small cups they called '*finjals*' with a little local water to make it go round further. Most of the elderly women who tried it didn't like it, but the men were delighted to have tasted the drink of those 'never smiling people who speak through their noses.' That was a reference to the stereotypical view of the British soldiers who occupied Eritrea from 1941 to 1951.

Once the visitors had gone, Teame's father called him over and told him how proud he was of him that he had not forgotten the village tradition. They discussed many things together. Mainly his father wanted to talk to Teame about his responsibilities to his family and the village and to the world. There were also subtle rebukes for not bringing his lovely wife and children with him to 'where they belonged' and not forcing his three daughters to marry Eritreans.

He described his son as one 'who lived a life of privilege' but thanked him and his family for supporting relatives in Eritrea in their 'time of need'. And he urged Teame to never allow his privileges to blind him to the problems of the ordinary villagers or those of poor children everywhere. He said that just as Teame had given him hope, all children had the power to pull their parents from a crisis of hopelessness.

They were wise words. Teame recognised that much of his own appreciation of the needs of humanity came from his father's approach to life and his care for others. Mebrahtu Beraky may have been uneducated but he had a deep understanding of people and a wisdom that many of greater learning did not possess.

During his time in the village he also met some of his relatives who told him that they had heard him being interviewed on the liberation radio service, Voice of the Masses, when he was at the Zero School. A few of them criticised him because they thought he could have put the life of his father, who was then living in occupied Eritrea, in danger. But other relatives said they had been proud of him braving the war zone. Teame replied that he had simply been experiencing what the fighters in the area experienced. He told his critics that he was only talking about the peaceful educational work he was doing at the Zero School.

Whilst in the village Teame also heard about the brave action of two villagers from Adi Ghehad who had captured two armed Ethiopian soldiers fleeing from the battlefield. They had seen the two soldiers, exhausted but well-armed, walking near the village and had followed them. When they caught up with the two and confronted them, although they had no arms themselves, the soldiers gave themselves up. The villagers became local heroes and were also interviewed on Voice of the Masses radio. It was a story that Teame was proud to hear about residents of his home village especially as he knew the two individuals concerned.

Teame met many people but one who he had not expected to meet was the President, Isias Afwerki, who had been in charge of the provisional government and was now at the head of the new administration following the referendum. Teame was approached and encouraged by a member of the Government to go and see him.

Needless to say he considered it an honour and was soon on his way to the President's office in the Government Headquarters in Asmara. He was ushered in to see him in his huge office. The President rose from his chair and came across the room to greet him and gave him an embrace. Teame congratulated him on his victorious leadership.

The President clearly knew all about Teame and what he had been doing for the liberation cause at the Zero School and elsewhere. As some of his Ministers like Haile Woldetensae had in fact been quietly in the background at the Zero School, and as the President was believed to be fed detailed accounts of what is being done when and by whom, Teame was certain that Isias knew a lot more than he cared to say.

He told Teame the country needed well educated people like him. Teame, who had heard rumours that he would be offered a job in the

Ministry of Education, was careful not to appear to be seeking an appointment, which he was not. He was aware that there was a lot of positioning for posts in the government and was determined not to be involved in any manoeuvring. But he told the President it was his duty to serve the country and, if the government wished, he would do all he could in the field of education.

As the meeting came towards its end the President asked Teame if he had any advice to offer him. This took Teame by surprise as the President did not appear to be one who sought advice. So, instead of giving direct advice, Teame decided to tell him a proverb in Tigrigna which went, '*Ade kinfiz ndeqki kemey gierki tehaqfiyom? Kekem getsom.*' It was about a mother hedgehog which was asked how she embraced all her spiny offspring. Her answer was to position them carefully with their faces towards her belly so as to accommodate them all and not be touched by their prickly spines.

Teame explained the proverb as illustrating the need to accommodate everyone. He had in mind the diverse ethnic groups and differing views of the Eritrean population and how best they could be bound together.

The President, who was making notes of the meeting in a small diary, listened carefully and admitted that he did not know the proverb. Teame said he hoped he would reflect on it. The meeting ended with a big smile from the President and the two embraced again in the Eritrean way before Teame left, saying he was sure he had many others waiting to see him. He felt it was a privilege to have spent a short time with the man who was to run the country as it was rebuilt after the war. He could only hope that in the years to come the country and its people would prosper in his charge.

Before he left to return to Bristol he was also able to meet up again with Beraki Ghebresellasie who had been Head of the Department of Education in the war zone during one of Teame's visits to the Zero

School. He was now Eritrea's new Minister of Education. Teame respected him and looked upon him as a genuinely committed member of the teaching profession.

Beraki had a request. He asked Teame to address 3,000 teachers in Asmara. The meeting would be in the city's huge Cinema Capitol in a few days. It was chance for Teame to carry out his promise to the teachers at the Zero School when he had told them he would return to the country after liberation as long as it could be on the outskirts of Asmara. Well, this invitation would bring him into the heart of the city and he had no hesitation in accepting.

The Minister said he would not impose a subject on Teame's talk but would like him to share something of the concept of local management of schools. i.e. providing better education through improved management.

Teame was glad to have the opportunity to have some further input into the creation of the kind of schools and teachers who could take the country's education system forward.

Using a loud hailer to address the huge audience he did not mince his words. He said he would identify the requirements needed for a successful locally managed school and then discuss whether the Eritrean education system in 1993 was ready to meet such a challenge.

After outlining the kind of education system the new country needed – schools well resourced, teachers adequately trained, supported by the local authority and the community – he then outlined, in no uncertain terms, what was needed to achieve it.

He recommended an increase in the education budget to provide better resources including higher pay for teachers and improved pensions. Teacher qualifications should be improved too. One way of achieving these aims would be to cut spending on arms, he suggested.

Teame said he wanted to see an education system in Eritrea where teachers helped students to grow in understanding, knowledge, self-awareness, moral development and the qualities where students learned how to survive in a complex and uncertain world. He wanted students to foster a love of mankind and a passion for world peace.

They were strong words. But Teame had been determined to hold nothing back. He hoped his vision of what Eritrea's education system needed would hit home with the people who could make it happen. The reaction of his audience was encouraging. They warmly applauded him.

At the end of his talk he gave his audience the chance to ask questions and provide some feedback. Many of them, having been teachers at the Zero School, expressed gratitude for Teame's service there. Some of them told him that the notes they took from his lectures were still used by them in their new positions as urban school teachers.

Others questioned whether Eritrea had the ability to pay teachers more. Teame said it was an important issue but doubted it would be possible at that time in the country's history, to raise teachers' salaries. But he added that government policies need not be cast in stone. If enough Eritreans appreciated the value of education in national development, then it would be hoped that their views would be listened to and budgets increased. He ended by pointing out that 'you get what you pay for'.

He knew this was a debate that would continue. But for him it was enough to know that he had played, what he would describe, as a small part in the development of the new Eritrea. There was however more work to do and he would soon be returning to the country.

CHAPTER THIRTY-EIGHT

Building Anew

With the country devastated by war Eritrea's schools had suffered. Buildings had been destroyed or damaged from bombing attacks by the Ethiopian MiG jets. The Zero School along with other initiatives like the Wina Technical School which were all set up in caves in the liberated areas, had provided education for some children as well as adults. But the schooling of many others had been disrupted by the conflict. There was an illiteracy rate in some areas of 80%. The suppression of Eritrean culture and the imposition of Amharic to replace the native Tigrigna or Arabic of the pupils had hindered learning.

There was much work to be done. As the joy of freedom turned to the reality of rebuilding the country, Teame made good on his commitment to help plan an education system in liberated Eritrea and to train the teachers and administrators. He had discussed his return to the country after liberation when he was at the Bologna Festival. By then he had already promised the teachers he trained at the Zero School that he would see them in Asmara once the liberation war had been won. So he had a sense of mission and was to return many times over the next ten years performing a variety of tasks along with other academics, both Eritrean and European, wishing to support the work of revitalising the battered Eritrean education system.

He felt there had been a positive start to the new post-referendum administration, known as The Peoples Front for Democracy and Justice (PFDJ) led by President Isias Afwerki. There was a fairly rapid growth in the economy. Eritreans from the diaspora moved back from other countries to run the National Bank and take senior positions in some of the Ministries including Agriculture. A number of Eritrean Academics also took sabbatical leave to temporarily return to the University of Asmara. New houses were built – both state owned and private enterprise. A new Medical School was established to train more doctors. And there was a series of Question and Answer sessions in which the new President interacted with members of the public. It all helped to reassure the population that they were living in a democratic state. In those early days after liberation these were hopeful signs. There were also optimistic words from many public figures that Eritrea would learn from the mistakes of other African states.

It was amidst this atmosphere of a country being rebuilt that in 1994 Teame was invited to give a paper at a conference in Asmara on The Challenges of Education in Eritrea, a subject close to his heart. It was sponsored by Norad, the Norwegian aid organisation, and organised by the Faculty of Education at Asmara University – the very department which Teame had been head-hunted to run as an assistant professor before it was shut down by the Mengistu regime.

The conference was attended by education and aid experts from Norad as well as Sida, the Swedish aid organisation, teaching staff from Asmara University and representatives from a number of Eritrean Ministries.

Teame, who was among a number of speakers, chosen to speak on 'What is a good or effective teacher?' He was glad to do so because he believed one of the greatest challenges facing the Eritrean education system so soon after liberation – and still faces today – was an acute shortage of good teachers.

He described the attributes of a good teacher as having the ability to think critically and analytically and to use multiple learning styles. They should look upon education as a basic human right. He concluded that one of the greatest qualities of an effective teacher was a sensitivity to the differences between learners and their varying abilities and needs, which was something that was acquired over time and with the help of feedback from colleagues and the students themselves.

Teame, like others at the conference, considered it timely and relevant. But there were some sensitive issues. One of them was the concept of aid, how it should be implemented and where the money went. The question became more complicated when the President of Asmara University, Dr Woldeab Isahak, declared that money from any of the aid agencies should be paid direct to the government to spend as they saw fit.

Teame, who had lectured extensively on the subject, and understood the possibility of aid benefitting the donor more than the recipient, had some sympathy with the President's position. But he felt that such an approach was not right at that time. He considered that it would be better to foster a good rapport with the aid agencies like Norad and Sida before trying to lay down how aid would be handled.

It seemed that the Norwegian and Swedish aid agencies also took this view since both of them rejected the President's proposal apparently, having doubts over how their aid money would be spent. The failure to strike a deal, which would have brought much needed investment in the cash and staff-starved Asmara University, did not go down well with Teame and many of the other delegates. It raised doubts about the future of the University which, as events turned out, were to prove prescient some years later.

It did not go unnoticed that Teame was among the first ex-patriot Eritrean academics to return to his homeland wanting to help the war-torn country get back on its feet. Dr Negusse Araya, who had worked with him on developing a distance education programme at Asmara University where he was Dean of Social Sciences, and later became Director of the British Council in Eritrea, praised his commitment to the educational development of Eritrea and the Eritreans. (He was later rusticated along with other academics by the Eritrean government who claimed that they were incompetent – a decision which many, including Teame believed was false and politically motivated.)

In 1997 Teame was invited to launch an In-Service programme designed to help school directors and administrators to run their schools more efficiently. There were modules on school governance and managing finance. Improving relations with their staff and including them in efforts to improve efficiency, were also on the agenda. Teame wanted to see school resources managed more effectively and to create a professional ethos.

He also aimed to see all school staff, teachers and administrators, becoming 'change agents' who understood and appreciated the role of education in national development. He wanted them to set an example as 'fair and disciplined' leaders who were also 'nation builders and paragons of learning'.

Teame had spent a great deal of time recruiting the team of educational trainers who would work with him to run the courses. They came from amongst his colleagues in Bristol but also further afield. They were all experienced educationists – one of them had an OBE for services to education. As well as extensive experiences in the UK some of them had worked in Africa, the Middle East and Asia.

After first ascertaining their suitability for the task in hand and their commitment to it, Teame put them through a rigorous programme of familiarisation with Eritrea, a country which hardly any of them had visited before or knew much about. The induction process included sessions on the climate, geography, culture, religion and history of Eritrea and the kind of clothing they would need. They were also told something about the structure of the In-Service programme and the people they would be training. Teame told them they would have to work hard in trying conditions.

Although they were paid, the fees were not high. But as Teame discovered in discussion with the trainers, they were more interested in taking part in the rehabilitation of the education system in Eritrea. He was impressed and heartened by their commitment.

Once in Eritrea the trainers all stayed at the Sunshine Hotel in Asmara which became a centre for weekly staff meetings. Teame also found it useful that the trainers could have meals together, getting to know each other and discussing the training programme. It was a cosy working base – albeit rather noisy at weekends when wedding celebrations were often held in the hotel. Evening meals were often at the popular Castello Restaurant known for its beef steaks.

Among those who joined him were some he had known and worked with in Bristol such as John Hayter and Ray Harris. The latter had been instrumental in assisting his work for the Eritrean refugees in Sudan during the liberation struggle. Ray would later remark on the 'pure joy' shown by everyone they met in Eritrea as they participated in the programme to rebuild the country after thirty years of war. He was impressed to see secondary school students planting trees and helping to build roads during their summer holidays.

The first of the In-Service programmes was held in the summer of 1997 at the former Comboni College in Asmara – the same college where Teame had obtained his textbooks to study for his School Certificate so many years previously. The programmes lasted for six weeks with the courses for about 250 directors, supervisors and district education officers run by trainers from Britain who would stay for three and half weeks before being replaced by another set of trainers. Teame, the co-ordinator, would stay eight weeks. He was not only directing the programme but also took courses in School Governance and Financial Management. He would spend many hours in Bristol preparing for the summer programmes wishing to ensure they answered the particular needs of the Eritrean staff.

Such were the numbers being trained that the day was split up into morning and afternoon sessions. The day would start at 8.00 am with the lesson continuing until 1.00 pm. But on Fridays they would start at 7.30 am and finish at 12.30 pm in order to allow Muslim participants to go to the Mosque. The afternoons would be devoted to watching educational videos and debating professional issues such as school performance data, setting targets for school improvement and leadership.

The trainees were selected by the Eritrean Ministry of Education who set a minimum qualification of five years' service, possession of a teaching certificate and a recommendation from their superiors as to their conduct and professionalism.

There was a democratic flavour to the way the courses were run. Teame, always a strong advocate of a democratic approach to the teaching-learning process, invited the participants to elect class repre-sentatives to pass on their suggestions on how the courses should be run. He also asked them to raise any issues they were concerned about. Teame would have a regular meeting with the class representatives every Friday.

One of the problems that he had to deal with was having to run extra sessions because some of the trainees were delayed getting to their classes due to transport facilities being disrupted by the rainy season. Some of them were disabled from injuries sustained during the liberation war and needed sensitive support. Others were separ-ated from their families and Teame found himself providing pastoral care as an alternative to allowing them to go home during the weekends which would not have been practical.

There were other practical difficulties to overcome. When the Ministry of Education photocopiers they were allowed to use were out of order – they were old and in need of replacement – the Director of the British Council Library in Asmara, Dr Neguse Araya, came to the rescue offering use of his photocopiers. With textbooks scarce it was essential to have facilities to copy material for the lessons. Another time two of the trainers' boxes of teaching resources went missing at Asmara Airport. In spite of a supporting letter from the Ministry of Education it took Teame and a Ministry official two more visits to the Airport warehouse before they eventually turned up.

One Bristol University colleague in Teame's team admired his tact in dealing with his fellow countrymen and his being aware of the sensitivities and the expectations. The colleague also noted that he took an abnormal load of responsibility but also went out of his way to see that his colleagues in the training team enjoyed the experience.

Keen to show accountability and transparency Teame invited the Minister of Education and other high ranking Ministry officials to come and see what they were doing. They witnessed the British trainers in action, saw their methods and preparation, the interaction with students and the way classroom debates were structured.

Teame worked himself and his team hard. Most spare hours were spent preparing lessons or marking assignments. But in their occasional free time he would take a group of the trainers out to experience the 'real Eritrea'. On a number of occasions he would invite them to come with him to the house of his Uncle Ghebremichael in Asmara – where he had lived during his student days – and to enjoy some Eritrean hospitality. His uncle, who spoke fluent English, would entertain the group, and Teame's aunt Woizero Azieb Ghebrehiwet, would provide dish after dish of delicious

Eritrean food. They may not have been used to the chillies and other spices in the salads but it was a happy time much enjoyed by the trainers.

One Saturday evening at about 9.30 pm when the day's work was over and lessons preparation for the next day completed, Teame decided to take the trainers to a traditional Eritrean wedding. It would allow them to see what actually went on amidst the incessant drum beating at weekends which was a feature of their stay in the hotel. Their arrival in the wedding hall raised a few eyebrows among the guests, who were all dressed in traditional Eritrean robes, unlike the trainers attired like most Westerners in shirts and slacks. But they were welcomed by the families of the bride and groom and offered food and drink. It was an experience of the real Eritrea which the trainers much enjoyed and appreciated.

Teame also organised trips to other parts of Eritrea during the weekends including a trip to Massawa where they swam in the Red Sea. The area is extremely hot in the summer. When they arrived at the beach they all changed into swimming costumes and ran towards the sea. But they did not have sandals and the sand was so hot it burnt the soles of their feet. They ran into the water to cool off, Teame among them, shouting excitedly and forgetting for a moment they were distinguished academics!

He also took them to Keren, 90 kilometres from Asmara, which has a huge British cemetery for the dead of the Second World War. They were shown a shrine for the 'Black Madonna' inside a baobab tree – a huge tourist attraction which is regularly visited by Eritrean women hoping to bear children.

Keren is the town where Teame's wife, Teblez, was born and he took one of the groups to her home in the town. By then it had been converted into an orphanage supported by Teblez and others. It had started with five girls aged from six to ten and now had modern facilities including a television. A local young woman called Terhas looked after the children like a mother helping them with their studies. The visitors were impressed at how clean the premises were kept. The girls were doing well at a local school and their good behaviour and robust health impressed others in the town. On another occasion a colleague of Teame's, Roger Deeks, visited the orphanage and taught some of the girls to count up to ten in English in return for being taught to do the same in Tigrigna. But he had trouble with his Tigrigna counting which led one of the young girls to exclaim: 'How come the old Taliano [which means white] cannot count up to ten?' The incident caused much amusement.

Sadly, the orphanage later closed after it was visited by local officials who decreed that looking after orphans was a government responsibility and the money raised for it should be given to them. Teame was sorry to hear that the girls were returned to the poor conditions in which they had been found.

There was also a trip to the archaeological site at Quohaito near the town of Adi Keyh where Teame had his first teaching post in 1960 more than thirty years earlier. Quohaito was the scene where he had the near disastrous experience with a large group of his school pupils and he had learnt valuable lessons about health and safety. He related the story to his group which raised a few smiles.

He also told them of another scary moment during his time there as a teacher when he and his friend Mohamed were walking in a wood near Quohaito by moonlight to reach a village where Mohamed's mother, Adey Halima, lived and where she was bitten by a poisonous snake. Discovering her they had managed to get her to a doctor in time to save her life. The experiences would no doubt have given the British trainers an insight into Teame's life as a young man in Eritrea.

The group, including Dr Bob Langton and Mrs Viv Casteel, were entertained to lunch at his sister Tekea's home in Adi Keyh which not only gave the opportunity to enjoy more Eritrean cooking but allowed Teame to see her for the first time in many years. It was a happy occasion when he not only introduced Tekea to his colleagues, but was able to catch up with her and share family news.

On one of his trips to Asmara Teame met up again with his cousin Fasil Ghebremichael who he had last seen at the Zero School. Fasil was the youngest brother of one of Eritrea's most renowned singers and songwriters, Yemane Ghebremichael – otherwise known as Yemane Baria. He had become an iconic figure during the liberation struggle as he reflected Eritrea's experience during the war in his writing and music. Yemane had sadly died prematurely in his fifties from natural causes in 1997. Teame accompanied Fasil to his grave in Asmara to pay their respects to a man who had also been known as the 'Eritrean caretaker' for his generosity and support towards his fellow countrymen. While at the graveside the two of them also spent a few minutes paying their respects at the adjoining grave of Ato Woldeab Woldemariam, the esteemed Eritrean nationalist who Teame had met in Bologna in 1989.

Teame had first got to know the Ghebremichael family during the traumatic time when, as a sixteen-year-old in 1955, he lost his boarding place at the Haile Selassie Secondary School and was offered a home with his Uncle Ghebremichael, Yemane and Fasil's father. So he had known Yemane since he was nine years old and would often take his young cousin to school and play football with him in the courtyard of their home in Asmara.

Later, when Yemane expressed an ambition to become a singer, Teame had vehemently disagreed with him believing that education was more important. As Yemane held fast to his determination to fulfill his musical ambitions, Teame's relationship with him had soured. He remained convinced that Yemane should go to university and have a successful career like his father. But, when Yemane followed his heart and then excelled as a musician, as well as becoming an influential figure in the independence struggle, Teame realised he had been wrong. His conviction about the value of education remained as strong as ever but he realised that, as in Yemane's case, there are sometimes other routes to success in life. Before Yemane died, Teame apologised to him and asked for his forgiveness.

The summer programme in Asmara was not Teame's only commitment to rebuilding the Eritrean education system. There was another dimension of the In-Service programme – this time in Bristol. At the request of the Minister of Education, Osman Saleh, he established a Bristol-Eritrea Link programme where Eritrean educators came to Bristol University to enhance their qualifications. It was a partnership between the Graduate School of Education, the Eritrean Ministry of Education and the Danish aid agency (DANIDA) who provided the funding.

It was a huge project which added to his work organising the summer programmes in Asmara. Teame found himself also coordinating the Link programme in Bristol. During the period it operatred, from 1994 to 2004, fifty Eritrean students completed courses at the university. Teame supervised the dissertations of many of them. The majority of the students are now holding down senior positions in the Eritrean Provincial Education Offices and the Ministry of Education.

Teame was responsible for the selection and recruitment of Eritreans for M.Ed, M.Phil and PhD programmes at Bristol – a job which he, as an Admissions Tutor, was well equipped to handle. He served as the Selection and Recruitment Officer for the group ensuring that they complied with the University's criteria for international students.

He also ran short educational visits to Bristol for officials of the Eritrean Ministry of Education. It was aimed at showing them how schools, colleges, teacher training institutions and teacher centres were run in Britain. Teame expended a lot of energy in organising the school visits in different parts of England and Wales. The officials had to write reports on their placements which Teame would also supervise. There were practical responsibilities too. Sometimes he would be called upon to pick them up from the station on their arrival or from one of the schools they visited.

It was hard and demanding work but Teame took it all in good part. He was, after all, pursuing his aim to assist a free Eritrea to have an education service that was fit for purpose.

One other project, though, proved more problematic. Tailor-made by Teame it was a two year programme in Bristol for twenty-four young men and women educators representing the diverse ethnic groups in Eritrea. The Ministry of Education in Asmara had selected the group as part of an initiative for their schools and colleges to be more inclusive. Teame had accepted the group rather hastily, fearing that another university might otherwise take them.

Teame believed it was a worthy objective. But it was not without its problems. The request to run the course came rather late and just as Teame was deeply involved in the induction of the international students at the Graduate School of Education. But despite his other responsibilities Teame hired a mini bus and picked up the twenty-four students from Heathrow Airport. Knowing they probably would not have local currency he took some with him, along with food and drink to facilitate their arrival in Britain. Then he dropped each one off at their assigned hall of residence in Bristol. It was midnight before the last one was settled in. Some of them were disabled former liberation fighters who needed sympathetic support. The group were supportive of each other and Teame was heartened to see one of the able bodied among them helping another, who had lost a hand in the fighting, to cook his meal.

A distinctive feature of the group was their varied cultural background from the different ethnic groups in Eritrea. In addition to learning how to live together, it meant that they could perform the many different Ethnic dances from Eritrea on the country's Independence Day on May 24th. Teame also organised a supply of Eritrean food and drink from a supplier in London. The Eritrean Ambassador at the time, Ato Ghermay Ghebremariam, attended the event where he was introduced to university officials as well as the Eritreans.

But, although Teame understood and sympathised with the aims of making the group inclusive of all Eritrea's ethnic peoples, he felt that 'political correctness' had meant that not all of the group were necessarily the best candidates available. It was, he thought, a case of 'sacrificing quality at the altar of equal ethnic opportunity'. He also took to task those members of the group who insisted on earning extra cash by working in the local supermarkets during their free time – a practice which Teame disapproved of as he wanted them to concentrate on their studies.

So it was not a smooth ride. But despite his earlier reservations Teame was glad, and a little relieved, to see that most of the group performed well and many of them took up key positions in the provincial Education Offices of Eritrea. He felt he had achieved the major *raison d'être* of the Bristol-Eritrea Link programme – enabling and assisting the MoE to meet its manpower demands. He also appreciated the support and understanding he received back in Eritrea from Ato Osman Seleh, the Minister, Ato Petros Hailemariam, the Director-General, Ato Abraham Tecle and Ato Tedros Seyoum.

In fact, because of the performance of the group, Teame decided that their graduation ceremony should be held not in Bristol but back in Asmara where relatives and friends could celebrate their achievements. Teame went to Asmara for the ceremony taking with him graduation gowns from Bristol University for the proud graduates to wear. They received their degrees and diplomas from Roger Deeks representing Bristol University and the Minister of Education Ato Osman Saleh. Among those receiving degrees were M.Ed students who had graduated in earlier years but returned to the country before the graduation ceremony in Bristol.

There was one hitch which Teame resolved in a novel way. He had been unable to find a PhD gown for one of the recent graduates, a young woman. So, he took off his own gown he was wearing for the occasion, and placed it round her shoulders. It was a touching gesture which drew loud laughter and applause from the audience.

Teame and his team carried out another In-Service programme in the summer of 1998. But shortly after it was completed the dark clouds of war had again appeared over the region. A festering border dispute resulted in Eritrean forces entering the Badme region along the border of Eritrea and Ethiopia's Tigray region setting off a two year war which was to cost thousands of lives on both sides and put back Eritrea's rebuilding plans after the liberation conflict. It meant the next planned session of the In-Service programme had to be postponed.

CHAPTER THIRTY-NINE

Badme War

Eritrea's invasion of the Badme border region in 1998 was to spark off a wider conflict with Ethiopia which was to continue for the next two years. The Eritrean government had clearly not heeded the warnings of the then Ethiopian Prime Minister, Meles Zenawi, at the Liberation ceremony five years earlier when he urged them to 'stop scratching old wounds' and to look towards building a peaceful and neighbourly future between their two countries.

Teame, who had been at the ceremony and heard the Ethiopian Prime Minister speak, was dismayed at the turn of events and feared for the affect it would have not only on the plans to revitalise the Eritrean education system, but also on the country as a whole. Not one to involve himself in politics – preferring to seek change through dialogue and education – he would have liked to have seen a peaceful solution to the long running border dispute.

But it was not to be. The two governments, allies in the liberation war against the Mengistu regime, could not reach agreement on the border between their two countries, which, when Eritrea had been part of Ethiopia, had not been contentious. Then the border was no more than a demarcation line between two federated provinces. Now it was different.

According to a ruling by an international commission in The Hague,

Eritrea broke international law and triggered the war by invading Ethiopia.

Badme is in the province of Tigray, the area where many members of the Ethiopian government originated – including Meles Zenawi. The Ethiopian government came under pressure to meet force with force and mobilized for a full assault on Eritrea. First World War style trench warfare along the border areas became a feature of the conflict.

It was to prove a costly struggle with the two sides spending millions of dollars on the war and there being tens of thousands of casualties. By the end of May 2000, Ethiopia occupied about a quarter of Eritrea's territory displacing 650,000 people – massively escalating the refugee problem – and destroying key components of the country's infrastructure. There was widespread looting of houses and shops, as well as the deportation of thousands of Eritreans from Ethiopia back to their homeland.

There was a ceasefire on June 18, 2000 after the warring parties accepted a comprehensive peace deal under the Algiers Agreement. Ethiopian forces had to withdraw from areas they occupied. A 25-kilometre-wide Temporary Security Zone was established patrolled by United Nations peace keeping forces. Despite the ruling that Eritrea had broken international law by invading Ethiopia, the Eritrea-Ethiopia Boundary Commission, a body founded by the UN, decreed that Badme does in fact belong to Eritrea. The border area between the two countries remains heavily militarised, with instances of armed conflict, and a no-man's land between the two armies.

For Teame the outbreak of war had caused deep frustrations as it meant that his carefully laid plans for the next In-Service programme in the summer of 1999, the third and last in the series, had to be put on hold. He had selected the trainers who all had busy schedules and had in many cases made sacrifices to make the time. There would have to be some tricky rescheduling when it became possible to continue the programme.

Teame had tried to keep to the original schedule despite the outbreak of war. The Eritrean Ministry of Education were also keen for it to happen and pointed out that the fighting was 1,000 kilometres away from Asmara. But the British Foreign Office, who Teame kept in constant contact with by phone and letter, were adamant that no British national should go to Eritrea while the war was going on.

The Ministry officials in Asmara were unhappy at the non-appearance of Teame and his team having already selected the participants for the latest In-Service programme. But there was nothing Teame could do. He understood the frustration in Asmara, but felt the officials had not fully taken on board the Foreign Office advice which he had to abide by.

He kept in touch with the Ministry in Asmara throughout the war, anxiously reading news reports of the way the conflict was going, and awaiting the moment when he could return. Eventually, after the end of the conflict in 2000 he was finally able to begin planning. He ran what would be the last In-Service programme the following year. It meant re-booking the trainers. Some could not change their plans and new trainers had to be found. But in the summer of 2001 he and his team flew to Asmara. This time he was accompanied by his youngest daughter Zeb, now a medical student, who had been given a placement at one of the hospitals as part of her training.

He arrived in a very different country than the one he had left three years earlier. Although Asmara had not been in the war zone, so there were no visible signs of the conflict, he felt he had come back to a sadder place. Many families had lost sons and daughters in the war – a burden which they might have thought they would not again experience after the trials of the war of independence. The cost of living had also shot up as the country grappled with reviving the economy after spending many millions on the war effort.

It was during Teame's final time with the In-Service programme in 2001 that there were ominous signs that the relationship between the new regime and Asmara University was deteriorating.

First the government asked the university students to help with the harvesting in the rural areas of the country. It brought back memories of a similar call to the students during the Mengistu regime in the 1970s when Teame was an assistant professor at Asmara University. He and his colleague, Dr Petros, who was later assassinated, had been ordered to convey Mengistu's message to the students and had advised them to exercise caution in their response. But the students had revolted over the call to the farms and refused to do it on the grounds that it was 'politically motivated'.

This time, nearly thirty years later, the Asmara University students were similarly disinclined. They refused on the grounds that the university was an autonomous body where freedom of expression reigned and where they had the right to be consulted on decisions affecting them. Therefore, they claimed, the government had no right to intervene. But the government disagreed. Some of the student leaders were arrested.

Then the government arrested and imprisoned the G15 – mostly former ministers and ambassadors who had challenged its stance on the Badme War. Finally, on the pretext of restructuring the country's higher education system, the government effectively closed down the university when its staff were assigned to hastily built colleges. One of them, Mai Nefhi, was run on military lines with an army colonel in charge.

Teame saw the closure of the university as a retrograde step which discouraged many Eritrean academics from the diaspora from return-ing to work in Eritrea. They were planning to offer their services free to Asmara University during their sabbatical years claiming only living expenses. Teame believed that an opportunity had been lost for these highly valued academics to share their experiences and to help with the running of the University. He knew that, like him, they were only interested in the development of Eritrea and its people.

The university closure was also a blow to Teame as he had been hoping to establish a link programme with his own Bristol University. He considered the programme could have played a significant role in the professional development of the younger staff of Asmara University. With this in mind he had already invited Dr Belaynesh Araya, the then Acting Dean of the Faculty of Education at Asmara University, to visit Bristol as a precursor to further co-operation. The visit went ahead but the collaborative projects that it was hoped would follow never transpired. It had not helped that the then President of Asmara University, Dr Isahak, did not appear supportive.

Teame viewed these developments with growing dismay. He felt that such drastic action did not augur well either for the university or the country as a whole. In fact the events proved a harbinger of what Teame perceived as even worse developments for the country of his birth.

The National Constitution, established at Liberation in 1997, was set aside and, in 2002, the National Assembly was dissolved. And then came the introduction of indefinite national service leading to the calling up of the country's young men and women with no idea when they would return to civilian life. It would have been of little surprise to Teame to hear that conscription was described as 'national slavery'. The indefinite call up is continuing to this day and has been blamed for adding to the flow of young men from Eritrea joining the increasing flood of migrants desperate to leave the country.

Teame saw these actions, along with the setting up of secret prison camps and a government controlled media after the banning of a free press, as signs that there had been a 'breakdown in communication between the State and its citizens'.

But the travails of the country did not stop Teame and his trainer colleagues from commencing the third and final In-Service programme. Teame, ever the pragmatist, was convinced – no doubt rightly – that his job was to concentrate on areas that he had some control over. So rather than worrying about national issues which he saw as the responsibility of 'those in authority' he focused on the In-Service programme. He and his trainers arrived in Asmara a few days in advance. The participants, mostly school directors, turned up on time on the first day.

As the training got under way again in 2001 Teame could not help noticing the sombre demeanour among those sitting in the class-rooms. It was very different from the joyful scenes the training team witnessed when they first arrived in the country before the Badme War erupted. He suspected the trainees were deeply affected by the ongoing traumas of the War and, perhaps, the effects of work pressures too. But it was not something he and the other trainers discussed with the participants. They understood the war was a taboo subject and kept their discussions to purely professional matters.

With the course nearing completion it was time to assess how effective it had been. Had it achieved its aims of helping school directors and administrators to run their establishments more efficiently?

In their own evaluation forms most of the trainers concluded that the programme had been well planned and implemented. It had succeeded in the tricky task of transferring best practice from Western countries, and more experience in educational management issues, to educational professionals in a new and growing State. The trainers along with Teame were particularly impressed with the positive state of mind of the school directors in view of the difficult conditions in the country after the war.

The training included a vigorous system of examination. But the trainers acknowledged the incongruity of aiming to help the participants to develop professionally whilst also subjecting them to the exams. There was a danger of the stress involved stultifying the learning process. It was difficult to see how else the trainers could properly assess their students. But Teame recognised that it was a matter of concern that needed addressing in the future – perhaps by reducing the frequency of tests although not abandoning them altogether.

At the end of every module the school directors being trained would be asked to complete an evaluation form providing feedback on how they thought the course had gone. Teame was glad to discover that the majority view was that they felt the training had been of direct relevance to their roles as school directors. They particularly appreciated the interactive sessions in the afternoons when they had a chance to ask questions and input their own ideas and discussed the relevance or otherwise of educational videos.

There were a few critical comments. Many felt the course was too intensive – something Teame was aware of but felt was inevitable in view of the limited time available and the need to squeeze so much into the timetable.

Language difficulty was another issue. Some of the school directors on the courses had trouble understanding the concepts outlined by their trainers because of their limited English. Another problem that emerged was the late payment of travel expenses and daily allowances. It was likely to be a knock-on effect of the financial problems in the country following the Badme War. Teame did not consider that was an issue he should get involved in. In any case the matter was later dealt with satisfactorily by Ato Abraham Tecle, Eritrea's Chief Supervisor of the programme.

But, overall, Teame was satisfied that the three summer programmes – albeit interrupted by the Badme War – had gone well and achieved their objectives. There were positive responses from both the Ministry of Education in Eritrea and Bristol University who were both given detailed reports at the end of each summer programme.

Confirmation of how well the programmes had been received came in the feedback submitted by the school directors and administrators on the course. One of them, a man with a physical disability, described how he left home very early in the morning taking two taxis to get to classes on time, so keen was he not to miss any lessons.

Another said he was 'ever grateful' to Teame for his decision to 'serve your people' in spite of his responsibilities to Bristol University and to his family. Others highlighted the 'respect and pride' he gave to the teaching profession and how he built up their morale and confidence.

Teame's natural modesty was challenged by one man who said: 'Don't under-estimate the importance of what you are doing for us and the country.' The man added: 'You keep undermining your efforts.'

Teame's reputation as an educationist meant that, whenever he was in Asmara, he would often find himself being asked to perform duties other than those demanded by his busy schedule with the In-Service Programme. He was regularly asked to gives lectures and take part in seminars. His time there in 2001 was no exception.

One such occasion was an invitation to address the Asmara Rotary Club. And, much to his delight, his daughter Zeb was able to take time off from her medical duties to sit beside him. Teame took great pride that she had come with him to Eritrea, giving her own service to the country, working in the local hospital as part of her medical training.

The Rotary Club event gave Zeb a chance to see a new side to her father. She was impressed when one of the members of the audience, a former pupil of Teame's at Asmara Teacher Training Institute, rose to thank him for the way he had taught him discipline and motivation. The man, Dr Tsegay Ghebregziabeher (the last name means Servant of God) had gone on from teaching to become a leading pharmacist and entrepreneur with businesses in America and Asmara.

During his series of visits to Asmara since liberation in 1993 Teame gave no less than five lectures to the Eritrean Teachers Association. He was keen to encourage the Association to concentrate on improving the professional standards of their members instead of getting side-tracked by issues like salary scales. He had also known a number of the leading officers who were former students at the Asmara Teacher Training Institute. One of the presidents of the Eritrean Teachers Association was Ato Zehaye Tsegay, a class mate of Dr Tsegay Ghebregziabeher. Apart from honouring their invitations, Teame's aim was to help them avoid the antagonism between education ministries and teaching associations that he had seen in other African countries.

During this last visit in 2001, before the In-Service programme finished, Teame gave another public lecture to the Institute of Secretarial, Management, Auditing and Pedagogic Courses at the Eritro-German building in Asmara. It had been at the invitation of the Head of the Institute, Dr Tesfay Haile. The Institute was a rising centre of higher learning and something of a trend-setter in the country. He addressed its staff members on how they could best serve the country by minimizing the number of untrained and undertrained secondary school teachers – an issue Teame felt strongly was vital to the future of Eritrea's education system.

There was more fulsome praise for Teame from a member of the audience, Ato Woldu Seyoum, who had known him when he was a student teacher in Asmara in the 1960s. Teame's shield of modesty was somewhat dented when Ato Woldu told the audience how he had been a role model as a student who took his studies seriously and had bought second hand books from him and his friends in order to sit the Oxford School Leaving Certificate Exam as a private candidate. It might have been an embarrassment for Teame to be reminded of this moment, but the fact is that getting through the Oxford exam with the help of those second hand books had been essential to completing his eventual journey to university. So it represented an important stage in his academic life.

Another lecture he was asked to give was at a seminar on the subject of 'Teachers as Professionals' to a group of teachers at religious schools. The request had come from a Norwegian academic also working in Asmara, Dr Arve Brunvoll from Bergen University, who Teame had known and worked with earlier.

Teame was interested to discover that his audience of eighty teachers at the St Mary's Orthodox Church Hall in Asmara included those from all the traditional church schools in Asmara and embraced not just Orthodox, Catholic and Protestants, but also the teachers (*ustazs*) at the *madrassas*, the Muslim schools.

Not having dealt with such a mixed group of elderly educators before, Teame was glad to have the opportunity to learn from them as well as imparting his own knowledge and experience. He was both moved and impressed to see this learned group of educators of different faiths sitting next to each other discussing how the term 'professional' could apply to them.

He was pleasantly surprised to find they all agreed that a 'professional' was someone whose activities were governed by morality, the wish to serve humanity and to instil a quest for wisdom and knowledge in those they taught.

In his summing up Teame told his audience that they should not allow others to under-estimate their contribution to the development of education in the country or to civilisation in general. He reminded them that their forerunners as educators had been monks and sheikhs, who taught in the monasteries and mosques for centuries before, and they had also served their communities by diagnosing illnesses and dispensing herbal medicines.

All in all Teame found his time with the elderly teachers from different religious schools a very fulfilling experience. He and Professor Brunvoll were both given silver crosses by the workshop organisers in thanks for their contributions – a gift that Teame still treasures.

Just as he was about to leave to return to the UK at the end of the final session Teame was persuaded to do an interview for Eritrean national television on the In-Service programme. The reporter who had conducted the interview, Ato Eyasu Teweldemedhin, had been very persistent, accosting him in his hotel on three separate occasions. Despite Teame's reluctance because he did not have time to prepare in view of the imminence of his departure, he finally agreed to do the interview. It was to be on the theme of improving the quality of education in the country.

The interview was split up into three episodes over the succeeding weeks. Teame got positive reports from both family members and colleagues who had seen the episodes. There were messages from friends all over the world including Canada, USA, and Germany. He was both pleased and relieved, to hear that the interviewer had kept a promise to make it clear that he had not had time to do any preparation for the interview and so had been speaking off the cuff.

So, his efforts with the In-Service Programme were at an end. He would leave Eritrea with a deep sense of concern at what he perceived as dark clouds appearing over the horizon as the government tightened its grip on power. He was alarmed at the apparent disdain for democracy and the perception that the government was above the law. He thought it made independence look like a poisoned chalice.

There was a shortage of housing, erratic supply of water and electricity and incidents of corruption among some provincial administrators who were acting in their own interests. He felt the country was engulfed by grief and despair. He saw that many hard working Eritreans, the elderly among them, were reduced to leaving their villages and going into the towns under the cover of darkness to beg on the streets.

Even some of the ex-fighters he met told him they were not happy. They regretted that the kind of 'independence' they saw around them was not what they had fought for.

One of the most telling conversations he had was with a woman in her eighties who he came across begging in the streets of Keren outside St Mary's Church. She exclaimed, '*Meenti Kidiste Mariam,*' 'In the name of the Blessed St Mary,' as she begged. Teame gave her the little money he had in his pocket and asked what had brought her to this sad state.

As he sat beside her and asked how he could help, she told him she was from the Highlands of Eritrea – the area where Teame also came from. She had lost her only grandson in the Badme war and had packed up her few belongings and decided to leave the area and travel to a part of the country where she was not known.

Teame asked her if she would like to return to her home village if someone could pay for the transport. But she replied that she did not feel there was hope any more. She told Teame: 'Just pray for me so that my Maker can collect me sooner rather than later.'

It was a sad reflection on the state of the country. Teame considered what he had heard from the old woman and others he had talked to cast serious doubts on the future of the country that had been liberated at the heavy cost of its children's lives.

CHAPTER FORTY

Father's Funeral

In January 2012, on hearing that his ninety-eight-year-old father was ailing and unlikely to live much longer Teame hastily made arrangements to fly out to Asmara and see him one last time before he died.

He considered the fact that he was able to go something of a miracle. In the previous year he had been undergoing treatment for liver cancer and, at one point his own life seemed in danger. In fact the family had been told that all that was left was palliative care as his life slipped away. It was a particularly devastating blow since it followed Teblez's own cancer diagnosis and treatment six month earlier.

Teblez and her daughters, with Zeb now qualified as a doctor using her own medical knowledge, sought other advice from a specialist centre in London. Then they heard of a young surgeon who had just joined the Bristol Royal Infirmary where Teame was being treated, who might be able to perform a life-saving operation to remove the tumour on Teame's liver.

The surgeon, Mr Reyyed Abadi, offered to carry out the operation although he warned them of the risks involved. Putting their faith in him the family asked him to go ahead. When the day of the operation arrived, the family anxiously waited for news of the outcome. So it was with great joy, and considerable relief, that they heard the tumour had been safely removed. Their faith in Mr Abadi's skill had been justified. No doubt a few prayers had gone up too. Teame, from being close to his end, was now on the road to recovery.

Teame had had to face his own mortality. But, as one of his daughters later remarked, he did so with self-effacing humour and courage and was sustained by his religious faith. During his life-threatening illness he had made friends with the ward staff lifting their spirits and even spent time talking to the overworked porters and nurses asking about their countries of origin. If he sensed they were missing their families in a far off land, he would attempt to raise their morale. It was little wonder that, glad as they were to see him restored to health, they were sorry to see him go.

He was recovering at home when he got the call about his father. He was desperate to go to him and, much to his relief, his doctor cleared him to travel. As the first-born son it was, under Eritrean custom, his responsibility to organise the ceremonies for burial after his father had died. There was a huge amount to do and Teame, along with his brothers and sisters, took the responsibility very seriously.

It was not an auspicious arrival in the Eritrean capital. There was a power cut with no lights at the airport and when he got to his hotel in Asmara there was just one candle in reception as he arrived tired and stiff after his long flight. He was still weak from his major operation, used crutches to walk, and had been given help carrying his heavy baggage by his old friend Ato Girmay Araya and his brother Anghesom.

His father was staying with Anghesom in Asmara. He knew he was not long for this world and was glad to see his eldest son. Teame was able to spend many hours of quality time with him over the next few days. He was amazed at how mentally agile his father still was despite his frailty.

Teame and other members of the family including his siblings and cousins sat around Mebrahtu Beraky's bed as they reminisced with him about his life and sought advice on family matters they might have to deal with when he was no longer with them. It was a precious time when they talked of serious issues as well as laughing together about some of the lighter moments from his long life.

One of the most pressing matters they wanted to talk to him about was that of his younger brother Seltan Beraky, who had disappeared from the village fifty years previously and neither Mebrahtu Beraky nor any other member of the family had seen or heard of him since. Teame remembered him as a big man – much taller and broader than his slight framed father – who was prone to get into arguments. He wondered if this might have been one reason why he had disappeared and also suspected it was unlikely he was still alive.

Teame, and his siblings, knew that their uncle's disappearance had always been a source of distress to their father. It was the custom in Eritrea, on the death of a family member, to perform what was known as 'closing the mouth' of the deceased. It was not a literal closing of the mouth but a ceremony when the dead were properly celebrated with a fee paid to a priest to ensure it was done according to tradition. Believing the brother to be dead, Teame and the rest of the family wanted to know if Mebrahtu Beraky would like him to be included in his 'closing the mouth' ceremony. It would be a way, they thought, of giving Beraky closure on his concerns about the disappearance of his brother.

However, Mebrahtu Beraky was not in favour of the idea. He said he appreciated why they were offering to undertake to put his brother's soul to rest. But he was concerned that such an action might offend his brother's many children (he had been married three times) if his life was commemorated at the same time as his own. Their pride, he thought, might be hurt and they would not thank them for their help. It was typical of him to put the feelings of others first. The idea was quietly dropped.

Another question asked of Teame's father was whether he had any outstanding debts that needed settling. His firm response was that anyone who knew him would know that he did not live beyond his means. But he did say he was owed money by others although he declined to say how much. He would often lend sums to needy villagers and friends. But he was adamant that his family should not seek settlement of the debts, or to accept repayment if it was offered out of a sense of honour. Teame promised to abide by his wishes.

Another important matter discussed was where would Mebrahtu Beraky like to be laid to rest. He declared he wanted to be buried in the church yard of his home village of Adi Ghehad next to his older brother Dimtsu and his wife Wagaye.

There were some lighter reminiscences too. Teame's cousin Aya Berhane reminded Mebrahtu Beraky of the time he beat him for losing one of his heifers when it was eaten by a hyena whilst he was supposed to be looking after the animal. And Teame's brother Anghesom related how he and his father had gone to a site, some distance from their village, where there were hot springs. They had plunged into the waters not knowing there were local protocols to go through first. Anghesom was pelted with stones by a group of very large villagers annoyed at their ignorance (they left Mebrahtu Beraky alone apparently respecting his greater maturity). The story brought a smile and the comment: 'Yes, I almost lost my son that day.'

Teame playfully asked him why, when he was a fourteen-year-old schoolboy in Dekemhare, he had made him wear his only pair of long trousers and a pair of borrowed shoes to go with him to visit an Italian Signora who grew and sold paw paws, mangoes and oranges in Mai Aini. His father replied that he had hoped that he might be given a job there to help the family budget which was ailing that year because the harvest had been hit by a plague of locusts. But his efforts were to no avail. No job was forthcoming.

Teame was grateful that he had been able to spend such a valuable time with his father alongside others from the family. His father finally urged them all – sons, daughters and daughter-in laws (Ghenet and Nebiat) – to stick together and respect each other and offer their help and service to others whenever it was required. It was as though, knowing he did not have long to live, he wanted to pass his own philosophy of life on to those he was leaving behind.

He died a few days later. Teame was not at his bedside, although his brothers and sisters were. He had been sent from the room as he was still weak from his operation and needed to rest.

It was a sad although not unexpected moment. Teame was both relieved and pleased that he had been able to see and talk to his father one last time. He remembered the time, when he was ten, that they had travelled together on a mule across the mountainside in search of a new school and how he had realised how much his father cared for him despite his tough exterior.

Although he had rarely seen him since seeking asylum in Britain, they had kept in touch via the erratic telephone system. Teame has always seen his father as a wise and loving man whose counsel he valued. He may not have been an educated man, like his son, but his wisdom, experience of life and sense of service to the community had been a strong influence on Teame.

A villager told him that his father had been seen ploughing one of the local fields with oxen the previous year at the age of ninety-seven. And he frequently walked the 14 kilometres from his village to Quoatit, where the bus to and from Asmara stopped. But he had said he did not expect to be in this world beyond January. In fact he died peacefully on January 31st.

At 6.00 am the next morning, at Anghesom's house, the family started the official period of mourning which included erecting a huge tent in the compound to accommodate the big crowds who would want to pay their respects.

Meanwhile Teame had to start planning the funeral and all that followed. First he hired a land cruiser to take his father's body back to his home village of Adi Ghehad when he would be accompanied by a priest and his younger brother Habte. As the land cruiser drove through the villages on the way to the family home, it stopped periodically for letters to be distributed to the villagers telling them of Mebrahtu Beraky's passing and that the funeral was to be the next day.

Teame had been unsure how many people would be able to get to the funeral because of the short notice and distances involved. So he was astonished by the huge numbers that turned up. There were several thousand of them. It was a sign of the respect in which his father was held. As a leading village Elder he was well known and much loved for his thought and care for others.

Every one of the fourteen villages in the region, known as Eghela Hatzin, sent three elders. Friends and relatives came from many miles away. Three of Teame's sisters had to come from villages on the other side of the country. One, his sister Tekea along with her husband Abraha Bahlibi, brought two bus-loads of friends and relatives from Adi Keyh. The others, Letteberhan and Meleite, walked for seven hours, along with other relatives and local villagers, to be at the funeral. In fact the service had to be delayed to await their arrival. There were also three bus-loads of mourners from Asmara.

A total of forty-eight priests in full regalia came to keep an overnight vigil. They spent the night praying over the body and then conducted the service the following day. It all made for a huge gathering assembled to mourn and pay tribute to a man who was much admired for his selfless work and leadership in the community. Teame, like other male mourners, wore the traditional black overcoat and a shawl around his shoulders. The women, led by close female members of the family, were wailing – part of the ritual lamenting of the dead common among the Coptic Christian community.

After the church service the body was taken back to the family home in the village for the final goodbyes. Then followed a procession, with Teame and other family members at the head, to the centre of the village, a circular area known as the *Bayto*, where all important events take place. Village elders joined the family in moving through the assembled throng standing around the circle to thank them for coming. Later the mourners were entertained at the homes of other villagers who had specially prepared food for the occasion, and given something to eat and drink.

Finally, a highlight of the proceedings was the arrival of a mule which Mebrahtu Beraky had sold to a local villager some years previously. The mule had been a favourite of his despite proving a bit too lively at times. He had several times fallen off and once broken his shoulder. The mule, covered in traditional regalia, was paraded round the cere-mony three times – and seemed to be saying her own goodbye to her former master. 'A wonderful moment for all the family,' says Teame.

While there was an overnight vigil for his father's body, Teame found himself having to conduct some delicate negotiations to ensure his father's wish to be buried in the local church yard were complied with. Some of the villagers wanted the church, which was crumbling down, to be relocated along with the graveyard to another site further away from the village. They said they wanted Mebrahtu Beraky to be the first man buried in the new graveyard as he was such a respected member of the community. But Teame was determined to follow his father's instructions on the matter. As well as wanting to be buried alongside his brother and wife his father also wanted the church to remain in the village. It was closer for the elderly, many of them blind, to walk to.

Teame and family eventually managed to persuade the Elders to respect their father's wishes. With agreement finally reached, the family had to arrange for the grave to be dug. Teame was much moved that the work was largely done, during the night, by one of his younger brothers, Habte, helped by some of the other relatives and friends.

Twelve days after the burial came the traditional ceremony of respect and remembrance. Two thousand people came, including the forty-eight priests. The family had to organise feeding and looking after them. Many of the guests had walked for eight hours or more and needed overnight accommodation. So tents had to be obtained and food and water supplied. The village had no running water or electricity and the only vehicles that could enter the village were land cruisers or minibuses.

Much of the food, plates, glasses and cutlery needed for the ceremonial feast had to be transported from Asmara. The meal needed 80 kg of onions, 45 kilograms of peppers and spices and 150 litres of the local mead known as *Mies*. Water had to be carried from the local well. A goat from Teame's wife Teblez's family was slaughtered as their gesture of respect.

Teame's father had already asked that one of his oxen was to be slaughtered for the feast. A second oxen was paid for by another of Teame's brothers, Zerom Mebrahtu, who was then living in Israel and unable to come to the funeral. The feast also included several sheep. The women, including Teame's sisters, sisters-in-law and other female relatives, worked long into the nights getting everything ready. They brewed the local *suwa* beer, baked the *enjera* bread and produced the many sauces that accompanied the food.

The feast was held at the family home in Adi Ghehad with tents erected in the compound. Guests were milling about on the verandah which was covered by tree branches to provide shelter from the heat. There were family members, villagers, local elders and priests. For the meal everyone was placed in groups of eight according to age, gender and status. Custom dictated that each guest was given half a litre of mead, two or three glasses of beer and a share of the food on offer. But the priests, who had their own separate place in another building to eat, demanded, and got, a whole leg of an ox in addition to the food everyone else had.

As Teame mingled with the crowd of people wanting to celebrate his father's life he was struck by some of their comments. He heard him praised for his honesty, a man who believed that 'truth would make you free', a firm believer in 'Haki Yehaysh' – better tell the truth. The expression became his nick-name.

As he talked to the mourners Teame learnt things about his father he had never known. One man in his fifties got up at the ceremony and said he felt compelled to say something about him which he had never spoken of before. He said that Teame's father had saved his life when he had been under a sentence of execution from one of the Eritrean liberation fighters in the early 1970s. He had persuaded them to release him. 'But for him I would not be alive now' he said.

Another man said how he had been an orphan and had been taken in by Mebrahtu Beraky and treated as one of the family. He had even arranged and organised his wedding with as much care as if he had been one of his own children. He wanted to do something for the family in gratitude. So all he had was a camel which he used to gather wood for cooking the huge meal which was being prepared. As Teame said, it saved them a large sum which would otherwise have gone on buying the wood.

A third man, who was blind, told how Mebrahtu Beraky used to take him away after church services but, instead of taking him straight home, would take him to the family house for breakfast (the services were in the early morning) before then taking him to his own home.

As Teame reflected on his father's service to the community, he remembered how he was asked by one of the former *Msliene*, or District Administrators of the fourteen villages of Eghela Hatzin, Kegnezmatch Tedla Ogbu, to act on his behalf in holding local courts because of his knowledge of Heghi Endaba – the traditional law of the region. It was a sign of the high esteem in which Mebrahtu Beraky was held. But, although he obeyed the call, he was annoyed that it took him away from his personal duties to the family, as he would spend most working days at the court in the *Bayto* – the circular area in the village used for meetings.

Teame had also admired the love and respect his father had shown for his mother, Teame's grandmother, by returning to the village to help her run the smallholding after she was widowed. When she died he and his brother Dimtsu had conducted a fitting celebration. It included brewing mead from the honey produced by the bees which were descendants of the swarm Teame had collected as a schoolboy many years earlier.

He recollected the story, told him by his father, of the two 'lion killers'. The first one, a man from outside the village, boasted of his lion killing skills and even wore a lion's mane as proof of his prowess. But a distant relative, known as 'Uncle Buru' took offence because he claimed to be a lion killer too! A fight ensued between the two of them because there was a prize of a heifer to be bestowed upon a man who killed a lion with a shield and a spear. Teame wondered what his grandmother would have thought of such an unseemly sight. Years after, the story was one which was still talked about among the villagers with some amusement.

There was another amusing incident when his father met with his cousin, Menghis Ghebremedhin in Asmara, after many years when they were both elderly. He was told by his cousin in Italian – a language they both spoke, '*Io sono com un ferro; ma, tu sei com un acciaio,*' 'I thought

I was as strong as a piece of iron, but you are as strong as a piece of steel!' He laughingly replied, '*Si, Si, guisto*,' 'Yes, yes, right.' It was a reference to the fact that although Menghis was younger than Mebrahtu, the latter looked fitter.

Teame also remembered his father as a man with a determination to do what he felt was right. He was prepared to fight for justice for anyone, not just family members. Once, when he was a policeman in Dekemhare, while Teame was still a young schoolboy, he had been impressed when his father had taken up the case of villagers who had been cheated out of their money by one of the groups of street gangsters who operated in the town on market days. It was a not uncommon practice and the culprits would often get away with their crimes. Not every policeman would have bothered to follow it up. But, when the villagers sought him out at his home to complain about the crime, Mebrahtu Beraky went out of his way to find the gang and retrieve what was left of the money they had stolen and return it to the victims.

Although not a schooled man himself, he was revered as someone with a love and respect for education, something which he demonstrated by becoming the first man in the village to send his son – Teame – to school. Teame had much later helped to achieve his father's desire to send two of his other sons, Anghesom and Habte Mebrahtu, to school by paying for their living expenses in Dekemhare. He saw it as a continuation of his father's commitment to education.

It had been an exhausting time for Teame. His visit might have been a sad one but it had immersed him once again in the Eritrean culture instilled in him since childhood and in which his father, in no small measure, had been his mentor. He had a huge sense of respect and gratitude for the values his father had lived by which had influenced him so much in his own philosophy of life. Above all he was relieved that, despite still feeling the effects of a serious operation, he had performed his duty to his father. He had been able to say goodbye to him and to ensure that, along with his siblings and other family members, all the traditional funeral procedures, including erecting the headstone, were carried out. He could have done no more.

CHAPTER FORTY-ONE

Living with a Difference

Starting a new life in a strange land, with a different culture and customs to those you have been brought up in, can undoubtedly be a daunting experience for those who seek safety from oppressive regimes in their own country. During his time in Britain, first as an asylum seeker and refugee, then working to establish himself as an academic, Teame had known the realities of this new life. So he understood the challenges that face newcomers to a new country, the potential problems that could arise and how they might be resolved.

Firstly, as he had embarked on a new start for him and his family in 1978, he considered he had a duty of loyalty to his second country. That, to him, implied that he should do his best to integrate with the British community in which he now found himself. It was not always easy though.

On the whole he felt accepted. But there were times when he was reminded that he was 'different'. Filling in forms, when he had to identify himself as 'Black African', was one such occasion. Or there was the time when he was called 'Mandela' by drunken youths. After living in Britain for forty years and serving the country and his community well, he still finds it puzzling to be reminded that he is a 'foreigner'.

He understood such things as a kind of racism which had to be understood and confronted in the right way. His students would often come to him with stories of abuse they had received by virtue of their skin colour or their accent. Comments like: 'Hi jamba – did you just come off the banana boat?' Followed by, 'Banana is good isn't it? The monkeys love it.'

Another time a group of mature and experienced Pakistani academics, in Bristol to take a year-long professional training course, were playing football on The Downs, a huge area of protected parkland near their Hall of Residence, when they came across another form of racism. There was a corner kick. One of the watching spectators called out to the Pakistani players: 'Hey guys, you have a corner. Are you going to build a shop there?'

The students were offended saying, but we don't own any shops. When he heard about the incident Teame couldn't help smiling at the spectator's joking reference to the number of corner shops run mainly by Asians. He understood the discomfort of the Pakistani students but urged them not to take it to heart.

It was yet another example of racial stereotyping. The spectator clearly saw all Pakistanis as shop keepers. (Although, truth to tell, their shops are now a valued and accepted part of British life). Such stereotyping was, he felt, at the heart of many of the problems faced by those newcomers to the country who looked and sounded different from the majority population.

Teame asked himself: 'Why do we have these stereotypes, why do we have hatred when we are all members of the same human family?' He reasoned that the differences of skin colour or language were purely superficial and that genetically there are no other differences between members of the human race. But he viewed the stereotyping and mistrust that existed as people wanting to highlight the differences to prove their superiority. It was human nature. He had seen it all over the world, including Eritrea where the racial mix – between the Eritreans and the Ethiopians for example – could result in one group feeling superior to another. Similar feelings could also be found when there were marriages between different ethnic groups.

Is there an answer? Teame is convinced the process of understanding and getting on with people of a different background, a different race, is beginning to understand where the other person comes from. It was part of his deeply held belief in the value of multicultural, as well as global, education.

If differences were celebrated rather than a source of division it could unite people rather than divide them. Diversity, he believes, should enrich us as members of the human family. But first we need to make the effort to get to know someone else – by walking in the other person's moccasins as the Native Americans would put it.

A key function of education, he would say, is to help children to know each other – particularly in the West where there is a multiplicity of ethnic groups. In talks on the subject he would say: 'Knowing each other. That is what we fail to do. We just don't want to know each other.' One reason for people failing to do so, he believed, was that it elevated the other person to their status.

He knew from his own experience living in the Bristol community that smiling and putting out the hand of friendship – even to those who treated him and others like him with suspicion – can break down barriers and create understanding and appreciation of differences. A prime example was the way he and Teblez had made friends in their street in the Bristol suburb where they live.

He remembered the lesson he had learnt when he was lecturing at the Teacher Training Institute in Asmara and had lost his temper with some of his trainees who failed to submit their homework on time. Then he had been taken aside by a wiser and older colleague from the Philippines who quoted him an old Japanese proverb: 'He who smiles, rather than rages, ends up a winner.' They were wise words and had remained with him.

Teame understood that he, like other newcomers to the country arrived with deeply ingrained values and beliefs. There was a clash of cultures which could, and often did, result in division and mistrust. The attitude to women of some immigrant communities was one example.

Teame was never one to tell others what to do. But he was convinced that sometimes it was necessary to adapt, or at the very least, understand and accept that attitudes in the host country were different and should be respected.

He believed that there was much to learn from the British way of life. And sometimes that could mean embracing change.

He did in fact change his own views on the traditional Eritrean attitude to women which was based on a patriarchal society where women were secondary. Teame had been brought up in an environment where the role of women was looking after the home and doing the cooking. They would rarely, at least in the rural areas, go to school. He realised he had been complicit in that environment, encouraging his father to send his two younger brothers to school – and helping maintain them – but not his sisters. That was a battle he could not win.

But arriving in Britain he recognised the rightness of equal opportunity for men and women and became a firm advocate of the idea not just in Britain but the rest of the world. He recognised that there was a different style of living where women could equally contribute to society. It was one reason why he was able to make such an effective contribution to the work of ABANTU for Development (AfD), the non-governmental organisation that seeks to empower African people, especially women, to have a say in the policies and decisions of their countries. On a personal level the fact that his three daughters all went to university and have successful professional careers was testament to his embracing of equality for all. He also got a more enlightened view on Female Genital Mutilation (FGM) which was a common and accepted practice in the Coptic Church in Eritrea when he lived there.

A product of the Orthodox Christian church in Eritrea, he arrived in Britain steeped in their traditions and teachings. But, as he experienced a multicultural and multi-faith Britain, he realised that he needed to be less sectarian and more ecumenical. He joined a non-conformist church and supported freedom of worship whatever the branch of Christianity or, for that matter, other religions.

His thinking also changed from the provincialism of his upbringing in the Highlands of Eritrea, where you would die for your village, to a loyalty to his adopted country and a wider understanding of the global picture. It was a fundamental shift in his way of looking at the world.

As he became, by his own admission, a 'global citizen' he rejected his old ideas of fatalism which he saw as accepting what comes in life rather than fighting to change it. In the Eritrean culture there is a proverb which proclaims: 'Whoever becomes the King is our ruler.' With his eyes open to the need for all sort of changes in the world, Teame now had no wish to accept the status quo along with its baggage of inequality and injustice. As an active 'global citizen', he embraced the right to highlight inequalities and injustices at local, national and global levels.

All these things represented a sea change in his thinking which he felt was both right and necessary to integrate into his new environment in the West. But, as well as embracing change, he also held on to the basic values of the culture he left behind which remained an important part of his life and his contribution to the country.

One of the most important was respect for elders. He has never forgotten the old priest who ran the church school he first went to as a young boy in Dekemhare. He told his pupils to obey the

Commandment, 'Respect your father and mother.' Service to neighbours, especially those in need, was another tenet of life in an Eritrean community. He was committed to both these social requirements which were powerful influences in his life in Britain. As were his belief in 'bridge building' between different cultures – with teachers being a vital conduit for getting the message across.

His belief in the 'connectedness of humanity' – that we are all human beings irrespective of external appearance – also coloured his relationships. He was always happy and willing to accept anyone as 'his brother', regardless of their background, colour, race or religion. He looked upon them as just like him. That was 'connectedness'.

He felt that if he had a positive attitude to others, especially the host society in which he now found himself, they would respond positively to him. A negative approach, looking in an angry way, being unwelcoming would inevitably provoke them to reciprocate in a like manner. They are just human beings like me Teame would say to himself. A smile was always better than an angry look. He looked upon himself as an optimist who tried to build bridges. To promote understanding through the way he lived but also through education.

His advice to any new migrant was, 'Learn to adapt.' And that, he would point out, did not mean abandoning their culture, faith and way of life. But they did need to realise that if they chose to live in the United Kingdom then their first loyalty should be to that country which, after all, had given them shelter and a new life as well as the freedom to practice their religion.

Refugees did have the opportunity of being positive citizens in the host society, Teame would declare. He was a great believer in the maxim, 'Light a candle rather than curse the darkness.' If their fear was that they would be made to 'feel inferior' by virtue of their diverse identity, they needed to remember that no-one could make them feel inferior without their consent. They had the chance of changing their perspective. Bt to do that they had to be wise and also humble enough to learn how to tame their frustrations and fears – even when they felt undeservedly slighted.

They needed to break down barriers, to understand and be prepared to be assimilated into, the culture of the host nation. They should respect the society that welcomed them even if they had differences. Although he could see that the relationship between the Scots and the English over devolution showed that even in the United Kingdom there are differences.

Another piece of advice he would offer new migrants was to recognise that the world is governed by rights and responsibilities which applied to them as newcomers to the country. He felt some of them concentrated on getting something for themselves rather than giving something back to their host society. They would become more accepted, and their life would be easier, if they thought about their responsibilities to their new country.

In fact, he considered there were purely pragmatic reasons for participating in the local society. It could present opportunities for improving the lot of all citizens, including the migrants, by becoming part of the decision making process or serving in some other way – as Teame himself had done by becoming a Magistrate.

He would urge migrants not to think of themselves as victims. His message to them was: 'My brothers, you are not victims. You have a choice because you can become a constructive member of your new society.' They had rights and entitlements under the law, but it did not mean that every person they passed on the street would smile at them. They had to recognise that rights did not necessarily mean acceptance. They may have to offer a hand of friendship first.

They should not 'put up a wall around themselves', or fail to learn the language of the majority. That resulted in a parallel life with the mainstream of society going one way and them the other. That way they were bound to be marginalised.

But he would also be the first to say that integration was a two-way process. The incomers have to try and understand and embrace the new but unless the host community embrace and understand them, there will be no assimilation. So embracing the new is a dual process. It has to be undertaken by both the minority and the majority populations. This can lead both to understand each other's alternative world view and to learn from each other. That way both of them benefit from the richness that comes from diversity. That, he believes, is the key to successful integration.

Teame took the view that everyone has a 'multiplicity of identities', depending on where they were and what they were doing at a particular time. In his case, he would say, he was a man, husband, father, grandfather, Justice of the Peace, an academic, a Christian, an Eritrean and, as long as he lived in Britain, British. So, he reasoned, perception of one's identity can be fluid, evolving and, at times, contradictory.

He had no trouble integrating himself into the British community. In fact it would not have occurred to him to do anything else. His attitude was influenced by his belief in the need for tolerance and understanding – both on the part of newcomers to the country and, the long-time residents who made up the majority of the population.

So he would answer critics, who feared the impact of immigrants, by urging them not to think every asylum seeker or refugee was a 'parasite' or someone responsible for 'dumbing down' the quality of their education system. And he would encourage the immigrants to integrate themselves as much as possible, rather than keep themselves to themselves by recreating, for instance, a little Pakistan or a little Eritrea in the UK.

They were in danger of becoming marginalised especially if they made no effort to learn and speak the language. Everybody should make the effort to learn, he believes. After all, he points out, English is an international language and they could benefit from learning it. In other countries people pay to learn English.

But whilst advising immigrants to grasp the opportunities of their new life, he was also mindful of the heartbreak felt by many of those who had fled their countries, leaving behind homes and, in many cases, good jobs as doctors, lawyers and engineers. It could be a lonely time, cut off from the support of their extended families which, in many African, Asian and Middle Eastern cultures, play such a vital role in people's lives, not just in a material sense but by providing emotional support and guidance. It was a comfort blanket and they could feel lost without it.

After all, uprooting oneself, or being uprooted, was a harrowing experience as it automatically denied an individual the basic requirements of survival as defined by academic Adam Curle as the 'Four S's' – sustenance, security, satisfaction and stimulus.

There was also a loss of self-esteem. At home they might have been professionals with a position in society. In their new country each was just another refugee. They had lost their identity. For some the name they had been known by in the local language, such as *Abboy Keshi* (Priest/Father) or *Abu Ali* (the father of Ali), which represented their place in society and their cultural values, was replaced with plain 'Mr' in their new home. It may sound like a small thing, and members of the host community were merely using the accepted form of address in Britain, but to the immigrants it could be yet another blow to their self-esteem and confidence as their view of the world was turned upside down.

So Teame hoped that the host community, including those processing asylum applications, understood and were sensitive to the traumas that refugees had experienced and the difficulties they faced in their new surroundings.

Differences in social attitudes could sometimes cause misunderstandings. A prime example, which Teame had come across during his years of mentoring students from Africa and Asia, was their eye contact when talking to others. Whereas in the culture of the West it is considered good manners and a sign of confidence to look a person in the eye when talking to them, in some other countries the opposite is true. There a younger person would never look their elders in the eye. They would avert their gaze away as a sign of respect. Indeed to do otherwise could cause offence.

Here in the UK, as Teame would explain to his students, making and holding eye contact was the norm. Not to do so could be wrongly construed. Did they have something to hide? Were they lacking in confidence? He would advise migrants not to make this mistake when, for instance, talking to officials about their status in the country, in a job interview or just conversing with someone they met in the street. Teame realised that issues such as these further highlighted the need for mutual understanding between immigrants and the host community.

Teame is of the opinion that, whether belonging to the majority population or the minority, life is a journey of self-discovery. This, he says, can mean a new attitude which reflects the reality of uncertainties of life in our globalised world. Such self-discovery can prepare us all to be interested in the beliefs and ways of thinking of other individuals or groups.

He believes everyone, the minority and the majority, should learn to make concessions for the sake of peace and harmony. They both need to identify and cherish the traits, attitudes and habits they share in common, so that they do not need to look inwards, to see their differences, or to search for stereotypes.

To him religion of any sort is not in itself a cure for hatred and contempt unless the deep-seated root behind these emotions are resolved. Arrogance and insensitivity, he says, are among the main causes of misunderstanding. So people need to find an answer to their differences through dialogue and education which is, or can be, an effective instrument for changing behaviours.

There are questions, raised by those who view immigration negatively, which need to be confronted. Will the presence of migrants lead to the end of patriotism? Are immigrants coming to Europe to conquer? Should Europeans be tolerant towards Muslims who may not be tolerant to them in their own countries? He sees concerns like these as being a fear of the unknown, of being swept away by change. He believes this is one of the underlying dreads of human beings, irrespective of colour or creed.

Change, he believes, could have a major psychological impact on the mind. To those who are fearful, change is threatening and it could lead to a worsening situation. But if one had hope then change could lead to something better. One thing that is certain is that there will always be change because nothing remains static. New immigrants need to understand this.

But he acknowledges the fears are genuine and need to be confronted. The attitude of the immigrants themselves could, he believes, do much to allay such fears. However, he also sees an irony in the fact that some of the immigrants come from countries colonised by Europeans in the 19th century which produced changes which were 'bitter, irrational and divisive'. Now, he says, the immigrants see Europe as a place of refuge and a haven of democracy and justice. Is this, he asks, really so surprising?

After all, he points out, most European countries with a colonial past would do well to remember that their history is intrinsically linked to those of Africa, Asia and the Middle East where the refugees currently flooding into Europe are coming from.

To those who condemn the immigrants he points out that this may only lead to some of them turning against their country of safe haven.

Ideally, if Europe has the desire to embrace them as its own people and the imagination to help them become the best they can, then, this will lead to a win-win situation for asylum seekers and those who give them sanctuary.

There is, he believes, much at stake. Effective integration in a multiracial society can provide immigrants with the tools to become effective change-makers, both in the West and back in their own countries, should the conditions which had forced them to leave improve and they wished to return. That, he believes, would be a worthwhile legacy of multiculturalism and a priceless contribution to a more peaceful world.

We live in a shrinking world in an age of super mobility and complex diversity. So, he believes, the sooner we learn how and why we need to live with an understanding and acceptance of our differences, the better for humanity.

CHAPTER FORTY-TWO

Dreams of a Global Educator

'I have a dream.' Those historic words of American civil rights campaigner Martin Luther King in 1963, when he called for an end to racism in the United States, had resonated with Teame. Now, more than half a century later, he has his own dreams about the future of a world beset by an immigration crisis, poverty, inequality and wars.

He would admit that he feels the need to dream of the kind of world he would like to see because, in reality, there are parts of it which are more of a nightmare. And to have a dream is to have hope. He is encouraged that the iconic Martin Luther King address, and the dreams he expressed, have sparked a change in policies and attitudes – albeit a still ongoing process – which led to the first black American President, Barack Obama. Who would have suspected that in 1963?

He does not compare himself with the great civil rights leader but feels that to have dreams of a better and more just world might be the first step toward achieving it, however unlikely the outcome might appear. He challenged himself to think: 'What are the areas where change is needed?' He considered it one of his duties as an educator to highlight them.

A vision at the heart of the hopeful aspirations in Teame's dreams is changes in the effects of globalisation when a shrinking world makes it easier to move from one country to another. It is a subject on which he had regularly lectured and had also co-edited a book, *Globalisation, Educational Transformation and Societies in Transition*, which was published in 2000 and is still widely read and cited today. One of his co-editors, Professor Michael Crossley, has paid tribute to Teame's work on the issues surrounding globalisation saying it has had 'a wide international influence'.

The book pointed out that the globalisation process was currently having a powerful and far-reaching influence upon all societies world-wide. At the same time, many communities were ever more forcefully acknowledging their distinctive characteristics and celebrating their cultural differences.

Teame feels passionately about the subject and has studied it closely. He concludes that the effects of an increasing 'Westernisation' across the world and the material benefits of improved economic ties had its good side, but there were limitations too. Globalisation is the dominant feature of the 21st century. But, he believes, it is part of a 'lop-sided world' where 15% of the global population owns 85% of the available resources and wealth.

He questions the policies of multinational corporations who encourage farmers, mostly in the South, to produce cash crops, on land which had previously been used to feed their families, but then could barely make a living from the proceeds. And part of the 'lopsidedness' of globalisation is, he considers, aid policies which 'protected the interests of the rich North rather than the poor South'. So globalisation is, to all intents and purposes, Westernisation because it represents the expansion of Western values and ideas. That does bring benefits which are to be welcomed. But there is still a 'yawning gap' between the social and economic realities of the rich and the poor which means 'we live in a massively unequal world'.

He likens the two sides of that unequal world to a story he often used in his lectures to students on the subject of globalisation. It revolved around two mules who were supposed to walk together to pull a heavy cart. But instead they would pull in different directions so the job would never get done. That, he would say, is what is happening in our global situation. So we are not getting the best out of our material and human resources.

Sometimes, to make the same point, he would use a different analogy about people in a boat during a heavy storm which was in danger of sinking. Some of the stronger passengers wanted to throw weaker ones overboard to lighten the load, but there would be too many others on the boat who would stop them. So the only way to survive was to collaborate and weather the storm.

He feels that 'morals have become elastic'. The moral boundaries of previous generations, which had formed the basis of societies all over the world, are being 'adapted according to circumstances'.

So he concludes that the process of globalisation is not yet complete. As he looks at this globalised and unequal world, what are his hopes of a better future for all mankind? He looks back at his own experience and the difficulties he had overcome – to get an education, to escape a brutal regime, to start a new life – and tells himself that nothing is impossible.

Firstly, he is convinced of the need for the reform of global governance. He freely admits that he does not know all the answers but, as an educator, considers it his job to highlight the issues and encourage debate which could hasten change.

To that end he calls for a fresh look at the mechanisms of our globalised world which control aid, the flow of capital and is responsible for human safety, immigration and the effects of climate change.

He would like to see more rigorous scrutiny of the roles of influential key players like the United Nations Security Council and especially, the World Bank, the International Monetary Fund and the

World Trade Organisation, the three pillars of the economic structure, which *The Economist* described in October 2015 as 'all in bad repair'.

Teame also believes smaller nations should have a greater say in the UN Security Council instead of decisions being in the hands of a small group of powerful nations. He wants global governance to be unfettered by capitalism and to work towards redressing the balance between rich and poor countries.

He has harsh words for those leaders in the South who 'cannot control the egomania that comes with power'. These, he says, are individuals who neither inspire nor empower their own people. They do not lead or move aside for others and are 'neither creditable or accountable'. Their vision does not 'go beyond accumulating millions of dollars in foreign banks'.

Why not, he asks, change the parameters of assessing global well-being from calculating Gross National Product (GNP), concerned only with economic growth, to a 'Human Development Index' which concentrates on the development of people rather than a country's wealth? He would like to see a multi, or inter-disciplinary study which could rethink the definition of globalisation, what it was meant to achieve and how it could be made sustainable. Such a study should identify the negative consequences of globalisation like fragmentation, chaos and even the weakening of nation states.

He believes that the 21st-century needs a new gospel which is not based on consumerism. Instead he dreams of a gospel that could lead humanity to formulate a way of life that was 'inwardly rich and outwardly simple'.

He questions the veracity of those who claim that globalisation (a complex set of interrelated processes – economic, social, political, technological and environmental) is drawing together the peoples of the world. Does that, he asks, mean that there is a single entity of global culture – where all cultures merge into one? Or does it refer only to the culture of the West? He is concerned that, if the latter, does that not foster the growth of inequality between rich and poor nations?

He is convinced there is a moral dimension to many of the questions relating to globalisation. For instance, is there a link between global connectedness – the links between countries – and moral responsibility? In other words, the connections, at every level, between different countries could lead to the development of some but the underdevelopment of others. So there is a moral responsibility needed in narrowing the gap.

Materialism, he feels, has been elevated to a 'pseudo-religious level'. There is a new disease, 'affluenza', which is in need of a vaccine. Encouraged by advertising and the mass media it affects peoples' aspirations and view of life. And it gives birth to 'stuffocation' – the acquiring of yet more possessions. 'To have' had become more important than 'to be'. He has seen both diseases afflicting people around him – and admits to being tempted by them himself – but also knew they could lead to depression and anxiety. If that dream of a cure to 'affluenza' and 'stuffocation' came true, it would usher in a new value system of sharing which could improve well-being.

Another of his dreams is to see an exorcism of the 'curse of colour'. It reminds him of the 'Mandela' jibe he received crossing a street in Bristol from someone reacting to a black face. He knew this was something that people of a different colour from the majority – no matter which colour or which country they were in – might experience. It is an issue that could serve to separate people. Education, he considers, is how it could be confronted. It is part of his philosophy of introducing multicultural education into schools which would celebrate differences.

And the ignorance of the one who called him 'Mandela' was ironic since the great South African freedom fighter Nelson Mandela who became South Africa's first black president – after years of imprisonment – was acknowledged all over the world for his leadership and ability to bring people together. Teame admires, in particular, Nelson Mandela's belief in forgiveness. He also believes it is an essential ingredient of a new world.

He marvels at the comparatively peaceful transformation from the apartheid years to democratic government which had been marked by a Truth and Reconciliation Commission where perpetrators of some of the most gruesome atrocities were given amnesty in exchange for being honest about their crimes. So instead of revenge and retribution the new nation, led by Mandela, chose to tread a different path of forgiveness and reconciliation. Could Mandela's example be repeated in other troubled parts of the world? Now that was a dream worth having.

Teame has never forgotten the power of forgiveness in his own life after he had felt liberated by putting aside the bitterness he felt towards his Ethiopian masters and the American he had an altercation with.

A subject inevitably close to his heart is the need for the development of educators. He does not believe that educational reform, along with expert opinions and public consultation, is a complete answer to the shortcomings of any education system. His philosophy has always been to develop the teachers first. He believes that without a coherent and ongoing people development programme for teachers at all levels, from kindergarten to university, improvements could not be made. Educators need to constantly update their skills to keep up with the rapid pace of change. That is a dream which he made real during his career and he will always advocate other teacher-educators to do the same.

With his own background of seeking asylum and building a new life in Britain, and with the flow of hopeful and desperate immigrants into

Europe likely to continue indefinitely, he also sees the need for a collaborative and comprehensive study on refugee related issues.

Whilst he recognises the refugee issue – not least how many the UK and other European countries could or should accept – is a hot political topic, he believes that immigrants could contribute much to the countries that accept them. However, if they are to be helped to integrate successfully, their needs must be understood. Issues like the reasons why they were forced to leave their country, their experiences at the hands of human traffickers, and the fears for the family they may have left behind. But he was encouraged by the words of the then Prime Minister, David Cameron, who said: 'Our migrant communities are a fundamental part of who we are and Britain is a far richer and stronger society because of them.'

He advocates that the education system could play a role in bringing an understanding by introducing art and drama into schools depicting the issues refugees face. This, he believes, would challenge some of the prejudice and stereotypical attitudes which prevail in some homes and communities in the UK and other European countries. It would be an extension of the work he had undertaken first with the Rowntree Trust when he toured schools talking about Africa and later involved some of the pupils in supporting Eritrean refugees in camps in Sudan.

As any historian knows mass immigration is nothing new. It had happened before in the 19th century when about 45 million Europeans emigrated comparatively unhindered to different corners of the world without having to face the barbed wire or dangerous seas of today. Even today, according to some studies, there are 200 million people living outside their countries of birth. So, the mass migration of peoples from the poorer countries to the richer ones is not going to go away. It was after all a natural reaction for people with empty stomachs, or whose lives were at risk from war or despotic regimes, to be prepared to take any risk – such as crossing the Mediterranean in small boats in winter – to improve their lives or, in many cases, to save them.

He acknowledges that there is a difference between economic migrants, who want a better life, and migrants fleeing from war zones. So he has no doubt that those refugees from conflict areas should be given priority.

Teame also wants proper controls for economic migrants. That could, he proposes, take the form of legislation both in their home-land and the country where they seek to resettle which would govern their length of stay – perhaps five years. Then there could be some incentives in their home countries, such as housing and pensions, to encourage them to return with new skills and experience which would benefit their homeland. Meanwhile the countries receiving the immi-grants could contribute to improving the infrastructure of the nations they come from, investing in education for instance.

Perhaps a more practical way of reducing the flow of refugees to Europe would be for countries there to find ways of tackling the root causes of the problem, collaborating over reforms in the conflict zones – although he acknowledges the latter is easier said than done.

He sees one of the most critical challenges humankind faces in the 21st century is a failure to appreciate our common humanity. There are, he believes, more things that unite us than divide us. Embracing diversity can serve as a bridge between people rather than a wall separating them.

The futures of the rich North and the poor South are, he believes, intricately linked and dependent on each other. So Teame's dream is that the North will have the humility to learn from the South who could for their part have the magnanimity to forgive the past as they enlist support from their wealthier global neighbours.

Part of that dream is to see the dawn of a New Age driven by the 'Family of Man'. He remembers the children in the Bristol school, which he had visited during his days with the Rowntree Trust, who had impressed him by singing the song of that name. He felt at the time, and still feels, that it is a microcosm of the kind of world he would like to see.

His idea of the family of mankind is influenced by the African proverb, often used by the American writer and civil rights activist Maya Angelou: 'I am a human being. Nothing human is foreign to me.'

Teame sees the proverb as challenging some of the stereotypical views associated with 'blackness' and 'whiteness' in many European languages, including English. For instance 'whiteness' was often associated with positivity and 'blackness' with negativity. As a black British, he finds offensive the association of his colour with words for 'black' in various dictionaries describing it as 'dirt', 'evil', 'deadly', 'sinister' or 'wicked'.

So a cherished dream is to see an all-embracing civilisation where the colour of one's skin, be it black, brown, yellow or white, is not a trigger for division or intolerance, but a sign of a diverse world where everyone has a contribution to make and the right to live.

But the greatest dream of all is seemingly the most unattainable, the establishment of a Culture of Peace. He sees peace as having a number of agents at its disposal, education being one of them. Others include the communication tools of mass media, the exchange of ideas and knowledge, and the United Nations systems for conflict prevention and resolution. He remains convinced that if these are utilised wisely and systematically it is possible to sow the seeds of peace. But above all education, in all its forms, could have a key role if only governments could avoid conflicts.

But he is also aware of the threat to human rights from 'self-centred dictators'. He feels the thoughts of German theologian Martin Neimöller, imprisoned by the Nazis during World War Two, still ring true. Neimöller, who died in 1984, said:

First they came for the Socialists, and I did not speak out –
  Because I was not a Socialist.
Then they came for the Trade Unionists, and I did not speak out –
  Because I was not a Trade Unionist.
Then they came for the Jews, and I did not speak out –
  Because I was not a Jew.
Then they came for me – and there was no one left to speak for me.

Teame admires Neimöller's views and believes that it is sometimes necessary to take difficult steps to follow one's conscience. From his own experience one such occasion was when he braved the angry and armed mob of Ethiopian secondary school students and villagers as he accompanied the body of one of his trainees who had accidentally drowned – despite being warned it was too dangerous. Or when he dreamed up and spearheaded the South-North conference which attracted international attention and sharpened the debate about the world's rich-poor divide.

As he looks back on his life as an educator – with experience in both the developed North and the underdeveloped South – Teame remains convinced that education is the future, and that the future belongs to those who prepare for it today. He takes great pride in seeing many of his former students take up top positions such as Ministers of Education in their countries in the developing world.

Aware of the calibre of his former students he is optimistic that they will utilise education, in all its forms, in the development of their countries. He believes in President Barack Obama's maxim: 'Change will not come if we wait for some other person or some other time. We are the change we seek.'

He was inspired too by Australian Gill Hicks, who lost both her legs in the 7/7 bombings in London in 2005. She has become an ambassador for the charity Peace Direct, whose primary objective is that, 'we are all responsible for peace in our world ... let us do what we can for each other, let's not wait for tragedy to do that.' A globalised world – one that is inter-connected – has the potential for self-destruction unless it is based on safer, saner and fairer traditions than are currently the case. His belief is that humanity can get better if we all accept our differences and cherish what we have in common.

So Teame's dreams are about the changes he would like to see in humanity. He wants to make a difference in a world of indifference. That, he believes, is his duty as an educator, a conviction that has motivated him since his early days as a young teacher in Eritrea.

He believes everyone has a personal responsibility to shine a light, however small, on the injustices of an imperfect world. Small chinks of light can move beyond a dream and become beacons of hope. And hope is the one thing that can never be extinguished.

Acknowledgements

In producing this account of the remarkable life of Teame Mebrahtu there are a number of people whose help and support have been invaluable. But without the active, honest and willing co-operation of Teame himself nothing would have been achieved. I am grateful to him for allowing me to delve into his life with no areas out of bounds.

From the very outset our work together, over a period of two and half years, has been a collaboration in which it has been a privilege to discover so much about Teame's life journey. The fact that we remain on good terms is a tribute to his gracious nature.

But like me, Teame would also want to thank his wife Teblez, who as he says, has 'contributed to this book much more than she knows'. Without her wisdom, support and encouragement, the task of tracing details that span over seven decades would have been neither possible nor meaningful.

And, as Teame would also point out, but for Teblez's ability to run the day-to-day life of the Mebrahtu household, and her determination to bear stoically any responsibility that came her way, he would not have been able to undertake his many professional adventures.

His three daughters, Aida, Esther and Zeb, have been pillars of strength providing insights that enhance the narrative. They also ensured their father did not neglect the many meetings with his biographer that were necessary to complete this multi-tiered story of his life.

There are others too who have played their part. High among them has been Professor Malcolm Johnson whose wise counsel and continuing encouragement played a vital part in bringing Teame's story to a wider audience.

Teame's close friends, John Hayter and Ray Harris, who have been both colleagues and participants in some of his adventures, deserve thanks for sharing their memories. Other valued friends, Jim and Sally Baynard-Smith, whom he first met in Asmara in the 1960s, have been a source of constant support.

There have been many others who have contributed their memories of Teame and encouraged him, and me, in this literary exercise. Among them Dr Negusse Araya, Les Fry, Stuart McFarlane, Professor Michael Crossley, Bridgette Blackmore, and former students Cheryl Brathwaite, Mesfin Gebremedhin and Zemikael Habtemariam.

My thanks also must go to Anthony Werner of Shepheard-Walwyn Publishers whose empathetic support and assistance in preparing this book for publication was invaluable.

And I am grateful to Karl Dallas's wife, Gloria Dallas, for permission to use those wonderful lyrics from Karl's inspirational song, 'Family of Man'. It encapsulated Teame's ethos of bringing cultures together and he encouraged children to sing it during his school visits with the Rowntree Trust. Sadly, Karl died aged 85 in June 2016, but his song lives on.

Finally, I could not have completed this work without the support of my wife Jill who has been a constant source of encouragement, an eagle-eyed proofreader, and provided valuable feedback when I bounced ideas off her.

For my part, helping Teame to revisit the experiences of his time in Eritrea and his new life in Britain, with all its different aspects, has been exhilarating and enjoyable. I have learnt a great deal – but Teame is, after all, an educator with a global perspective. If this book has opened minds and provided inspiration it is entirely the result of Teame's passionate belief in the power of education and the capacity of the human spirit to change and adapt for the better. That is no small achievement for a boy from Adi Ghehad.

SH

Index of Names

Following the convention for Eritrean and Ethiopian names they are listed alphabetically by their forenames. All others are indexed by surnames.